SCIENCE FUN IN CHICAGOLAND

SECOND EDITION

D1713379

Companion Book by the Author

SCIENCE FUN WITH TOYS

SCIENCE FUN IN CHICAGOLAND

SECOND EDITION

A Guide for Parents and Teachers

Describing Over 1,000 Resources,
Including Over 600 from Around the Country

THOMAS W. SILLS

Prepared with the Support of
Wilbur Wright College
One of the City Colleges of Chicago

Dearborn Resources
P. O. Box 59677
Chicago, IL 60659

SCIENCE FUN IN CHICAGOLAND - SECOND EDITION

Published by Dearborn Resources, P. O. Box 59677, Chicago, IL 60659.

SECOND EDITION   ISBN 0-9644096-1-5

Cover design by Dickinson Associates

Publisher's Cataloging-in-Publication
(Provided by Quality Books, Inc.)

Sills, Thomas W.
      Science fun in Chicagoland : a guide for parents and
teachers : describing over 1,000 resources, including over
600 from around the country / Thomas W. Sills. -- 2nd ed.
      p. cm.
      Includes bibliographical references and index.
      ISBN: 0-964496-1-5
      1. Science--Study and teaching--United States--Bibliography
--Catalogs. 2. Science--Study and teaching--Illinois
--Bibliography--Catalogs. 3. Science--Study and teaching
--Bibliography--Catalogs--Juvenile literature. 4. Scientific
recreations--Bibliography--Catalogs. I. Title.

Q158.5.S54 1999   507'.0773'1
                          QBI99-86

Library of Congress Catalog Card Number: 99-72233

ACKNOWLEDGMENTS

A countless number of people helped with the production of the second edition. They gave suggestions, answered telephone inquires, and made this book possible. It would be impossible to acknowledge everyone here who contributed to the information contained in this book.

A few individuals were more than generous with their time and energy to help the author. It is appropriate to list their names: Kathy Fishback, AAAS; Dave Bayless, Dana Kesse, Judy Kolar, Bryan Wunar, Adler Planetarium and Astronomy Museum; Harold Myron, Argonne National Laboratory; Karen Perinunzi, Cernan Earth and Space Center; Kathleen Berg, Jean DeHorn, Phil Parfitt, Kara Tourville, Chicago Academy of Sciences Sheryl Cash, Tamara Marks, Chicago Botanic Garden; Ginger Kranz, Elizabeth Lach, Rosanna Mendez, Barbara Unikel, Chicago Children's Museum; Jane Sorensen, NatureConnections, Chicago Public Library; James Cowden, Judith Foster, CPS Teachers Academy for Professional Development, Chicago Public Schools; Clifton Burgess, Nijole Mackevicius, Melanie Wojtulewicz, Department of Curriculum and Instruction, CSI, Chicago Public Schools; Allan Reisberg, Student Science Fair, Inc., Chicago Public Schools; Michelle DeHaven, Sarah Wolf, Discovery Center Museum; Phil Hanson, Johanna Krynytzky, The Field Museum; Lisa Roberts, Garfield Park Conservatory; Susan Dahl, Lederman Science Education Center; Dorothy Asher, Lizzadro Museum of Lapidary Art; Sarah Solsvig, The Morton Arboretum; Donna Kinimer, Carolyn Wilson, Motorola Museum; Nancy Dove, Museum of Science and Industry; Stephanie Blaser, NCREL; Karen Baker, National Science Teachers Association; Lori Defiore, Karen Farina, Power House; Olivia Diaz, Karen Gleason, SciTech; Elizabeth Ban, Jennifer Oltroggy, Bert Vescolani, John G. Shedd Aquarium; Joe Frattaroli, Teachers Academy for Mathematics and Sciences; and Joan Bieler, TIMS Project.

Thanks! Your efforts will be a great help to the parents, teachers, students, and science fans who read this book.

TABLE OF CONTENTS

TABLE OF CONTENTS

Dedicated to

Students of Science Everywhere

SCIENCE FUN IN CHICAGOLAND

SECOND EDITION

Chapter

1

Introduction

Short History of this Guide

As a professor of college-credit science-methods courses for pre-service and in-service teachers in the mid 1980's, I was obligated to produce a short list of science resources in the Chicago area. When I asked these future teachers of science what they wanted in this resource list, they shouted: "Telephone numbers."

A small hand-size 14-page booklet of 85 resources resulted with easy-access accurate telephone numbers. This small booklet gained popularity, but aged with time. In 1994, my initial search for an estimated list of 300 resources resulted in the first edition of *Science Fun in Chicagoland* that contained over 800 resource listings for all age levels: preschool, elementary school, middle school, high school, college, and adult. It was published in 1995 and with little promotion became an unexpected success. Schools and parents purchased this first edition in equal quantities.

This second edition was produced during a sabbatical from my teaching duties at Wright College, one of the City Colleges of Chicago. This sabbatical allowed time for a thorough updating, purging, and adding of resources so that now this book includes over 1,000 resource listings. From the first edition to the second, many telephone area codes changed. And a new technology called "Internet web sites" evolved, providing great quantities of instant information. Over 600 web sites are included in this second edition.

Chapter Names

The chapters in this guidebook grew almost organically on their own. A natural list of categories evolved into chapter names for the huge data base that resulted. Many individuals provided information. Teachers, teachers of teachers, school administrators, science organization members, manufacturers, distributors, and students of science continued to be generous with what they like and what they know makes science fun. As a very large data base grows, it almost sorts itself.

It must be stated, however, that the chapter names were selected by the author. They were affected by his 30 years experience in science education. And, sometimes a resource is in more than one chapter.

The chapter on science toy sources from the first edition grew into another book, *Science Fun with Toys*, a companion to *Science Fun in Chicagoland - Second Edition*. This new guide to unique and educational science toys has a foreword by Judith Q. Iaccuzi, Executive Director of the USA Toy Library Association. In her foreword she gives the history of toy library development across the country. Just like book libraries, these libraries loan toys to children and one of these libraries likely is near you. *Science Fun with Toys* describes hundreds of toys and their sources, including manufacturers, distributors, and retail mail order sources. If you like this guide, you will also enjoy *Science Fun with Toys*.

How Readers Use this Guide Book

With more than 1,000 annotated references, including addresses, phone numbers, and web sites, plus 14 chapters devoted to books, computers, education, events, excursions, groups, instruments, libraries, materials, periodicals, safety, science fairs, and video, this book provides something for science lovers of all interests.

This guide is used beyond the Chicago area. Do not let the regional title mislead you. This resource guide is sold in book stores nationwide. Included are over 600 resources from around the country, helping parents, teachers, and students find science awards, competitions, events, science groups, mail order suppliers, fun Internet web sites, science magazines, and much more.

Teachers use it for planning classroom lessons and field trips, or locating educational material. A teacher used the first edition to find an agency that funded her school's science festival. Teacher organizations from the Nebraska Science Teachers Association to the National Science Teachers Association requested copies of the first edition for distribution. The Illinois Association of School Boards sold copies to its members attending a conference.

Parents can select science museums and nature centers for family excursions or find quality educational materials for their children. Plan a fun weekend around a visit to a museum or nature center. Parents benefit from activity books described in this guide. These activity books are favorites with countless fun science experiments that can be performed with common materials in the home or outdoors. Popular and educational Internet web sites are described for the home computer. Resource descriptions of periodicals for parents and children guide parent purchases of fun magazines.

Students can create winning science projects with resources indexed by science subjects. *Chicago Books in Review* says, "This rich resource for adults and children will come in handy, especially for those all-encompassing science fair projects ." One book reviewer called the first edition, "a great gift for children and parents."

Science fans can find science groups to join and can locate Chicago area science libraries. Did you know that Chicagoland has 50 quality science libraries? National and Chicago area science organizations range in group interest from kiting and astronomy to future scientists and women in engineering. You can find sources of quality mail-order science books for sale by 800-numbers in catalogs or via the Internet, putting science at your fingertips.

University courses in science education require this reference for their college students. Schools buy this guide for distribution to their teachers, libraries, and counselors. The first edition of *Science Fun in Chicagoland* is in many public and school libraries at the reference desk.

Many who purchased the first edition said they read this book like a novel, cover to cover. But, who would want to read a book with hundreds of addresses, telephone numbers, web sites, and annotated descriptions cover to cover? Surprisingly, it appears even seasoned science educators find new sources and ideas in *Science Fun in Chicagoland*. Perhaps this is the reason several universities require teachers-in-preparation to purchase a copy for use in their future careers.

Ultimately this guide benefits children. And quality education benefits our future.

Use the Index

I once asked the private librarian to a famous founder of a large pharmaceutical company, "What makes a good book?" She quickly responded with an easy answer, "It's the quality of the index." With this wisdom, each resource in this guide is alphabetically listed in the index. The index also lists resources under science subject areas, or relevant topics, like earth science, zoology, arts & science, special needs, and teacher development.

The index makes *Science Fun in Chicagoland - Second Edition* a science education telephone book.

Thomas W. Sills
Author

Chapter

2

Books

Resource Reference Books

These helpful resource lists and bibliographies are in libraries or may be purchased where indicated.

AAAS RESOURCE DIRECTORY OF SCIENTISTS AND ENGINEERS WITH DISABILITIES

American Association for the Advancement of Science, 1200 New York Ave, NW, Washington, DC 20005-3920 800-222-7809 http://www.aaas.org/ehr 1995 254 pages $ 20.00

For science teachers, curriculum developers, program directors and counselors, a listing of more than 600 scientists, mathematicians, and engineers--from all disciplines and with a wide spectrum of disabilities.

ASTC DIRECTORY

Association of Science-Technology Centers, 1025 Vermont Ave, NW, Suite 500, Washington, DC 20005-3516 202-783-7200, ext 140 Fax 202-783-7207 Email pubs@astc http://www.astc.org Published Annually Nonmembers $ 40.00

The "yellow pages" of the science-center field. Science centers, museums, institutions of informal science education.

BEST BOOKS FOR CHILDREN 1992-1995
American Association for the Advancement of Science, 1200 New York Ave, NW, Washington, DC 20005-3920 800-222-7809 http://www.aaas.org/ehr 1996 286 pages $ 24.00
This bibliographic resource book lists and describes over 800 science books for children categorized under seventeen different science subject areas.

BEST SCIENCE BOOKS & AV MATERIALS FOR CHILDREN
by O'Connell, Montenegro, and Wolff 1988 Out of print
This bibliographic reference work lists resource books under sixteen different science subject areas. Look for this book in your local library.

CONSERVATION EDUCATION CATALOG
by the Conservation Education Advisory Board Illinois Department of Energy and Natural Resources, 524 S Second St, Springfield, IL 62071-1781 217-782-7454 79 pages
This extensive catalog lists resources under the topics of Agriculture & Land Conservation, Atmosphere, Ecology & Interdisciplinary, Energy, Fauna, Flora, Geology & Geography, Outdoor Recreation & Safety, Waste, Recycling & Pollution Control, and Water. Over 80 resource publications and many agency addresses are also listed.

DIRECTORY OF STUDENT SCIENCE TRAINING PROGRAMS
Science Service, Inc., 1719 N St, NW, Washington, DC 20036 202-785-2255 Fax 202-785-1243 Email youth@scisvc.org http://www.tss-inc.com/sciserv/ 1994 $ 3.00 per copy.
This directory lists extra-curricular opportunities in science for high ability precollege students.

EDUCATORS GUIDE TO FREE SCIENCE MATERIALS
38th Edition by Mary H. Saterstrom Contact Kathy Nehmer Educators Progress Service, Inc., 214 Center St, Randolph, WI 53956-1497 920-326-3126 888-951-4469 Fax 920-326-3127 1997 256 pages $ 29.95
This book lists and describes free science materials, including films, filmstrips, slides, videotapes, and printed materials by category of science subject area. Revised annually.

ENERGY EDUCATION RESOURCES - KINDERGARTEN THROUGH 12TH GRADE
National Energy Information Center, EI-231, Energy Information Administration, Room 1F-048, Forrestal Building, 1000 Independence Ave, SW, Washington, DC 20585 202-586-8800 1992
Ask for a copy of this 31-page booklet listing 86 different sources of educational materials from both public and private institutions and companies. Each source usually offers a catalog listing free materials.

EVERY TEACHER'S SCIENCE BOOKLIST
by the Museum of Science & Industry, Compiled and Edited by Bernice Richter and Pamela Nelson Scholastic Professional Books, Scholastic Inc., 2931 E McCarty St, Jefferson City, MO 65102 800-325-6149 1994 182 pages $ 12.95
This extensive bibliography of science literature for children lists and describes trade books by science topic. It also describes resource books for adults.

THE GUIDEBOOK OF FEDERAL RESOURCES FOR K-12 MATHEMATICS AND SCIENCE
Eisenhower National Clearinghouse for Mathematics and Science Education, The Ohio State University, 1929 Kenny Rd, Columbus, OH 43210-1079 800-621-5785 614-292-7784 Fax 614-292-2066 Email editor@enc.org http://www.enc.org
A directory of federal resources for mathematics and science education.

HANDBOOKS AND TABLES IN SCIENCE AND TECHNOLOGY
Third Edition Edited by Russell H. Powell Oryx Press, P O Box 33889, Phoenix, AZ 85067-3889 800-279-6799   Fax 800-279-4663   Email info@oryxpress.com http://www.oryxpress.com 1994 368 pages $ 95.00
This comprehensive reference lists over 3,600 scientific and technical handbooks. Look for this book at the reference desk of your library.

IDEAAAS: SOURCEBOOK FOR SCIENCE, MATHEMATICS, AND TECHNOLOGY EDUCATION
Directorate for Education and Human Resources Programs, American Association for the Advancement of Science, 1200 New York Ave, NW, Washington, DC 20005-3920 800-222-7809 http://www.aaas.org/ehr 1995 256 pages $ 24.95
Listings of more than 1,000 organizations and their 10,000 resources and programs.

INFORMATION SOURCES IN SCIENCE AND TECHNOLOGY
Third Edition   by C. D. Hurt   Libraries Unlimited, Inc., P. O. Box 6633, Englewood, CO   80155-6633   800-237-6124   Fax 303-220-8843   Email lu-books@lu.com http://www.lu.com 1998 ca. 350 pages Hardcover, $ 55.00 Papercover, $ 45.00
This bibliography lists reference and resource books and is in the Library Science Text Series. Resource books are listed under the following categories: History of Science, Multidisciplinary Sources, Astronomy, General Biology, Botany, Chemistry, Geosciences, Mathematics, Physics, Zoology, General Engineering, Civil Engineering, Energy & Environment, Mechanical & Electrical Engineering, Production Engineering, Transportation Engineering, and Biomedical Sciences. Includes web sites.

MILESTONES IN SCIENCE AND TECHNOLOGY

The Ready Reference Guide to Discoveries, Inventions, and Facts by Ellis Mount and Barbara A. List Oryx Press, P O Box 33889, Phoenix, AZ 85067-3889 800-279-6799 Fax 800-279-4663 Email info@oryxpress.com http://www. oryxpress.com 1994 216 pages $ 34.50

Readers of all ages can easily find facts, history, names, and dates surrounding the 1,250 most important events in sci-tech history. Look for this book at your library.

THE NATURE OF CHICAGO

by Isabel S. Abrams Chicago Review Press, Inc., 814 Franklin St, Chicago, IL 60610 800-888-4741 1997 278 pages $ 14.95

This resource guide is for those who enjoy and study nature in the Chicago area. It is full of resource listings.

NSTA SCIENCE EDUCATION SUPPLIERS

A Supplement to: Science & Children, Science Scope, and The Science Teacher, National Science Teachers Association, 1840 Wilson Blvd, Arlington, VA 22201-3000 800-722-NSTA http://www.nsta.org Published annually. 165 pages $ 5.00 per copy.

List of science textbook and trade book publishers and distributors. The most current and comprehensive list of manufacturers, publishers and distributors of science education materials. See Textbook Publishers, Trade Book Publishers.

REFERENCE SOURCES IN SCIENCE, ENGINEERING, MEDICINE, AND AGRICULTURE

by H. Robert Malinowsky Oryx Press, P O Box 33889, Phoenix, AZ 85067-3889 800-279-6799 Fax 800-279-4663 Email info@oryxpress.com http://www.oryxpress.com 1994 368 pages $ 39.95

Written by a bibliographer of science and technology. More than 2,400 entries of complete bibliographic information are described. Every source is indexed by author, subject, and title. Look for this book at the reference desk of your library.

RESOURCES FOR SCIENCE LITERACY:
PROFESSIONAL DEVELOPMENT

Oxford University Press, 200 Madison Ave, New York, NY 10016 / Oxford University Press, Order Department, 2001 Evans Road, Cary, NC 27513 800-451-7556 1997 CD-ROM & 120-page companion book. $ 39.95 includes computer disk with book.

Contents include Comparisons of Benchmarks to National Standards, Science Trade Books, Project 2061 Workshop Guide, Cognitive Research, College Courses, and Full text of Science for All Americans.

RESOURCES FOR SCIENCE, MATHEMATICS, TECHNOLOGY AND EDUCATION

by the Teachers Academy for Mathematics and Science (TAMS), 3424 S State St, Chicago, IL 60616-3834 312-808-0100 Fax 312-808-0103 8 pages

Names, addresses and telephone numbers are listed under categories: 1) Science Centers, Museums, and Zoos 2) Institutions/Organizations Promoting Science, Mathematics and Technology Education.

RESOURCES FOR TEACHING ELEMENTARY SCHOOL SCIENCE

by the National Science Resources Center National Academy Press, 2101 Constitution Ave, NW, Lockbox 285, Washington, DC 20055 800-624-6242 202-334-3313 Fax 202-334-2451 http://www.nap.edu 1996 312 pages $ 17.95 (Learning Team 800-793-TEAM $ 19.95)

A completely revised edition of the best-selling, Science for Children: Resources for Teachers. This extensive resource book lists and describes curriculum materials by science subject area, supplementary resources, and sources of information and assistance.

RESOURCES FOR TEACHING GEOLOGY FROM THE ILLINOIS STATE GEOLOGICAL SURVEY

Contact LeAnn Benner Illinois State Geological Survey, Natural Resources Building, 615 E Peabody Drive, Champaign, IL 61820-6964 217-333-4747 Fax 217-244-0802 Email benner@geoserv.isgs.uiuc.edu http://www.isgs.uius.edu 1997 2 pages Free

This brochure lists low-cost publications and maps useful for teaching Illinois' geology, landscape and mineral resources. The Geological Survey leads four free field trips to selected sites in Illinois each year. Ask for a current brochure about the field trips.

RESOURCES FOR TEACHING MIDDLE SCHOOL SCIENCE

by the National Science Resources Center National Academy Press, 2101 Constitution Ave, NW, Lockbox 285, Washington, DC 20055 800-624-6242 202-334-3313 Fax 202-334-2451 http://www.nap.edu 1998 ca. 400 pages $ 19.95

This volume describes more than 400 curriculum titles that are aligned with the 1996 National Science Education Standards. Authoritative, extensive, and thoroughly indexed.

SCIENCE & TECHNOLOGY IN FACT AND FICTION: A GUIDE TO CHILDREN'S BOOKS

by Kennedy, Spangler and Vanderwerf R.R. Bowker, New York, 1990 319 pages

This guide to children's books is divided into categories of science and technology and subcategories of fiction and nonfiction. Each book listed is summarized and evaluated. This reference includes author, title, subject and readability indices.

SCIENCE & TECHNOLOGY IN FACT AND FICTION: A GUIDE TO YOUNG ADULT BOOKS

by Kennedy, Spangler and Vanderwerf R.R. Bowker, New York, 1990 363 pages
This guide to young adult books is divided into categories of science and technology and subcategories of fiction and nonfiction. Each book listed is summarized and evaluated. This reference includes author, title, subject and readability.

SCIENCE ON THE WEB

by Edward J Renehan, Jr. Springer-Verlag New York, Inc., P O Box 2485, Secaucus, NJ 07096-2485 800-SPRINGER Fax 201-348-4505
Email sales@springer-ny.com 1996 382 pages $ 19.95
A connoisseur's guide to over 500 fun web sites.

SCIENCE SOURCES 1998

Compiled by the News and Information Office, American Association for the Advancement of Science, 1200 New York Ave, NW, Washington, DC 20005-3920 202-326-6408 http://www.aaas.org
This international directory of colleges and universities, corporate and industrial research organizations, federal agencies and laboratories, museums of science and technology, and scientific and professional societies lists nearly 1200 science and science-related organizations in 26 countries, with primary focus on the U.S.

SCIENCE TRADEBOOKS, TEXTBOOKS AND TECHNOLOGY RESOURCES WITH ANNOTATIONS

Anne Grall Reichel, Science Coordinator, Lake County Educational Service Center, 19525 W Washington, Grayslake, IL 60030 847-223-3400, ext 240 Fax 847-223-2415 Email areichel@lake.k12.il.us 55 pages
This resource list includes over 700 Illinois Science Literacy Grant Publisher Gifts and Purchases. Listed alphabetically each resource is classified into subject area with a brief annotation.

Books on Activities and Methods of Teaching

These books on teaching ideas are just a few from hundreds of similar publications available. Teacher recommendations and quantity of book sales to teachers determined selection for this list. Each book in this list has exciting ideas for science learning activities.

700 SCIENCE EXPERIMENTS FOR EVERYONE - REVISED AND ENLARGED

Compiled by UNESCO Doubleday & Company, Inc., Garden City, New York 1956, 1962 250 pages

This classic reference lists science activity experiments by categories of science subject area. Look for this book in your library.

AMUSEMENT PARK PHYSICS: A TEACHER'S GUIDE
by Nathan A. Unterman J. Weston Walch, Publisher, 321 Valley St, P. O. Box 658, Portland, ME 04104-0658 800-341-6094 Fax 207-772-3105 http://www.walch.com 159 pages $ 20.95 (800-722-NSTA $ 20.95)
This guide provides tutorials, practice problems, and lab exercises appropriate for studying the motion of amusement park rides.

THE ART AND SCIENCE CONNECTION
- HANDS-ON ACTIVITIES FOR INTERMEDIATE STUDENTS
by Kimberley Tolley Distributed by the National Science Teachers Association 800-722-NSTA 1994 206 pages $ 19.95 Grades 5-10.
Activities include drawing, painting, sculpture, bas-relief, printmaking, collage, graphic arts, and mixed media.

THE ART AND SCIENCE CONNECTION
- HANDS-ON ACTIVITIES FOR PRIMARY STUDENTS
by Kimberley Tolley Distributed by the National Science Teachers Association 800-722-NSTA 1993 160 pages $ 19.95 Grades K-6.
Activities include drawing, painting, sculpture, bas-relief, printmaking, collage, graphic arts, and mixed media.

BIOLOGY ON A SHOESTRING
National Association of Biology Teachers - NABT Publications 11250 Roger Bacon Dr, #19, Reston, VA 20190-5202 800-406-075 703-471-1134 Fax 703-318-0308 Email NABTer@aol.com http://www.nabt.org $ 18.00
This publication contains hands-on investigative laboratory activities for high school students that require little or no money. Ask for publications brochure.

BOTTLE BIOLOGY
by Department of Plant Pathology, University of Wisconsin - Madison Distributed by the National Science Teachers Association 800-722-NSTA 1996 127 pages $ 17.95
Activities that explore science and the environment with soda bottles, film cans, and other recyclable materials.

CLASSROOM CREATURE CULTURE: ALGAE TO ANOLES - REVISED EDITION
by Carol Hampton, Carolyn Hampton, and David Kramer Published and distributed by the National Science Teachers Association 800-722-NSTA 1994 96 pages $ 12.95

Ideas for collecting, caring for, and investigating plants and simple animals in the science classroom grades K-9. This book is dedicated to understanding the respect and care living things need.

CRIME LAB CHEMISTRY
by Jacqueline Barber Distributed by the National Science Teachers Association 800-722-NSTA 1985 24 pages $ 9.00
This activity challenges student "detectives" to use paper chromatography to determine which black ink pen was used to write a ransom note. Grades 4-8.

CRIME SCENE INVESTIGATIONS: REAL-LIFE SCIENCE LABS
by Walker and Wood Center for Applied Research in Education, P O Box 11071, Des Moines, IA 50381-1071 800-288-4745 http://www.phdirect.com $ 28.95 For grades 6-12.
Contains 68 crime scene investigations for the classroom from fiber analysis to evidence from the soil. Activities grouped by life science, earth science, physical science, and critical thinking.

DECISIONS -- BASED ON SCIENCE
Produced and distributed by the National Science Teachers Association 800-722-NSTA 1997 144 pages $ 19.95
This book guides students to not just memorize information, but use scientific was of thinking to make everyday decisions.

DEMONSTRATION EXPERIMENTS IN PHYSICS
Edited by Richard Manliffe Sutton, Ph.D., Prepared under the Auspices of The American Association of Physics Teachers McGraw-Hill Book Company, Inc., New York 1938 545 pages
Out of print and hard to find. Perhaps the best compendium of classroom demonstrations for physics yet published.

DEMONSTRATION HANDBOOK FOR PHYSICS - SECOND EDITION
Edited by Freier and Anderson American Association of Physics Teachers, One Physics Ellipse, College Park, MD 20740-3845 301-209-3300 Fax 301-209-0845 Email aapt-memb@aapt.org http://www.aapt.org 320 pages $ 33.00
This handbook contains hundreds of apparatus demonstrations that require only low-cost, everyday materials.

EARLY CHILDHOOD AND SCIENCE
compiled by Margaret McIntyre Published and distributed by the National Science Teachers Association 800-722-NSTA 1984 136 pages $ 12.95
Skills of observation, identification and exploration are the focus of this book for the preschool child. It has application for the young gifted child as well as the slow learner.

**Children learn about energy and science at ComEd's Power
House, an interactive science museum in Zion, IL.**

Photo Courtesy of Power House/ComEd

EARTH CHILD 2000 WITH TEACHER'S GUIDE
by Kathryn Sheehan and Mary Waidner Council Oak Books, 1350 E 15th St, Tulsa, OK 74120 800-247-8850 Fax 918-583-4995 Email oakie@ionet.net 478 pages 1998 $ 26.95
A classic treasury of resources for teaching young children ages three to ten about the environment and Earth Sciences. Includes activities, stories, songs, resources, Internet web sites.

EARTH: THE WATER PLANET
by Gartrell, Crowder, and Callister Distributed by the National Science Teachers Association 800-722-NSTA 1992 204 pages $ 18.50
Middle school activities that use readily available materials to investigate many science and environmental problems.

THE EVERYDAY SCIENCE SOURCEBOOK
by Lawrence F. Lowery Distributed by the National Science Teachers Association 800-722-NSTA 1985 438 pages $ 21.00
This book is filled with activity ideas for teaching science in the elementary and middle school.

EXPERIMENTING WITH INVENTIONS
by Robert Gardner Watts, New York 1990 128 pages $ 11.90
The process of inventing, the importance of the inventor's notebook, school invention clubs and fairs, and stories about inventors are topics in this book about inventing. This book is appropriate for parents and teachers, although it was written for junior high school students.

EXPERIMENTING WITH MODEL ROCKETS
Distributed by the National Science Teachers Association 800-722-NSTA 1989 86 pages $ 16.00 Teacher's guide.
Explains what influences a model rocket's flight and how to measure the flight's height.

EXPLORATORIUM SCIENCE SNACKBOOK SERIES
Exploratorium, 3601 Lyon St, San Francisco, CA 94123 415-563-7337 Fax 415-561-0307
Many "snacks" are available at the Internet web site, http://www.exploratorium.edu. Or in books, The Magic Wand and Other Bright Experiments on Light & Color, The Cheshire Cat and Other Eye-Popping Experiments on How We See the World, The Cool Hot Rod and Other Electrifying Experiments on Energy and Matter, and The Spinning Blackboard and Other Dynamic Experiments on Force and Motion. John Wiley & Sons, Inc. 1995-1996 Each $ 10.95 These books show how to build classroom interactive science exhibits like those found at the hands-on Exploratorium science center.

EXPLORE THE WORLD USING PROTOZA
edited by Anderson and Druger   Produced and distributed by the National Science Teachers Association 800-722-NSTA 1997 240 pages $ 29.95
This book shows you how to bring protozoan research into your classroom. Educational Press Association award winner.

FIELD MANUAL FOR WATER QUALITY MONITORING
by Mitchell and Stapp   Ninth Edition   Distributed by the National Science Teachers Association 800-722-NSTA 1994 272 pages $ 19.95
Developed for and field tested in high school biology and ecology classes. Includes water quality tests, explanations of tests, and a case study.

FLIGHTS OF IMAGINATION
- AN INTRODUCTION TO AERODYNAMICS
by Wayne Hoskings Produced and distributed by the National Science Teachers Association 800-722-NSTA 1990 56 pages $ 10.50
Eighteen projects transform trash bags, dowels, and tape into high-flying lessons. Grades 5-12.

FORECASTING THE FUTURE - EXPLORING EVIDENCE FOR GLOBAL CLIMATE CHANGE
Produced and distributed by the National Science Teachers Association 800-722-NSTA 1996 160 pages $ 21.95
Fourteen classroom activities and more than 40 extension exercises help students understand climate. Grades 6-10.

HELPING YOUR CHILD LEARN SCIENCE
U. S. Department of Education, Office of Educational Research & Improvement, Washington, DC 20208-5572 http://www.ed.gov 57 pages $ 3.25
This illustrated publication is full of activity ideas for the home and in the community. Science is described as observing, predicting and testing predictions. This book describes nine important concepts for science curriculum design recommended by the National Center for Improving Science Education.

INVENTING, INVENTIONS AND INVENTORS: A TEACHING RESOURCE BOOK
by Jerry D. Flack Teacher Ideas Press, A Division of Libraries Unlimited, Inc., P. O. Box 6633, Englewood, CO 80155-6633 800-237-6124 1989 148 pages $ 21.50
This book includes the process of inventing, methods of teaching, inventing competitions, and a resource bibliography.

INVENTORS WORKSHOP
by Alan J. McCormack Distributed by the National Science Teachers Association
800-722-NSTA 1981 84 pages $ 12.00
Activities that encourage kids to construct an intriguing invention or device from readily available materials. Grades 3-8.

INVITATIONS TO SCIENCE INQUIRY - SECOND EDITION
by Tik L. Leim Contact Jeanne Liem Science Inquiry Enterprises, 14358 Village View Lane, Chino Hills, CA 91709 909-590-4618 Fax 909-590-2881
(800-722-NSTA $ 45.00)
This popular book is filled with science teaching ideas.

KITCHEN SCIENCE
by Howard Hillman Exploratorium, 3601 Lyon St, San Francisco, CA 94123
415-561-0393 http://www.exploratorium.edu $ 9.95
Learn about the science behind cooking and about the physics and chemistry in your kitchen. This fun book includes experiments and recipes.

MR. WIZARD'S SUPERMARKET SCIENCE
by Don Herbert, Television's Mr. Wizard Distributed by the National Science Teachers Association 800-722-NSTA 1980 96 pages $ 10.00
In this book you will learn that your local supermarket is a resource of everyday items that can be used in over 100 hands-on science experiments.

MULTICULTURAL WOMEN OF SCIENCE
by Bernstein, Winkler, and Zierdt-Warshaw Distributed by the National Science Teachers Association 800-722-NSTA 1996 170 pages $ 11.00
The contributions of thirty-seven women in all areas of science and from diverse backgrounds are presented. Followed by activities and thinking questions.

MULTICULTURALISM IN MATHEMATICS, SCIENCE AND TECHNOLOGY: READINGS AND ACTIVITIES
Distributed by the National Science Teachers Association 800-722-NSTA 1993
206 pages with wall poster $ 32.00
This book is filled with activities keyed to the activity's cultural origin. The enclosed wall poster show a map of the world with pictures of famous scientists and inventors from all over the world.

ONE-MINUTE READINGS
by Richard F. Brinkerhoff Distributed by the National Science Teachers Association 800-722-NSTA 1992 136 pages $ 10.95
Gives students opportunities to carefully consider and apply real-world problems to science study. A pleasure to read.

PHYSICS OF SPORTS
Edited by C. Frohlich American Association of Physics Teachers, One Physics Ellipse, College Park, MD 20740-3845 301-209-3300 Fax 301-209-0845 Email aapt-memb@aapt.org http://www.aapt.org 124 pages $ 26.00
This collection of reprinted scientific journal articles presents the physics involved in today's popular sports including baseball, basketball, bowling, golf, tennis, and track and field.

PHYSICS OLYMPICS HANDBOOK
Edited by Agrusco, Escobar and Moore American Association of Physics Teachers, One Physics Ellipse, College Park, MD 20740-3845 301-209-3300 Fax 301-209-0845 Email aapt-memb@aapt.org http://www.aapt.org 26 pages $ 14.00
This handbook offers suggestions for organizing a physics olympics in your high school complete with rules, events, sample handouts, and schedules.

PROJECT EARTH SCIENCE
Produced and distributed by the National Science Teachers Association 800-722-NSTA 1994 Each $ 21.95 Series set $ 69.00
Ready to use middle school activities in four subject areas: Astronomy, Geology, Meteorology, and Physical Oceanography.

QUICK SCIENTIFIC TERMINOLOGY
by Kenneth Jon Rose John Wiley & Sons, Inc., New York 1988 267 pages Out-of-print
Learn scientific terminology with this self study guide by combining simple root words like megawatt or mega + watt means one million watts and creophagous or creo + phagous means flesh eating.

RISING TO THE CHALLENGE
by Ostlund and Mercier Distributed by the National Science Teachers Association 800-722-NSTA 1996 90 pages $ 20.00
Thirty-six activities are described that show you how to make use of the new science standards and encourage scientific inquiry in students.

SAFETY IN THE ELEMENTARY SCIENCE CLASSROOM
by Dean, Dean, Gerlovich, and Spiglanin Produced and distributed by the National Science Teachers Association 800-722-NSTA 1993 22 pages $ 5.95
Easy-to-read flip chart covers the important safety topics for the classroom.

THE SCIENCE EXPLORER OUT AND ABOUT BOOK
- AN EXPLORATORIUM SCIENCE-AT-HOME
Exploratorium, 3601 Lyon St, San Francisco, CA 94123 415-561-0393 Fax 415-561-0481 http://www.exploratorium.edu 125 pages 1997 $ 12.95

Family-oriented collection of experiments designed for parents and children to do together.

THE SCIENCE EXPLORER
- AN EXPLORATORIUM SCIENCE-AT-HOME BOOK

Exploratorium, 3601 Lyon St, San Francisco, CA 94123 415-561-0393 Fax 415-561-0481 http://www.exploratorium.edu 125 pages 1996 $ 12.95
Family-oriented collection of experiments designed for parents and children to do together.

SCIENCE HELPER K-8 CD-ROM

Contact Dimitri Zafiriadis The Learning Team, 84 Business Park Dr, Suite 307, Armonk, NY 10504 800-793-TEAM 914-273-2226 Fax 914-273-2227 Email learningtm@aol.com http://www.learningteam.com $ 195.00
At the touch of a button, a teacher can have access to 919 lesson plans that includes 2000 activities. Developed at the University of Florida under the direction of Dr. Mary Budd Rowe, this resource lists curriculum materials developed and tested over a 15-year period with millions of dollars in funding from the National Science Foundation.

SCIENCE ON A SHOESTRING - SECOND EDITION

by Herb Stongin Distributed by Thinking Works, P O Box 468, St. Augustine, FL 32085-0468 800-633-3742 904-824-0648 Fax 904-824-8505 1991 208 pages $ 18.95
This book describes fun experiments with inexpensive materials that are easily obtained. For grades K-8.

SCIENCEWORKS

by the Ontario Science Center Distributed by Thinking Works, P O Box 468, St. Augustine, FL 32085-0468 800-633-3742 904-824-0648 Fax 904-824-8505 Email thnkgwks@aug.com 1988 86 pages $ 11.95
Simple science experiments are presented in cartoon illustrations as fun mind-puzzling tricks. This book is a favorite of teachers and students.

SECRET FORMULAS

by Tilley and Willard Distributed by the National Science Teachers Association 800-722-NSTA 1996 150 pages $ 16.00
Students make their own paste, toothpaste, cola, and ice cream. Grades 1-3.

SOAP SCIENCE

by J. L. Bell Distributed by the National Science Teachers Association 800-722-NSTA 1993 64 pages $ 9.95 (Thinking Works 800-633-3742 $ 9.50)
Thirty-six fun experiments that use soap and suds.

STRING AND STICKY TAPE EXPERIMENTS

Edited by Ronald Edge American Association of Physics Teachers, One Physics Ellipse, College Park, MD 20740-3845 301-209-3300 Fax 301-209-0845 Email aapt-memb@aapt.org http://www.aapt.org 448 pages $ 33.00

Describes simple experiments that may be constructed with materials readily available from a discount store.

SUNLIGHT, SKYSCRAPERS & SODA-POP

American Chemical Society, Education Division, 1155 16th St, NW, Washington, DC 20036 800-209-0423 Fax 800-209-0064 304-728-2170 http://www.acs.org/edugen2/education/conted/conted.htm 64 pages $ 14.95

Book of poems and science activities for preschool to second grade.

TAKING CHARGE

by Larry E. Schafer Produced and distributed by the National Science Teachers Association 800-722-NSTA 1992 160 pages $ 18.95

These 25 teacher-tested, hands-on activities use readily available materials to study electricity. Grades 5-10.

TEACH THE MIND, TOUCH THE SPIRIT: A GUIDE TO FOCUSED FIELD TRIPS

The Field Museum, Education Department, Roosevelt Road at Lake Shore Drive, Chicago, IL 60605-2497 312-922-2497, ext 351 http://www.fmnh.org 80 pages $ 10.00

This book describes museums as educational opportunities, structuring your field trip, The Field Museum opportunities, and a reference bibliography.

TEN-MINUTE FIELD TRIPS

by Helen Ross Russell Produced and distributed by the National Science Teachers Association 800-722-NSTA 1991 176 pages $ 16.95

More than 200 short, close-to-home excursions in science for grades K-8 are described. Each excursion is categorized by science subject area and lists classroom activities with teacher preparation needs. Excursions are described for both rural and urban locations. Fun for both teachers and parents.

THE PILLBUG PROJECT

by Robin Burnett Produced and distributed by the National Science Teachers Association 800-722-NSTA 1992 110 pages $ 16.50

Students develop a sense of what science is all about. Grades 3-7 Educational Press Association award winner.

THE UNBELIEVABLE BUBBLE BOOK

by John Cassidy Distributed by the National Science Teachers Association 800-722-NSTA 1987 88 pages $ 12.95
Learn to make bubbles six feet tall and four feet wide that stretch across your lawn. Klutz bubble making apparatus included.

THOMAS EDISON BOOK OF EASY
AND INCREDIBLE EXPERIMENTS

by James Cook and the Thomas Alva Edison Foundation Distributed by the National Science Teachers Association 800-722-NSTA 1988 136 pages $ 14.95
This book includes descriptions of the most popular experiments and projects sponsored by the Edison Foundation.

TOYS IN SPACE: EXPLORING SCIENCE WITH THE ASTRONAUTS

by Dr. Carolyn Sumners, Project Director for the Toys in Space Program, NASA McGraw-Hill, 11 West 19th Street, New York, NY 10011 800-822-8158 1997 512 pages $ 29.95 (800-722-NSTA $ 29.95)
Many mechanical action toys were taken on a NASA shuttle mission to observe their motion in weightless space. These toys, how they move on Earth, and what happened to them in space are described.

WATER, STONES, & FOSSIL BONES

edited by Karen K. Lind Produced and distributed by the National Science Teachers Association 800-722-NSTA 1991 140 pages $ 18.50
Fifty-one fun hands-on science activities, listing background information, concept descriptions, and guided student discussion procedures.

Professional Books on Teaching Philosophy, Science History, and Science Reference

These books are very helpful references providing guidance, answers and encouragement to professional science teachers at all levels.

ACTIVE ASSESSMENT FOR ACTIVE SCIENCE

by Hein and Price Distributed by the National Science Teachers Association 800-722-NSTA 1994 156 pages $ 21.00
Provides practical information on developing, interpreting, and scoring new alternatives to traditional tests.

ASIMOV'S BIOGRAPHICAL ENCYCLOPEDIA OF SCIENCE AND TECHNOLOGY - SECOND EDITION

by Isaac Asimov Doubleday, New York, NY 1982 941 pages Out-of-print

This single volume chronologically describes the lives and achievements of over 1,000 great scientists from ancient times to the present.

ASIMOV'S CHRONOLOGY OF SCIENCE & DISCOVERY
Isaac Asimov Harper & Row, Publishers, 10 E 53rd St, New York, NY 10022
1989 707 pages Out-of-print
The history of science from 4,000,000 B.C. to the present, listed by calendar year.

AUTHENTIC ASSESSMENT
by Diane Hart Distributed by the National Science Teachers Association
800-722-NSTA 1994 120 pages $ 13.95
This book answers often-asked questions about student assessment and includes guidelines for all classrooms.

BLOCK SCHEDULING
Produced and distributed by the National Science Teachers Association
800-722-NSTA 1997 $ 9.95
This book shows you how to restructure the traditional school day to accommodate longer class periods for more thoughtful laboratory experiences.

CONNECTING WITH THE LEARNER: AN EQUITY TOOLKIT
North Central Regional Educational Laboratory (NCREL), 1900 Spring Rd, Suite 300, Oak Brook, IL 60523-1480 630-571-4700 800-356-2735 623 pages
This toolkit for educators provides numerous activities for promoting equity in math and science education. The toolkit also includes a section of activities for parents and community members.

CRC HANDBOOK OF CHEMISTRY AND PHYSICS
CRC Press, Inc., 2000 Corporate Blvd, NW, Boca Raton, FL 33431-9868
800-272-7737 Annually $ 99.50
This book often becomes the standard source for data and information about the physical properties of matter. It is available in most libraries.

DICTIONARY OF SCIENTIFIC BIOGRAPHY
Edited by Charles C. Gillespie Scribner, New York 1970-1980 16 volumes
This reference work can be found in major libraries and provides an excellent record of the history of science. It contains scholarly biographies of over 5,000 scientists from ancient to modern times.

AFRICAN AMERICAN SCIENTISTS
OF THE 20TH CENTURY DISTINGUISHED
by Kessler, Kidd, Kidd, and Morin Oryx Press, P O Box 33889, Phoenix, AZ 85067-3889 800-279-6799 Fax 800-279-4663 Email info@oryxpress.com

http://www.oryxpress.com 1996 392 pages $ 49.95
Each biographical profile is packed with personal as well as professional information
on 100 outstanding scientists. Look for this book at your library.

EDTALK: WHAT WE KNOW ABOUT MATHEMATICS TEACHING AND LEARNING

North Central Regional Educational Laboratory (NCREL), 1900 Spring Rd, Suite
300, Oak Brook, IL 60523-1480 630-571-4700 800-356-2735 69 pages
This booklet for teachers and parents answers some of the most frequently asked
questions about teaching and learning mathematics.

EDTALK: WHAT WE KNOW ABOUT SCIENCE TEACHING AND LEARNING

North Central Regional Educational Laboratory (NCREL), 1900 Spring Rd, Suite
300, Oak Brook, IL 60523-1480 630-571-4700 800-356-2735 95 pages
This booklet for teachers and parents answers some of the most frequently asked
questions about teaching and learning science.

ELEMENTARY SCIENCE METHODS: A CONSTRUCTIVIST APPROACH

by David Jerner Martin Distributed by the National Science Teachers Association
800-722-NSTA 1996 508 pages $ 44.00
This comprehensive text helps teachers encourage children to develop their own
investigations.

EXPLORING CHEMICAL ELEMENTS AND THEIR COMPOUNDS

by David L. Heiserman Distributed by the National Science Teachers Association
800-722-NSTA 1992 384 pages $ 19.95
Periodic table, including element discovery, historical background, economic use,
production, and physical properties.

EXPLORING SCIENCE IN EARLY CHILDHOOD - SECOND EDITION

by Karen K. Lind Distributed by the National Science Teachers Association
800-722-NSTA 1996 320 pages $ 32.00
A developmental approach, this book trains teachers to help children understand basic
science concepts through activities.

FACILITATING SYSTEMIC CHANGE IN SCIENCE AND MATHEMATICS EDUCATION: A TOOLKIT FOR PROFESSIONAL DEVELOPERS

North Central Regional Educational Laboratory (NCREL), 1900 Spring Rd, Suite
300, Oak Brook, IL 60523-1480 630-571-4700 800-356-2735
The toolkit includes activities to help those who support reform efforts deepen their

knowledge of math and science education and to help with dissemination, professional development, and the change process.

THE GUIDE TO MATH & SCIENCE REFORM - AN INTERACTIVE RESOURCE FOR THE EDUCATION COMMUNITY

The Annenberg/CPB Math and Science Project, 901 E Street, NW, Washington, DC 20004   Publication office: Toby Levine Communications, Inc., 7910 Woodmont Ave, Suite 1304, Bethesda, MD 20814 301-907-6510

Available in Macintosh and MS-DOS/Windows, this guide is an interactive computer data base of resources for the education community.

HOW TO ASK THE RIGHT QUESTIONS

by Patricia E. Blosser Produced and distributed by the National Science Teachers Association 800-722-NSTA 1991 16 pages $ 5.00

This booklet analyzes questioning techniques to classify and improve questions that teachers ask.

HOW TO WRITE TO LEARN SCIENCE

by Bob Tierney Produced and distributed by the National Science Teachers Association 800-722-NSTA 1996 24 pages $ 8.95

A science teacher for more than 30 years shares his secrets on how to use writing and drawing exercises to get students excited about science.

IMPROVING CLASSROOM ASSESSMENT:
A TOOLKIT FOR PROFESSIONAL DEVELOPERS: TOOLKIT 98

North Central Regional Educational Laboratory (NCREL), 1900 Spring Rd, Suite 300, Oak Brook, IL 60523-1480 630-571-4700 800-356-2735

This toolkit includes activities to promote the use of alternative assessments in mathematics and science education.

INTERMEDIATE SCIENCE THROUGH CHILDREN'S LITERATURE: OVER LAND AND SEA

by Butzow & Butzow Teacher Ideas Press, A division of Libraries Unlimited, Inc., P. O. Box 6633, Englewood, CO 80155-6633 800-237-6124 1995 193 pages $ 23.00 (800-722-NSTA $ 23.00)

Unique approach to science through children's stories. Grades 4-7.

ISSUES IN SCIENCE EDUCATION

Edited by Rhoton and Bowers Published and distributed by the National Science Teachers Association 800-722-NSTA 1996 240 pages $ 24.95

Essays by teachers, administrators, and other experts show you how to make use of the new science standards.

LEARNING AND ASSESSING SCIENCE PROCESS SKILLS
by Rezba, Sprague, Fiel, and Funk Third Edition Distributed by the National Science Teachers Association 800-722-NSTA 1995 269 pages $ 24.95
Ideas for adaptation of materials, activity suggestions, and resources that bring process skills to the preschool to sixth grade classroom.

MAGIC AND SHOWMANSHIP FOR TEACHERS
by Alan J. McCormack Distributed by the National Science Teachers Association 800-722-NSTA 1990 200 pages $ 21.95
Irresistible activities and presentations that delight students.

MATHEMATICS, SCIENCE, AND TECHNOLOGY EDUCATION PROGRAMS THAT WORK
U. S. Department of Education, Office of Educational Research and Improvement Programs for the Improvement of Practice, National Diffusion Network, Washington, DC 20208-5645 http://www.ed.gov 145 pages
A collection of 64 exemplary education programs and practices in the National Diffusion Network.

MC GRAW-HILL ENCYCLOPEDIA OF SCIENCE & TECHNOLOGY - 7TH EDITION
McGraw-Hill Inc., New York 1992 20 volumes
This excellent, international encyclopedia of science and technology covers topics alphabetically.

NATIONAL SCIENCE EDUCATION STANDARDS
National Research Council, 2101 Constitution Ave, NW, HA 486,Washington, DC 20418 202-334-1399 (800-722-NSTA $ 19.95) (800-793-TEAM $ 19.95) 1995 280 pages K-12
Ask to be placed on mailing list. Report prepared by the National Committee on Science Education Standards and Assessment, National Research Council.

NSTA PATHWAYS TO THE SCIENCE STANDARDS
High School, Elementary School, and Middle Level Editions Published and distributed by the National Science Teachers Association 800-722-NSTA 1996-1998 Each $ 29.95
These guide books show how the National Science Standards can be applied to teaching, professional development, assessment, content, programs, and system.

OPEN-ENDED QUESTIONING
by Freedman Distributed by the National Science Teachers Association 800-722-NSTA 1994 82 pages $ 13.95
Methods for using open-ended questions and for assessing student responses.

A family enjoys the Chicago Botanic Garden in Glencoe, IL, with
its 385 acres of display gardens, plant information service,
garden shop, cafe, and library.

Photo Courtesy of the Chicago Botanic Garden

PORTFOLIO ASSESSMENT - A HANDBOOK FOR EDUCATORS
edited by Barton and Collins Distributed by the National Science Teachers
Association 800-722-NSTA 1997 120 pages $ 13.95
Practical steps for using portfolios and examples of portfolios used in actual classroom
settings.

PROJECT 2061'S BENCHMARKS FOR SCIENCE LITERACY

Oxford University Press, 200 Madison Ave, New York, NY 10016 / Oxford University Press, Order Department, 2001 Evans Road, Cary, NC 27513 800-451-7556 1994 448 pages $ 35.00 includes computer disk with book.

This text of national standards identifies what all students should know and be able to do in natural and social sciences, mathematics, and technology by the end of grades 2, 5, 8, and 12. Project 2061, American Association for the Advancement of Science.

RESOURCES FOR SCIENCE LITERACY:
PROFESSIONAL DEVELOPMENT

Oxford University Press, 200 Madison Ave, New York, NY 10016 / Oxford University Press, Order Department, 2001 Evans Road, Cary, NC 27513 800-451-7556 1997 CD-ROM & 120-page companion book. $ 39.95 includes computer disk with book.

Contents include Comparisons of Benchmarks to National Standards, Science Trade Books, Project 2061 Workshop Guide, Cognitive Research, College Courses, and Full text of Science for All Americans.

SCIENCE FOR ALL AMERICANS

by Rutherford (AAAS) Oxford University Press, 200 Madison Ave, New York, NY 10016 800-451-7556 1989 272 pages $ 12.95

Goals established in this work for national science education standards were used in preparation of AAAS's Benchmarks for Science Literacy in Project 2061, a comprehensive list of what students should be able to do in science, mathematics, and technology. Prepared by the AAAS.

SCIENCE FOR ALL CHILDREN

by the National Science Resources Center National Academy Press, 2101 Constitution Ave, NW, Lockbox 285, Washington, DC 20055 800-624-6242 202-334-3313 Fax 202-334-2451 http://www.nap.edu 1997 224 pages

A guide to improving elementary science education in your school district.

SCIENCE FOR THE ELEMENTARY SCHOOL - SEVENTH EDITION

by Victor and Kellough Prentice Hall, Inc., One Lake Street, Upper Saddle River, NJ 07458 800-526-0485 Fax 201-236-7098 1993

This college textbook for science teaching methods courses contains a compendium of ideas and knowledge about teaching elementary school science. Contact university bookstores in your area.

SCIENCE PROCESS SKILLS

by Karen L. Ostlund Distributed by the National Science Teachers Association 800-722-NSTA 1992 142 pages $ 14.95

Assessment and year-end evaluation of six levels of process skills with materials lists, procedures, and worksheets. Grades 1-6.

SCIENCE THROUGH CHILDREN'S LITERATURE: AN INTEGRATED APPROACH
by Butzow & Butzow Teacher Ideas Press, A division of Libraries Unlimited, Inc., P. O. Box 6633, Englewood, CO 80155-6633 800-237-6124 1989 234 pages $ 24.50 (800-722-NSTA $ 24.50)
Unique primary school approach to science through children's stories.

STEPPING INTO THE FUTURE: AFRICAN-AMERICANS IN SCIENCE AND ENGINEERING
American Association for the Advancement of Science, 1200 New York Ave, NW, Washington, DC 20005-3920 800-222-7809 http://www.aaas.org/ehr 1996 24 pages $ 7.00
Biographies of 18 interesting African-American role models, targeted to young readers in grades 4-8.

STEPPING INTO THE FUTURE: HISPANICS IN SCIENCE AND ENGINEERING
by Estrella M Triana American Association for the Advancement of Science, 1200 New York Ave, NW, Washington, DC 20005-3920 800-222-7809 http://www.aaas.org/ehr 1992 24 pages $ 11.95
Biographies of 14 living Hispanic scientists and engineers, all printed in English and Spanish.

TARGETING STUDENTS' SCIENCE MISCONCEPTIONS
by Joseph Stepans Distributed by the National Science Teachers Association 800-722-NSTA 1994 232 pages $ 24.95
This book lists common misconceptions about physical science topics and ways to combat them.

TEACHING CHEMISTRY TO STUDENTS WITH DISABILITIES
Third Edition Contact Ronald J. Sykstus American Chemical Society, Chicago Section, 7173 N Austin, Niles, IL 60714 847-647-8405 Fax 847-647-8364 (Contact national ACS office for career pamphlets at 800-227-5558.) 1993 46 pages
Free Ask for this excellent information and resource booklet.

TEACHING SCIENCE THROUGH DISCOVERY
Sixth Edition by Carin and Sund Charles E. Merrill Publishing Company, Columbus, OH 1990
This college textbook for science teaching methods courses contains a compendium of ideas and knowledge about teaching elementary school science. Contact university bookstores in your area.

THE TIMETABLES OF SCIENCE

by Alexander Hellemans and Bryan Bunch   A Touchstone Book, Published by Simon & Schuster Inc., Rockefeller Center, 1230 Avenue of the Americas, New York, NY 10020 1988 660 pages Out-of-print

This chronology of science lists science and its discoveries from 2,400,000 B.C. to present time by calendar year.

WHAT IS LIGHT AND HOW DO WE EXPLAIN IT?

by Bill G. Aldridge Produced and distributed by the National Science Teachers Association 800-722-NSTA 1996 32 pages $ 7.95

Fourteen activities designed to guide teachers to successfully use models and theories that describe light.

Chicago Area Bookstores

These bookstores were selected for their exceptional offerings of science books. Retail bookstores sell either new or used books. Bookstores selling new books provide a source for science books currently available in-print from their publisher. Bookstores that sell used books are fine sources for out-of-print books where one searches for an unexpected treasure. For the easiest way to find a needed out-of-print book, or compare out-of-print book prices, see Internet listings under Mail Order Books for Sale.

Reference book listing Chicago area bookstores:

THE NEW BOOK LOVER'S GUIDE TO CHICAGOLAND

by Lane Phalen Brigadoon Bay Books, P. O. Box 957724, Hoffman Estates, IL 60195-7724 1996 312 pages $ 14.95

This handy reference describes 700 bookstores in the Chicagoland area including southern Wisconsin. Bookstores are categorized by geographic location and indexed by subject including science.

57TH STREET BOOKS

1301 E 57th St, Chicago, IL 60637 773-684-1300 Email books@semcoop.com http://semcoop.com 800-777-1456

New in-print books in all fields including science.

THE ADLER PLANETARIUM STORE

Adler Planetarium & Astronomy Museum, 1300 S Lake Shore Drive, Chicago, IL 60605 312-322-0312 http://astro.uchicago.edu/adler/

This store within the Adler Planetarium carries a good selection of books and educational materials on astronomy, astrophysics and space science.

ANDERSON'S BOOKSHOPS
123 W Jefferson Ave, Naperville, IL 60540 630-355-2665; 5112 Main St, Downers Grove, IL 60515 630-963-2665; and 176 N York Road, Elmhurst, IL 60126 630-832-6566 http://www.andersonsbookshop.com
These shops are a fine resource for educators and science.

B DALTON BOOKSELLER
(See your telephone directory for store locations.)
Retail outlets for current books-in-print.

BARBARA'S BOOKSTORE
1350 N Wells St, Chicago, IL 60610 312-642-5044; 700 East Grand, Navy Pier, Chicago, IL 60611 312-222-0890; 9500 S Western, Evergreen Park, IL 708-423-3456; and 1100 Lake St, Oak Park, IL 60301 708-848-9140
General new books including children's and science books.

BARNES & NOBLE BOOKSTORES
(See your telephone directory for store locations.)
Retail outlets for current books-in-print.

BOOKMAN'S CORNER
2959 N Clark St, Chicago, IL 60657 773-929-8298
Used out-of-print books in all fields including science.

BOOKSELLERS ROW
408 S Michigan Ave, Chicago, IL 60605 312-427-4242
General used and out-of-print books including a good selection of science books.

THE BOOKWORKS
3444 N Clark St, Chicago, IL 60657-1610 773-871-5318
General used and out-of-print books in all subject areas including science.

BORDERS BOOKS
(See your telephone directory for store locations.)
Retail outlets for current books-in-print.

BROOKFIELD ZOO - BOOKSTORE
3300 S Golf Rd, Brookfield, IL 60513 708-485-0263
http://www.brookfield-zoo.mus.il.us
The Brookfield Zoo Bookstore and Shop offers more than 5,000 titles on zoology topics and natural history.

CHICAGO CHILDREN'S MUSEUM SHOP
Navy Pier, 700 E. Grand Ave, Chicago, IL 60611 312-595-0600
This shop has many fun science items for children including a large book selection.

CHICAGO RARE BOOK CENTER
56 West Maple St, Chicago, IL 312-988-7246
A multi-dealer store featuring used, rare, and out-of-print books.

EVANSTON ECOLOGY CENTER - BOOKSTORE
Evanston Environmental Association, Evanston Ecology Center, 2024 McCormick Blvd, Evanston, IL 60201 847-864-5181
At this bookstore located in the Ecology Center you will find birdfeeding supplies, gardening books, puppets, children's books.

FIELD MUSEUM OF NATURAL HISTORY - MUSEUM STORE
The Field Museum, Roosevelt Road at Lake Shore Drive, Chicago, IL 60605-2497 312-922-9410 http://www.fmnh.org
The newly remodeled and expanded Museum Store contains a large selection of quality books about natural science and culture and a wide variety of museum related items.

GREAT EXPECTATIONS
911 Foster St, Evanston, IL 60201 847-864-3881
New books in-print in all fields including science.

ILLINOIS INSTITUTE OF TECHNOLOGY BOOKSHOP
3200 S Wabash Ave, Chicago, IL 60616 312-567-3120
Email 145_commons/iit_il@fcs.follet.com
This university bookstore has new in-print books on science and technology.

MUSEUM OF SCIENCE AND INDUSTRY STORE, "THE BIG IDEA^{SM}"
Museum of Science and Industry, 57th St and Lake Shore Drive, Chicago, IL 60637 773-684-1414 http://www.msichicago.org
This store sells science books, toys and novelties.

N. FAGIN BOOKS
459 N Milwaukee Ave, Chicago, IL 60610 312-829-5252
Listed at http://www.bibliofind.com
New and used books in anthropology, archeology, botany and zoology.

O'GARA & WILSON BOOKSELLERS, LTD.
1448 E 57th St, Chicago, IL 60637 773-363-0993
Established in 1882, this is Chicago's oldest bookstore. General out-of-print and used books including science.

POWELL'S BOOKSTORE
1501 E 57th St, Chicago, IL 60637 773-955-7780; 828 S Wabash, Chicago, IL 60605 312-341-0748; and 2850 N Lincoln, Chicago, IL 60657 773-248-1444
General out-of-print books and scholarly books in all fields including a very good science selection.

RAIN DOG BOOKS
404 S Michigan Ave, Chicago, IL 60605 312-922-1200 Fax 312-266-0081
Collectable books in all fields including a modest science collection.

SEMINARY CO-OP BOOKSTORE
5757 S University Ave, Chicago, IL 60637 773-752-4381
Email books@semcoop.com http://www.semcoop.com 800-777-1456
New in-print books in all fields including science.

THE STARS OUR DESTINATION
1021 W Belmont, Chicago, IL 60657 773-871-2722 Email stars@sfbooks.com
http://www.sfbooks.com
New and used books in science fiction. The largest used science fiction selection in Chicago.

THE TIME MUSEUM STORE
Clock Tower Inn, 7801 E State St, (Interstate 90 and business highway 20), Rockford, IL 61125 815-398-6000
The Time Museum is an extraordinary museum of timekeeping, from Stonehenge to the Atomic clock. The store within the museum includes a fine selection of books on horology, astronomy, physics and mathematics.

U. S. GOVERNMENT BOOKSTORE
401 S State, Chicago, IL 60605 312-353-5133
This bookstore sells books printed by Agencies of the U. S. Government.

UNIVERSITY OF CHICAGO BOOKSTORE
970 E 58th St, Chicago, IL 60637 773-702-8729
New books in-print in all fields including science.

UNIVERSITY OF ILLINOIS AT CHICAGO BOOKSTORE
750 S Halsted, Chicago, IL 60607 312-413-5500 http://www.uic.edu
This university bookstore is on the campus of UIC.

UNIVERSITY OF ILLINOIS AT CHICAGO
HEALTH SCIENCES BOOKSTORE

828 S Wolcott, Chicago, IL 60612 312-413-5500 http://www.uic.edu
This university bookstore is on the campus of UIC and sells new and used medical textbooks as well as other science subjects.

Mail Order Books For Sale

Some of these mail order sources sell used or out-of-print books as indicated. Most sources provide a catalog of books for sale. See Internet listings as an easy way to find a needed out-of-print book or to compare out-of-print book prices.

AMERICAN ASSOCIATION OF PHYSICS TEACHERS
- AAPT PRODUCTS CATALOG

American Association of Physics Teachers, One Physics Ellipse, College Park, MD 20740-3845 301-209-3300 Fax 301-209-0845 Email aapt-memb@aapt.org http://www.aapt.org
Ask for this 28-page catalog. The 1997-98 catalog lists 85 books on physics and physics education. It also offers Physics of Technology Modules, computer software, videodiscs, videotapes, materials for teachers, gift items, workshop materials, and posters.

AMERICAN GEOLOGICAL INSTITUTE

4220 King St, Alexandria, VA 22302 703-379-2480 AGI Publications Center, P. O. Box 205, Annapolis Junction, MD 20701 301-953-1744 Email agi@agiweb.org/
Ask for 6-page brochure listing publications available, including Earth Science Guidelines Grades K-12, Earth-Science Education Resource Directory, and Careers in the Geosciences.

ASSOCIATION OF SCIENCE-TECHNOLOGY CENTERS (ASTC)

1025 Vermont Ave, NW, Suite 500, Washington, DC 20005 202-783-7200, ext 140 Fax 202-783-7207 Email pubs@astc.org http://www.astc.org
Ask for 12-page catalog of publications. Publications include general topics: ASTC Basics, Education, Youth Programs, Exhibits, Collaboration, Administration, Planning, and Research. The ASTC Directory is the "yellow pages" of the science-center field.

BARRON'S MATHEMATICS AND SCIENCE CATALOG

Barron's Educational Series, Inc., 250 Wireless Blvd, Hauppauge, NY 11788 800-645-3476 ext 204 or 214 Fax 516-434-3217
Ask for 12-page catalog of mathematics and science books.

Visitors approach a pair of Tsavo lions on display at The Field Museum. These very two lions killed and devoured nearly 130 workers who were building a bridge over the Tsavo River in East Africa in 1898.

Photo Courtesy of The Field Museum
© 1996 George Papadakis

JOURNAL OF CHEMICAL EDUCATION
PUBLICATIONS/SOFTWARE CATALOG
University of Wisconsin-Madison, Department of Chemistry, 1101 University Avenue, Madison, WI 53706-1396 800-991-5534 (Software) 800-691-9846 (Subscriptions) Email jcesoft@chem.wisc.edu (Software) and jce@aol.com (Subscriptions) http://jchemed.chem.wisc.edu/
Request 47-page catalog of videos, CD-ROM, Online, Multimedia, Print, Software, and Books.

CRITICAL THINKING BOOKS & SOFTWARE
P. O. Box 448, Pacific Grove, CA 93950 800-458-4849   408-393-3288   Fax 408-393-3277 Email ct@criticalthinking.com http://www.criticalthinking.com
Ask for 54-page catalog of books on thinking and teaching skills, including 6 pages specifically on science.

EXPLORATORIUM STORE
3601 Lyon St, San Francisco, CA 94123 415-561-0393
http://www.exploratorium.edu
See web page that is filled with quality science toys and books.

FACTS ON FILE, INC.
11 Penn Plaza, 15th Floor, New York, NY   10001-2006 800-678-3633   Fax 800-322-8755 http://www.factsonfile.com
Ask for 50-page science books catalog.

I.C.E.
Institute for Chemical Education, Department of Chemistry, University of Wisconsin-Madison, 1101 University Ave, Madison, WI 53706-1396 800-991-5534 608-262-3033 Fax 608-265-8094
Email ice@chem.wisc.edu   http://ice.chem.wisc.edu/ice
The Institute of Chemical Education has books and tools to help you communicate the relevance and fun of doing chemistry. Ask for 7-page catalog: Publications, Kits and More.

IDEA FACTORY, INC.
Contact Fritz Schlichting 10710 Dixon Dr, Riverview, FL 33569 800-331-6204 Fax 813-677-033
Science and math resources for all levels, K-College. Ask for 16-page resource catalog filled with books and materials containing science teaching ideas.

INTERNET
http://www.abebooks.com
Advanced Book Exchange, Inc. World's largest source of used, and out-of-print books.

INTERNET
http://www.amazon.com
New books for sale.

INTERNET
http://www.bibliofind.com
Used and out-of-print books for sale.

INTERNET
http://www.ebay.com
Trading community for books, magazines, and records.

INTERNET
http://www.interloc.com
Large selection of used and out-of-print books for sale from dealers across the country.

INTERNET
http://www.nsta.org/scistore
Educational science books and posters.

J. WESTON WALCH, PUBLISHER
321 Valley St, P. O. Box 658, Portland, ME 04104-0658   800-341-6094   Fax 207-772-3105   http://www.walch.com
Ask for 115-page catalog, includes 21 pages of math and science books. Many of these books were written by teachers for teachers.

KEY CURRICULUM PRESS - SECONDARY MATH CATALOG
Key Curriculum Press, 2512 Martin Luther King Jr. Way, P. O. Box 2304, Berkeley, CA 94702-0304 800-995-MATH Fax 800-541-2442
Ask for 68-page catalog of innovative materials in math education.

KNOLLWOOD BOOKS
Contact Lee and Peggy Price   P. O. Box 197, Oregon, WI 53575-0197 608-835-8861 Fax 680-835-8421 Email books@tdsnet.com
Knollwood Books sells new, used and rare books on science, astronomy, meteorology, space and rocketry by mail order and at book fairs. Ask for a current catalog.

LAWRENCE HALL OF SCIENCE
University of California, Berkeley, CA 94720-5200 510-642-1016   Fax 510-642-1055 Email lhsstore@uclink4.berkeley.edu http://www.lhs.berkeley.edu
See web site filled with books, teachers' and parents' guides, science kits, videos, and ordering instructions. Known as Eureka!: Teaching Tools from the Lawrence Hall of Science.

LIBRARIES UNLIMITED/ TEACHER IDEAS PRESS
Attn: Dept. 9798, P. O. Box 6633, Englewood, CO 80155-6633 800-237-6124 Fax 303-220-8843 Email lu-books@lu.com http://www.lu.com
Ask for the 70-page catalog listing reference books and teaching ideas books. Many books by this publisher are about science.

MARTINTON BOOK COMPANY
Route 1, Box 148, Martinton, IL 60951 815-486-7252 Fax 815-486-7252
Retail mail order used/rare science and math books.

NATIONAL ACADEMY PRESS
2101 Constitution Ave, NW, Lockbox 285, Washington, DC 20055 800-624-6242 202-334-3313 Fax 202-334-2451 http://www.nap.edu
Ask for this publisher's catalog. The National Academy Press was created by the National Academy of Sciences. Its 50-page catalog lists publications about science and technology under twelve different subject area categories.

NATIONAL ASSOCIATION OF BIOLOGY TEACHERS - NABT PUBLICATIONS
Contact Kathy Frame 11250 Roger Bacon Dr, #19, Reston, VA 20190-5202 800-406-075 703-471-1134 Fax 703-318-0308 Email NABTer@aol.com http://www.nabt.org
Ask for publications and membership brochure that includes Favorite Labs from Outstanding Teachers, Biology Labs that Work: The Best of How-To-Do-Its, and Careers in Biology: An Introduction.

NATIONAL COUNCIL OF TEACHERS IN MATHEMATICS (NCTM) - EDUCATIONAL MATERIALS CATALOG
National Council of Teachers in Mathematics, 1906 Association Dr, Reston, VA 22091-1593 800-235-7566 Fax 703-476-2970 Email nctm@nctm.org http://www.nctm.org Fax on demand 800-220-8483
Ask for this 50-page catalog filled with quality books on the teaching of mathematics.

NATIONAL ENERGY FOUNDATION
Contact Gary Swan 5225 Wiley Post Way, Suite 170, Salt Lake City, UT 84116 801-539-1406 Fax 801-539-1451 Email info@nef1.org http://www.nef1.org
Ask for 15-page catalog of publications and science kits. Materials include Out of the Rock, a mineral resource and mining education program for K-8 produced in conjunction with the U. S. Bureau of Mines.

NSTA MEMBERSHIP & PUBLICATIONS CATALOG
National Science Teachers Association, 1840 Wilson Blvd, Arlington, VA 22201-3000 800-722-NSTA http://www.nsta.org/scistore Published annually
Ask for this 64-page catalog. In 1998 the NSTA publications catalog listed over 200 quality books for sale for teachers as well as posters and NSTA membership information. Both parents and teachers will find this the single best source for science activity books.

ORYX PRESS
P O Box 33889, Phoenix, AZ 85067-3889 800-279-6799 Fax 800-279-4663 Email info@oryxpress.com http://www.oryxpress.com
Ask for this publisher's 62-page catalog listing information books including guide books about science and technology.

PUBLICATIONS CATALOG FOR THE TECHNOLOGY TEACHER
International Technology Education Association, 1914 Association Dr, Suite 201, Reston, VA 20191-1539 703-860-2100 Fax 703-860-0353 Email itea@iris.org http://www.iteawww.org
Ask for 35-page catalog of publications, classroom materials, videos, resources, and computer software.

REITER'S SCIENTIFIC AND PROFESSIONAL BOOKS
2021 K St. NW, Washinton, DC 20006 800-591-7894 202-223-3327 Fax 202-296-9103 Email books@reiters.com http://www.reiters.com
Browse and order from entire database at web site. Request to be placed on mailing list for Chaos!, a monthly publication about books. Ask for 90-page Reiter's Scientific & Professional Books Catalog.

SHOWBOARD
Contact Mark Oleksak P O Box 10656, Tampa, FL 33679-0656 / 2602 W De Leon, Tampa, FL 33609 800-323-9189 813-874-1828 Fax 813-876-8046 Email sales@showboard.com http://www.showboard.com
Ask for 32-page resource catalog of materials for science fair projects and for running a local science fair, including project display boards, awards & ribbons, science fair quarterly newsletter, certificates of participation, idea books, and science fair videos.

SKY PUBLISHING CORP. CATALOG
Sky Publishing Corp., 49 Bay State Rd, Cambridge, MA 02138 / Sky & Telescope, P O Box 9111, Belmont, MA 02178-9111 800-253-0245 617-864-7360 Fax 617-864-6117 Email skytel@skypub.com http://www.skypub.com Since 1941.
Ask for 32-page catalog of products for professional and amateur astronomers. Products include maps, books, videos, globes, posters, software, CD-ROMs, slide sets, star atlases, and planispheres.

THE LEARNING TEAM
84 Business Park Drive, Armonk, NY 10504 800-793-TEAM Fax 914-273-2227
http://learningteam.org
Ask for 16-page catalog. Books and multimedia, including Investigating Lake Lluka, Exploring the Nardoo, Insects, The Dynamic Rainforest, and many more.

THINKING WORKS
P. O. Box 468, St. Augustine, FL 32085-0468 800-633-3742 Fax 904-824-8505
Email thnkgwks@aug.com
Ask for 48-page catalog of books on teaching and thinking, in all subject areas including science.

UNITED STATES GOVERNMENT PRINTING OFFICE
Public Documents Distribution Center, Pueblo, CO 81009   Email cic.info@pueblo.gsa.gov (Use words "SEND INFO") http://www.pueblo.gsa.gov
Request a free catalog of current publications or visit the U. S. Government Bookstore at 401 S State, Chicago, IL 60605, 312-353-5133.

Chapter

3

Computers

Resource References

If you are interested in learning about computers, the following list of computer information sources will be very helpful.

BOARDWATCH MAGAZINE: GUIDE TO ELECTRONIC BULLETIN BOARDS AND THE INTERNET

8500 W Bowles Ave, Suite 210, Littleton, CO   80123   800-933-6038 http://www.boardwatch.com Monthly $ 36.00 per year. $ 5.95 per issue.
This 150-page magazine covers current news about linking to electronic bulletin boards and the Internet. Available at retail stores selling magazines.

CHICAGO COMPUTER GUIDE

954 W Washington, Suite 510, Chicago, IL   60607 312-432-1662   Email ccg@ais.net Monthly $ 19.95 per year.
Chicagoland's business computer newspaper. Complimentary copies available at some local computer stores. Carries news stories and local advertising of computer stores.

CITY COLLEGES OF CHICAGO

Daley College 312-838-7500, Dawson Technical Institute 312-451-2000, Kennedy-King College 312-602-5000, Lakeview Learning Center 312-907-4400, Malcom X College 312-850-7000, Olive-Harvey College 312-568-3700, South Chicago Learning Center 312-291-6770, Truman College 312-878-1700, Washington College 312-553-5600, West Side Learning Center 312-850-7420, Wright College-North 312-777-7900, Wright College-South 312-481-8000. http://www.ccc.edu

Courses on computer training are available at most sites of the City Colleges of Chicago and at many community colleges in suburban areas. Inquire about current courses being offered usually at very reasonable fees.

COMPUTER CHRONICLES

2410 Charleston Rd, Mountain View, CA 94043 http://www.cmptv.com Program tapes $ 19.95 each, 888-310-2850

This television program is broadcast on WYCC/Chicago Channel 20 and summarizes current advances in personal computers and software.

EDUCATORS GUIDE TO FREE COMPUTER MATERIALS

15th Edition Contact Kathy Nehmer Educators Progress Service, Inc., 214 Center St, Randolph, WI 53956-1497 888-951-4469 920-326-3126 Fax 920-326-3127 1997 373 pages $ 38.95

This book lists and describes free computer materials available to educators. Revised annually.

I.C.E. CUBE

Computer Update Bulletin for Educators (CUBE), Illinois Computing Educators (ICE), 8548 145th St, Orland Park, IL 60462-2839 847-940-7132 http://www.iceberg.org Bimonthly $ 25.00 per year, includes membership.

This organization focuses on utilizing computer technology in the classroom. This newsletter includes information about computer bulletin boards, information on grants, reviews of software, announcements about meeting where public domain software is traded.

LEARNING AND LEADING WITH TECHNOLOGY

Contact Anita Best International Society for Technology in Education, 1787 Agate St, Eugene, OR 97403-1923 800-336-5191 541-346-4414 Fax 541-346-5890 Email anita_best@ccmail.uoregon.edu http://www.iste.org/publish/learning

This professional organization is dedicated to the improvement of all levels of education through the use of computer-based technology.

MACWORLD

Macworld Communications, P O Box 54529, Boulder, CO 80322 800-288-6848

http://www.macworld.com Monthly Single issue $ 7.00. $ 30.00 per year.
This 250-page magazine is dedicated to Apple computers. Macworld is a publication of Macworld Communications and is an independent journal not affiliated with Apple Computer, Inc.

MEDIA AND METHODS MAGAZINE

Contact Michele Sokoloff 1429 Walnut St, Philadelphia, PA 19102 800-555-5657 215-563-6005 Fax 215-587-9706 Email michelesok@aol.com
http://www.media-methods.com 5 issues per year. $ 33.50 per year.
The nation's magazine devoted to the practical applications of instructional technologies. For K-12 librarians, media specialists, teachers, computer coordinators, technology directors, curriculum chairpersons, and administrators. For those who influence the practical uses of multimedia tools, computers, CD-ROM, CD-I, presentation equipment, and library automation tools.

NEW TECHNOLOGIES FOR EDUCATION: A BEGINNER'S GUIDE

Third Edition by Barron and Orwig Libraries Unlimited, Inc., P. O. Box 6633, Englewood, CO 80155-6633 800-237-6124 Fax 303-220-8843
Email lu-books@lu.com http://www.lu.com 1997 295 pages $ 32.50
Updated look at the technologies that are profoundly affecting education, including LANs, the Internet, and multimedia. Try to find this book at the reference desk of your library.

NSTA SCIENCE EDUCATION SUPPLIERS

A Supplement to: Science & Children, Science Scope, and The Science Teacher, National Science Teachers Association, 1840 Wilson Blvd, Arlington, VA 22201-3000 800-722-NSTA http://www.nsta.org Published annually. 165 pages $ 5.00 per copy.
List of science educational software developers and distributors. The most current and comprehensive list of manufacturers, publishers and distributors of science education materials. See Computers/Software. In 1998, 181 distributors of computers and software were listed.

PC MAGAZINE: THE INDEPENDENT GUIDE TO PERSONAL COMPUTING

Ziff-Davis Publishing Company, L.P., One Park Ave, New York, NY 10016-5802 800-335-1195 212-503-3500 Fax 212-503-5335 Bimonthly Single copy $ 3.95. $ 49.97 per year.
This 400-page magazine is dedicated to all aspects of personal computing. Available where magazines are sold.

PC WORLD
Contact Luis Camus PC World Communications, Inc., 501 Second St, # 600, San Francisco, CA 94107 415-243-0500 Fax 415-442-1891
Email Luis_Camus@pcworld.com http://www.pcworld.com Monthly Single issue $ 3.95. $ 29.90 per year.
This 350-page magazine is dedicated to news about new products for computer needs and includes numerous reviews and resources.

SCIENCE & TECHNOLOGY INFORMATION SYSTEM (STIS)
National Science Foundation, 4201 Wilson Blvd, Washington, DC 22230 Voice 703-306-0214, Modem 7E1F 703-306-0212 or 703-306-0213
STIS is an electronic dissemination system that provides fast, easy access to NSF publications. There is no cost to you except for possible long-distance phone charges. The service is available 24 hours a day. Science education programs receive funding through the Division of Undergraduate Education, Directorate for Education and Human Resources, National Science Foundation.

SCIENCE ON THE WEB
by Edward J Renehan, Jr. Springer-Verlag New York, Inc., P O Box 2485, Secaucus, NJ 07096-2485 800-SPRINGER Fax 201-348-4505 Email sales@springer-ny.com 1996 382 pages $ 19.95
A connoisseur's guide to over 500 fun web sites.

T.H.E. JOURNAL (TECHNOLOGY IN EDUCATION JOURNAL)
Circulation Department, T.H.E. Journal, 150 El Camino Real, Suite 112, Tusin, CA 92680-3670
Request application for free subscription.

TECHNOLOGY AND CHILDREN
International Technology Education Association, 1914 Association Dr, Suite 201, Reston, VA 20191-1539 703-860-2100 Fax 703-860-0353 Email itea@iris.org http://www.iteawww.org Quarterly $ 40 per year.
Each issue is packed with practical, innovative, and creative articles and activities for the elementary teacher.

THE TECHNOLOGY TEACHER
International Technology Education Association, 1914 Association Dr, Suite 201, Reston, VA 20191-1539 703-860-2100 Fax 703-860-0353 Email itea@iris.org http://www.iteawww.org Monthly $ 65 per year.
Each issue provides ideas for the classroom, project activities, resources in technology, and current trends in technology education.

Science on the Internet

These Internet web sites, recommended by teachers as fun sources for both students and teachers, provide hours of science education activity.

ALFRED UNIVERSITY
http://nyscc.alfred.edu/college/summerinst/
Alfred University Summer Institute page with Slime Lab, the art of goop, sludge, and guk-making, complete with recipes.

ASK AN EXPERT
http://www.askanexpert.com/askanexpert/
PITSCO's web page is a directory of links to people who have volunteered their time to answer questions and provide webpages that provide information.

BEAKMAN'S WORLD
http://www.youcan.com
Beakman & Jax' web site with answers to questions, interactive demos, space photos, and more.

BIG PAGE OF INTERNET PROJECTS
http://www.mts.net/%7Ejgreenco/internet.html
Web page with classroom Internet projects.

BILL NYE THE SCIENCE GUY
http://nyelabs.kcts.org
Bill Nye the Science Guy's web site.

BROODING FROGS
http://www.csu.edu.au/faculty/commerce/account/frogs/brooding.htm
Web page of extinct(?) Gastric Brooding Frogs that lived primarily in water.

CHICAGO ACADEMY OF SCIENCES
http://www.caosclub.org
Home page of the Education Department of the Chicago Academy of Sciences.

CHICAGO PUBLIC SCHOOLS
http://www.cps.k12.il.us
Home page of the Chicago Public Schools K-12.

CITY COLLEGES OF CHICAGO
http://www.ccc.edu
Home page of the City Colleges of Chicago.

DRAGON FLY
http://www.muohio.edu/Dragonfly
The children's science magazine, Dragonfly, by the National Science Teacher's Association.

EARTHRISE
http://earthrise.sdsc.edu
Web site with many photos of Earth from space. These photos were taken by astronauts out the windows of the Space Shuttle.

ENVIRONMENTAL PROTECTION AGENCY
http://www.epa.gov/epaoswer/osw/kids.htm
Kids page from the Environmental Protection Agency.

EXPLORATORIUM
http://www.exploratorium.edu
Web site of the Exploratorium museum in San Francisco. Includes events, Exploratorium store, publications, programs, membership information, and more.

THE FIELD MUSEUM
http://www.fmnh.org
The Field Museum of Natural History in Chicago.

FOREFRONT CURRICULUM
http://www.4forefront.com/scimath.html
Forefront Curriculum's links to best web sites for the science and mathematics classroom.

FROGGY PAGE
http://frog.simplenet.com/froggy/
The Froggy Page is home to all kinds of frogginess, from the silly to the scientific.

THE GLOBE PROGRAM
http://www.globe.gov
Worldwide network of students, teachers, and scientists working together to study and understand global environment.

Students interacting with radio communications console at the Motorola Museum. This exhibit demonstrates the effectiveness of two-way communication between people on the move.

Photo Courtesy of the Motorola Museum

46 Science Fun in Chicagoland

HIGH SCHOOL CHEMISTRY
http://home.ptd.net/%7Eswenger/
Over 250 links to web sites for use in high school chemistry by Samuel E. Wenger.

INVENTING
http://mustang.coled.umn.edu/inventing/inventing.html
Web site on famous inventors where you learn more about inventing, including links to other web sites.

MAD SCIENTISTS NETWORK
http://medinfo.wustl.edu/%7Eysp/MSN/
Mad Scientists Network with Ask-A-Scientist. Scientists give answers to questions.

MARINE TURTLES
http://www.turtles.org
Web site about marine turtles and their survival.

MENDEL WEB
http://www.netspace.org/MendelWeb/
Mendel Web is an educational resource for teachers and students interested in the origins of classical genetics, introductory data analysis, elementary plant science, and the history and literature of science. University of Washington at Seattle and Brown University.

MINERALS MANAGEMENT SERVICE
http://www.mms.gov
Web page of Minerals Management Service.

NASA CORE
http://spacelink.nasa.gov/CORE/
Central Operation of Resources for Educators (CORE) is a national distribution center for NASA's audiovisual educational materials.

NASA INFORMATION MANAGEMENT SYSTEM
http://harp.gsfc.nasa.gov/v0ims/
Gateway to over 700 free Earth science data products and services.

NASA MARS PATHFINDER
http://entertainment.digital.com/mars/JPL/default.html
Images, science results, rover operations, engineering data and more about Mars expeditions.

NASA SHUTTLE IMPROVEMENT
http://quest.arc.nasa.gov/shuttle/events/improve/index.html
Students improve the Shuttle. An activity that challenges students to improve the Shuttle. NASA experts provide feedback.

NASA STARDUST
http://stardust.jpl.nasa.gov
Stardust plans to fly by comet Wild 2, and bring back samples of cometary material in January, 2004.

NASA STELLAR PROGRAM
http://stellar.arc.nasa.gov/stellar/
The Stellar Program is dedicated to all aspects of living in space.

NASA'S GODDARD SPACE FLIGHT CENTER
http://www.gsfc.nasa.gov
NASA's web site for the Goddard Space Flight Center.

NASA'S LEARNING TECHNOLOGIES PROJECT
http://learn.ivv.nasa.gov
The Learning Technologies Project uses the Internet to bring NASA technology to your classroom with more than 50 unique projects.

NATIONAL AUDUBON SOCIETY
http://www.audubon.org
National Audubon Society's home web site.

NATIONAL GEOGRAPHIC
http://www.nationalgeographic.com
National Geographic's home page.
See http://www.nationalgeographic.com/kids/index.html for kids page.

NATIONAL INSTITUTES OF HEALTH
http://science-education.nih.gov
Web site of the Office of Science Education at the National Institutes of Health.

NATIONAL OCEANIC AND ATMOSPHERIC ADMINISTRATION
http://www.noaa.gov
Home page of the National Oceanic and Atmospheric Administration. Programs include Adopt the Coast Action Kit, Weather Education, Teacher at Sea Program, Sea Grant Teacher Resources, Endangered & Threatened Marine Mammals, and Activities Using Research Data.

NATURAL HISTORY OF GENES
http://raven.umnh.utah.edu/
Natural History of Genes includes activities, experiments, and low-cost equipment. University of Utah School of Medicine.

NCREL PATHWAYS TO SCHOOL IMPROVEMENT
http://www.ncrel.org/pathways.htm
Pathways to School Improvement covers a range of educational issues, including math, science, technology, and assessment, with an overview of the latest research examples from classrooms, and links to other Web sites. North Central Regional Educational Laboratory, 1900 Spring Road, Suite 300, Oak Brook, IL 60523-1480 630-571-4700 800-356-2735

POTTER'S SCIENCE GEMS
http://www-sci.lib.uci.edu/SEP/SEP.html
Frank Potter's Science Gems web site by Frank Potter and Jim Martindale. Over 3000 selected resources.

PROJECT 2061
http://project2061.aaas.org
AAAS' web site for Project 2061 on reforming science education.

PUBLIC BROADCASTING SYSTEM
http://www.pbs.org
Public Broadcasting System (PBS) home page describing products and current television series.

RAINFOREST ACTION NETWORK
http://www.ran.org/ran/
Rainforest Action Network's web site with current information and science links.

RESOURCE DESK
http://www.realkids.com/tools.shtml
The Resource Desk's web site with links to many sites including science teachers lounge.

SCIENCE CENTRAL
http://www.scicentral.com
Award winning web site with science news, information, links, and more.

SCIENCE NETLINKS
http://www.sciencenetlinks.com
Designed specifically for teachers, parents, and librarians, Science Netlinks is a detailed

guide to the best science resources on the Internet. This on-line resource for science educators is a combined effort of the American Association for the Advancement of Science and MCI.

SCIENTIFIC AMERICAN
http://www.sciam.com
Scientific American's web site.

SPACE DAY
http://www.spaceday.com
Space day is celebrated each year in May.

TWINKIES PROJECT
http://www.owlnet.rice.edu/~gouge/twinkies.html
The T.W.I.N.K.I.E.S. Project. A series of fun experiments conducted and designed to determine the properties of that incredible food, the Twinkie.

U S GEOLOGICAL SURVEY
http://www.usgs.gov   http://www.nbs.gov
http://geology.usgus.gov   http://mapping.usgs.gov   and   http://water.usgs.gov
U. S. Geological Survey home pages.

WEB66
http://web66.coled.umn.edu/
Web66: A K12 World Wide Web Project by Stephen E. Collins. Click on "Science" for school site list, or type http://web66.coled.umn.edu/Schools/Lists/Science.html. University of Minnesota.

Education and the Computer

Here you will find several interesting educational applications, groups, and opportunities that use computers in science education.

AURBACH & ASSOCIATES, INC.
8233 Tulane Ave, St. Louis, MO 63132-5019 800-77G-RADY
http://www.aurbach.com
Offers the Grady student portfolio assessment program for the Macintosh. Ask for a free demonstration disk.

CAOS CLUB
The Chicago Academy of Sciences, Administrative Headquarters, 2060 N Clark St, Chicago, IL 60614 773-549-0606 Fax 773-549-5199 http://www.caosclub.org
CAoS Club, a distance-learning Internet service, provides teachers and students with relevant, fun science learning. Live science demonstrations and workshops broadcast over the Web, standards-based lesson plans, activities, curricular resources, and more are available to members.

CHANGING PERSPECTIVES
North Central Regional Educational Laboratory (NCREL), 1900 Spring Rd, Suite 300, Oak Brook, IL 60523-1480 630-571-4700 800-356-2735
This multimedia resource promotes systemic change and improvement in math and science education by challenging preconceived notions and allowing users to track their progress in a variety of areas. Multimedia: audio, video, CD-ROM, and print.

EDUCATIONAL NETWORKING CONSORTIUM (ENC)
Division of Educational Programs, Argonne National Laboratory, 9700 S Cass Ave, Argonne, IL 60439 630-252-5448 http://www.enc.k12.il.us
The Educational Networking Consortium (ENC) was formed in 1994 to provide low-cost dial-up access to the Internet for K-12 educators both at home and at school. The ENC is a collaboration of 22 dial-in access sites (school districts, ROEs, and other institutions) that provide full Internet access to the Chicago area. Using this low-cost access model, 7000 educators have gained quality access so they can learn to use the Internet at the highest possible rate. An account can be requested through Argonne or through a local trainer for about $ 5.00 per month. A CD installer is available to quick-connect new users.

THE GUIDE TO MATH & SCIENCE REFORM - AN INTERACTIVE RESOURCE FOR THE EDUCATION COMMUNITY
The Annenberg/CPB Math and Science Project, 901 E Street, NW, Washington, DC 20004   Publication office: Toby Levine Communications, Inc., 7910 Woodmont Ave, Suite 1304, Bethesda, MD 20814 301-907-6510
Available in Macintosh and MS-DOS/Windows, this guide is an interactive computer data base of resources for the education community.

ILLINOIS COMPUTING EDUCATORS (ICE)
Affiliate of International Society for Technology in Education, c/o Frada Boxer, 650 Appletree Lane, Deerfield, IL 60015 847-940-7132 Email frada@iceberg.org http://www.iceberg.org General membership $ 35.00 per year.
Membership includes programs, meetings, newsletter, network for resources, and Public Domain software. Various chapters of this organization meet in the Chicagoland area. Request a membership application.

LAP TOP COMPUTER EDUCATION
Contact Mary Charles Loyola University Chicago, 1041 Ridge Rd, Wilmette, IL 60091 847-853-3342 (Elementary School through High School)
Chicago area schools without computers can have lap top computers brought to their classroom for a fun hands-on introduction to computers.

LEON M. LEDERMAN SCIENCE EDUCATION CENTER - EISENHOWER NATIONAL CLEARINGHOUSE DEMONSTRATION SITE
Fermi National Accelerator Laboratory, P. O. Box 500 MS 777, Batavia, IL 60510-0500 630-840-8258 http://www.enc.org
At this science education center the visitor may preview the Internet, science education computer bulletin boards, and see multimedia materials. The Teacher Resource Center is a demonstration site for mathematics and science materials in the North Central Regional Educational Laboratory for the Eisenhower National Clearinghouse. Phone for an appointment.

NEWTON BBS
Division of Educational Programs DEP/223, Argonne National Laboratory, 9700 S Cass Ave, Argonne, IL 60439 630-252-6925, Telnet newton.dep.anl.gov, Modem 8N1F 630-252-8241, http://www.newton.dep.anl.gov
An electronic bulletin board system created for the expressed purpose of serving math, science and computer educators and their students. Six features of NEWTON include: 1) Ask A Scientist Service -- seven thousand (7000) math, science and computer questions have been addressed and can be found on the web (http://www.newton.dep.anl.gov) or by searching NEWTON BBS. 2) Discussion Forums -- NEWTON supports 53 forums for specific topics of discussion for education as well as a variety of other interests. 3) Web Server -- NEWTON BBS doubles as a web server. Teacher designed web pages for classroom activities are posted and available to all users at http://www.newton.dep.anl.gov. 4) Web Site -- Ask A Scientist Archives and the Cook County Forest Preserve District (Illinois) Nature Bulletins are available on line at http://www.newton.dep.anl.gov. 5) FTP Site -- NEWTON BBS offers data and freeware exchange with over 3000 downloads during an 18 month period. 6) Homework Help and Mentoring -- on-line homework help is available for students using live chat or by dropping notes for reply.

PHYSICS INFOMALL
The Learning Team, 84 Business Park Drive, Armonk, NY 10504 800-793-TEAM Fax 914-273-2227 http://learningteam.org $ 295.00
CD-ROM with a very large collection of physics resources.

POWERLAB STUDIOS, INC.
**616 Ramona Street, Suite 20, Palo Alto, CA 94301 800-843-8769 415-614-0900
Fax 415-614-0909   Email info@powerlab.com   http://www.powerlab.com
Manufacturer (Elementary School)**
Ask for brochure. PowerLab Electricity, a fully integrated curricular unit featuring multimedia software for grades 3 - 6.

PRODIGY
**Prodigy Services Company, 455 Hamilton Ave, H8B, White Plains, NY 10601
800-PRODIGY 800-776-3449, ext 176 http://www.prodigy.com**
Ask for information brochure about the Classroom Prodigy Offer offering teleconnecting a classroom. Includes one flat annual fee, the Internet E-mail, Internet Digest, bulletin boards, teacher's manual with lesson plans, projects that link up with classrooms all over the country.

TECHNOLOGY AND LEARNING
Available from the International Society for Technology in Education, 1787 Agate St, Eugene, OR 97403-1923 800-336-5191 541-346-4414 http://www.iste.org
This professional organization, ISTE, is dedicated to the improvement of all levels of education through the use of computer-based technology. This magazine is about technology in the classroom.

Chicago Area Suppliers of Hardware and Software

These retail stores compiled from computer educators' recommendations help you when shopping for your computer needs.

BEST BUY
(See your telephone directory for store locations.)
Retail source for both hardware and software. Inquire about software training classes.

CHICAGO COMPUTER EXCHANGE
**5225 S Harper Ave (Lower Level of Harper Court Shopping Center), Chicago, IL 60615 773-667-5221 Fax 773-667-6145 Email ccex@ripco.com
http://www.ccexhange.com**
For hardware needs this store buys and sells new or used computers, parts, and peripherals.

CIRCUIT CITY
(See your telephone directory for store locations.)
Retail source for both hardware and software.

COMPUSA
(See your telephone directory for store locations.)
Retail source for both hardware and software. Ask to be placed on mailing list.

COMPUTER DISCOUNT WAREHOUSE
(See your telephone directory for store locations.)
Retail source for both hardware and software. Ask to be placed on mailing list.

EGG HEAD SOFTWARE
(See your telephone directory for store locations.)
Retail source for computer software.

GEOBOOK
Contact Steve Turner Roselle, IL 800-252-2768 Email sturner@brother.com
Ask for brochure. GeoBooks is a low cost computer system by Brother International
Corporation. Includes Internet, Email, word processing, spreadsheet, file manager,
address book, and more.

MICRO CENTER
**2645 N Elston Ave, Chicago, IL 60647 773-292-1700 or 1100 Steelwood Rd,
Columbus, OH 43212 800-634-3478 http://www.microcenter.com**
This retail outlet in Chicago has competitive prices on computers, printers, multimedia
needs, and FAX machines.

MONTGOMERY WARDS ELECTRIC AVENUE
(See your telephone directory for store locations.)
Retail source for both hardware and software.

OFFICE DEPOT
(See your telephone directory for store locations.)
Retail source for both hardware and software.

OFFICEMAX
(See your telephone directory for store locations.)
Retail source for both hardware and software.

SEARS ROEBUCK AND CO.
(See your telephone directory for store locations.)
Retail source for both hardware and software.

Mail Order Suppliers

Computer educators recommended these mail order opportunities.

108 YEARS OF NATIONAL GEOGRAPHIC ON CD-ROM
National Geographic Society Member Catalog, 1145 17th Street, NW, Washington, DC 20036-4688 Orders: P O Box 400401, Des Moines, IA 50340-0401 888-225-5647 Fax 515-362-3345 $ 199.95
Ask for 24-page catalog. Gift catalog includes numerous National Geographic Videos, CD-ROMs, and gift items.

ACE SOFTWARE EXPRESS
666 Anderson Ave, Suite # 3, Cliffside Park, NJ 07010 800-377-9943 201-941-4949 Fax 201-941-5154 http://www.ace-soft.com
Ask for catalog of this software distributor. Significant discounts to students, teachers, and schools on latest versions of major software and CD-ROMS's.

ADAM SOFTWARE, INC.
Contact Alison Derreberry 1600 Riveredge Pkwy, Suite 800, Atlanta, GA 30328 800-755-2326, ext 3044 Fax 770-988-0611 Email aderreberry@adam.com http://www.adam.com
Ask for information about the Animated Dissection of Anatomy for Medicine scholar series. This multimedia application helps classrooms discover anatomy with dissections via computer.

AIMS MULTIMEDIA
9710 DeSoto Ave, Chatsworth, CA 91311 800-367-2467 Fax 818-341-6700 Email info@aims-multimedia.com http://www.aims-multimedia.com
Ask for 58-page Educational Technology Catalog. Distributor of video, CD-ROMs, Laserdisc, and teaching modules.

AMERICAN ASSOCIATION OF PHYSICS TEACHERS - AAPT PRODUCTS CATALOG
American Association of Physics Teachers, One Physics Ellipse, College Park, MD 20740-3845 301-209-3300 Fax 301-209-0845 Email aapt-memb@aapt.org http://www.aapt.org
Ask for this 28-page catalog. The 1997-98 catalog lists 85 books on physics and physics education. It also offers Physics of Technology Modules, computer software, videodiscs, videotapes, materials for teachers, gift items, workshop materials, and posters.

APPLE DIRECT - EDUCATOR ADVANTAGE PROGRAM
P. O. Box 3016, Lakewood, NJ 08701 800-959-APPL

Ask for price lists for software and computers at a significant educator discount. This program is not on Apple's web site http://www.apple.com/education/

APS TECHNOLOGIES
6131 Deramus, P O Box 4987, Kansas City, MO 64120-0087 800-374-5688 Fax 816-483-3077 Email sales@apstech.com http://www.apstech.com
Ask for 38-page catalog. Computer systems, drives, supplies and accessories.

ASSOCIATED MICROSCOPE, INC.
P O Box 1076, Elon College, NC 27244 800-476-3893 Fax 336-578-3897 http://www.assocmicroscope.com Distributor (High School)
Ask for brochure. Distributor of scientific software, including Rocks and Minerals, ScienceWorks, Computer Dissection, Ideal Gas, Circuits, Universal Gravitation, Optics, Gravity, Discover the Elements, All About Weather, and Everglades Journey. Also distributes balances, spectrophotometers, cameras and microscopes.

BELEW SPRUCE SOFTWARE
**806 Buchanan Blvd, # 115-164, Boulder City, NV 89005 702-565-8614 Email stargazer@belewspruce.com http://www.belewspruce.com
Manufacturer Distributor (High School)**
Ask for brochure. Star Gazer interactive educational astronomy software lets you discover your universe.

BRODERBUND SOFTWARE
500 Redwood Blvd, Novato, CA 94948 800-521-6263 415-382-4400 http://www.broderbund.com
Ask for catalog of this major software distributor. Source of "Where in the World is Carmen Sandiego?," and interactive, animated stories for children.

CARINA SOFTWARE
12919 Alcosta Blvd, Suite # 7, San Ramon, CA 94583 800-493-8555 510-355-1266 Fax 510-355-1268 http://www.carnasoft.com Manufacturer Distributor (High School)
Ask for brochure. Voyager II, Dynamic Sky Simulator; and SkyGazer software.

JOURNAL OF CHEMICAL EDUCATION - PUBLICATIONS/SOFTWARE CATALOG
University of Wisconsin-Madison, Department of Chemistry, 1101 University Avenue, Madison, WI 53706-1396 800-991-5534 (Software) 800-691-9846 (Subscriptions) Email jcesoft@chem.wisc.edu (Software) and jce@aol.com (Subscriptions) http://jchemed.chem.wisc.edu/
Request 47-page catalog of videos, CD-ROM, Online, Multimedia, Print, Software, and Books.

56 Science Fun in Chicagoland

CLASSROOM CONNECT
431 Madrid Ave, Torrance, CA 90501-1430 800-638-1639
http://www.classroom.com
Ask for 52-page catalog. Materials and guides for using the Internet in the classroom.

COMPUSA DIRECT
34 St. Martin Dr, Marlborough, MA 01752 800-215-8759
http://www.compusa.com
Ask for catalog. Retail mail order computer supplies.

COMPUTER CITY KIDS
800-538-0586
For more information on Education Sales Programs call 800-538-0586.

COMPUTER FRIENDLY STUFF, INC
Contact William Martens   312 N May St, Suite 4A, Chicago, IL   60607
888-FUN-BUGS 312-491-0424 Fax 312-491-0136
Email wmartens@computerbug.com   http://www.computerbug.com
Manufacturer Retail Mail Order (High School to Adult)
This computer screen saver, Monitor Morphs, is a face that comes on a CD-ROM and with movable arms that attach to the sides of a computer screen. A ten-inch plush computer bug, Computer Bug, is also available.

CUBIC SCIENCE, INC.
Educational Software Developer, 19433 E Walnut Drive South, City of Industry, CA 91748 800-383-6363 909-589-3277 Fax 909-598-3266
Email hrant@cubicsci.com   http://www.cubicsci.com
Manufacturer Distributor (High School)
Ask for brochure. The Virtual Physics CD-ROM Series with interactive 3-D experiments.

CYBER ED INC.
P. O. Box 3037, Paradise, CA 95967-3037 888-318-0700 Fax 530-872-2445
Email cybered@cyber-ed.com   http://www.cyber-ed.com   Distributor
Manufacturer
Ask for 18-page catalog. Multimedia biology courseware.

DAVIDSON & ASSOCIATES
P. O. Box 2961, Torrance, CA 90509 800-545-7677
Ask for 50-page School Catalog listing a variety of educational software, CD-ROM's, and teacher support materials.

Students enjoy hands-on exhibits and a technology classroom at the Leon M. Lederman Science Center near Fermilab. Teachers as well as students learn new ideas at this facility.

Photo Courtesy of Lederman Science Center

DEMCO
P. O. Box 7488, Madison, WI 53791-9955 800-356-1200 http://www.demco.com
Ask for 800-page school supply catalog that contains 32 pages of computer supplies for education.

DTP DIRECT
5198 W 76th St, Edina, MN 55439 800-311-7385 Fax 612-832-0052
http://www.dtpdirect.com
Ask for 74-page catalog. Retail mail order computer supplies.

EDMARK

An IBM Company, P. O. Box 97021, Redmond, WA 98073-9721 800-362-2890
http://www.edmark.com Manufacturer Distributor (Elementary School)
Ask for 120-page catalog. Software for all areas, including science.

EDUCATIONAL ACTIVITIES, INC.

Contact Alan Stern P. O. Box 392, Freeport, NY 11520 800-645-3739
516-223-4666 Fax 516-623-9282 Email learn@edact.com http://www.edact.com
Ask for science brochure including software, videos, and CD-ROMs.

EDUCATIONAL RESOURCES

1550 Executive Dr, Elgin, IL 60123 800-624-2926 http://www.edresources.com
Ask for catalog of this software distributor.

EDUCORP

7434 Trade St, San Diego, CA 92121 800-843-9497 http://www.educorp.com
Ask for catalog of this software distributor.

THE EDUTAINMENT CATALOG

5345 Arapahoe Ave, Suite #2, Boulder, CO 80303 800-338-3844
http://www.edutainco.com
Ask for 48-page catalog of educational software for children K-12, including DOS,
Windows, Apple, and Mac formats listed for disc and CD-ROM.

EGGHEAD COMPUTER

22705 E Mission, Liberty Lake, WA 99109-8553 800-EGGHEAD
http://www.egghead.com
Ask for 40-page catalog. Retail mail-order computer software.

FALCON SOFTWARE, INC.

One Hollis St, Suite 310, Wellesley, MA 02181 781-235-7026 Fax 781-235-1767
Email FalconInfo@falconsoftware.com http://www.falconsoftware.com
Ask for 12-page catalog. Software on general chemistry, organic chemistry,
environmental science, and electronics.

GATEWAY

800-424-1390 http://www.gateway.com/smbus
Formerly Gateway 2000, this company is a major mail order supplier of home computer
hardware.

INTERACTIVE PHYSICS
Knowledge Revolution, Prentice-Hall, Inc., Englewood Cliffs, NJ 07632 1995
http://www.prenhall.com
This interactive physics software with manual for students creates visual motion images and graphical analysis as the student selects the physical setting and parameters. This computer software has become the standard for modeling the physical world on the computer.

INTERNATIONAL SOCIETY FOR TECHNOLOGY IN EDUCATION
Contact Maia Howes 1787 Agate St, Eugene, OR 97403-1923 800-336-5191
541-346-4414 Fax 541-346-5890 Email ISTE@oregon.uoregon.edu
http://www.iste.org
This professional organization is dedicated to the improvement of all levels of education through the use of computer-based technology. Ask for a copy of ISTE's 50-page publications catalog offering special journals, books on computers in education, and educational software for educators and the classroom.

KNOWLEDGE REVOLUTION
66 Bovet Road, Suite 200, San Mateo, CA 94402 800-766-6615 415-574-7777 Fax
415-574-7541 http://www.krev.com
Ask for catalog. Innovative software applications for science education. Inquire about different products available.

LEARNING SERVICES
Contact Natalie Yarwood at nataliey@ls.learnserv.com P. O. Box 10636, Eugene, OR 97440-2636 800-877-9378, ext 107 (West) ...or Chelmsford, MA, 800-877-3278 (East) 541-744-0883, ext 107 Fax 541-744-2056 http://www.learnserv.com
Distributor of educational software, including Broderbund, Davidson, The Learning Company, Adobe, Roger Wagner, Optimum Resource, Microsoft, Visions, DK Multimedia, and many more.

MAC WAREHOUSE
1720 Oak St, P O Box 3013, Lakewood, NJ 08701 800-642-1297
http://www.warehouse.com
Ask for 146-page catalog. MacIntosch computer supplies.

MACCONNECTION
528 Route 13 South, Milford, NH 06055 800-800-2222
http://www.macconnection.com
Ask for catalog. Retail mail order computer supplies for the MacIntosch. See PC Connection.

MICRO CENTER

1100 Steelwood Rd, Columbus, OH 43212 800-634-3478
http://www.microcenter.com
Ask for 40-page catalog. This mail order retail distributor has competitive prices on computers, printers, multimedia needs, and FAX machines.

MICROSOFT PRESS

One Microsoft Way, Redmond, WA 98052-6399 800-MSPRESS
http://mspress.microsoft.com
Ask for 48-page catalog.

MICROWAREHOUSE

1720 Oak St, P O Box 3014, Lakewood, NJ 08701-5926 800-367-7080
http://www.warehouse.com
Ask for 186-page catalog. Retail mail order computer supplies.

MIDWEST VISUAL

6500 N Hamlin, Chicago, IL 60645 800-876-8298 847-673-4525 Fax 847-673-4528
Email thompsone@midwestvisual.com http://www.midwestvisual.com
Ask for 78-page catalog. This distributor of audiovisual and computer supplies sells software at an educator discount.

NSTA MEMBERSHIP & PUBLICATIONS CATALOG

National Science Teachers Association, 1840 Wilson Blvd, Arlington, VA 22201-3000 800-722-NSTA http://www.nsta.org/scistore Published annually
Ask for this 64-page catalog. In 1998 the NSTA publications catalog listed 14 CD-ROMs, including InventorLabs, Net-Lessons: Web-Based Projects for Your Classroom, Resources for Science Literacy: Professional Development, and What's the Secret from Newton's Apple.

PC CONNECTION

528 Route 13 South, Milford, NH 06055 800-800-5555
http://www.pcconnection.com
Ask for catalog. Retail mail order computer supplies. PC World Best Mail-Order Company Award. Secured on-line web site ordering. See MAC Connection.

PC MALL

2645 Maricopa St, Torrance, CA 60503-5144 800-555-MALL
http://www.pcmall.com
Ask for 92-page catalog. Retail mail order computer supplies.

PHYSICS ACADEMIC SOFTWARE
North Carolina State University, Box 8202, Department of Physics, Raleigh, NC 27695-8202 800-955-8275 919-515-7447 Fax 919-515-2682 Email pas@aip.org http://www.aip.org/pas/
Ask for 26-page catalog. Computer software for the physics classroom. American Institute of Physics (AIP).

PHYSICS CURRICULUM & INSTRUCTION
22585 Woodhill Dr, Lakeville, MN 55044 612-461-3470 Fax 612-461-3467
Ask for 18-page catalog of physics demonstrations and concepts on videocassette and laserdisc, as well as computer software.

PUBLICATIONS CATALOG FOR THE TECHNOLOGY TEACHER
International Technology Education Association, 1914 Association Dr, Suite 201, Reston, VA 20191-1539 703-860-2100 Fax 703-860-0353 Email itea@iris.org http://www.iteawww.org
Ask for 35-page catalog of publications, classroom materials, videos, resources, and computer software.

SCHOLASTIC SOFTWARE
P. O. Box 7502, 2391 E McCarty St, Jefferson City, MO 65102 800-541-5513 http://www.scholastic.com
Ask for catalog of this software distributor.

SCIENCE HELPER K-8 CD-ROM
Contact Dimitri Zafiriadis The Learning Team, 84 Business Park Dr, Suite 307, Armonk, NY 10504 800-793-TEAM 914-273-2226 Fax 914-273-2227 Email learningtm@aol.com http://www.learningteam.com $ 195.00
At the touch of a button, a teacher can have access to 919 lesson plans that includes 2000 activities. Developed at the University of Florida under the direction of Dr. Mary Budd Rowe, this resource lists curriculum materials developed and tested over a 15-year period with millions of dollars in funding from the National Science Foundation.

SCIENCE T.R.E.E.
North Central Regional Educational Laboratory (NCREL), 1900 Spring Rd, Suite 300, Oak Brook, IL 60523-1480 630-571-4700 800-356-2735
A standards-based CD-ROM for elementary science teachers that helps users plan individual units or an entire curriculum.

SCITECH ACADEMIC SOLUTIONS
SciTech International, Inc., 2525 N Elston Ave, Chicago IL   60647-9939
800-290-6057 Fax 773-486-9234 http://www.scitechint.com
Ask for 60-page catalog. Computing tools for science, engineering, research, and education.

SKY PUBLISHING CORP. CATALOG
Sky Publishing Corp., 49 Bay State Rd, Cambridge, MA 02138 / Sky & Telescope,
P O Box 9111, Belmont, MA   02178-9111   800-253-0245 617-864-7360   Fax
617-864-6117 Email skytel@skypub.com http://www.skypub.com Since 1941.
Ask for 32-page catalog of products for professional and amateur astronomers. Products include maps, books, videos, globes, posters, software, CD-ROMs, slide sets, star atlases, and planispheres.

SOFTCHOICE
625 W Jackson Blvd, Unit 102, Chicago, IL   60661-5610   800-268-7638 Fax
800-268-7639 http://www.softchoice.com
Ask for 114-page Software Sales Catalog.

THE SOFTWARE SOURCE CO., INC.
2517 Hwy 35, Bldg N, Suite 201, Manasquan, NJ 08736 800-289-3275
Ask for 20-page catalog listing software at large academic discounts.

SUNBURST
Contact Claire Kubasik   101 Castleton St, Pleasantville, NY   10570-0100
800-338-3457, ext 2175 914-747-3310 Fax 914-747-4109
Email ckubasik@nysunburst.com   http://www.sunburst.com
Ask for 88-page catalog of multimedia software programs for elementary, middle, and high school students in math, science and computing.

TASA GRAPHIC ARTS, INC.
9301 Indian School Rd NE, Ste 208, Albuquerque, NM 87112-2861 800-293-2725
http://www.swcp.com/~tasa
Ask for brochure. Interactive CD-ROM software on The Theory of Plate Tectonics, Topographic Maps, Explores the Planets, Rock & Minerals, Rain Forest, Wetlands, Minerals, and How the Earth Works.

TEACHER'S DISCOVERY
Science Division, 2741 Paldan Dr, Auburn Hills, MI 48326 888-97-SCIENCE Fax
888-98-SCIENCE 248-340-7220 Distributor (Elementary School to High School)
Ask for 68-page science catalog. Materials to make "teaching more exciting and fun."
Classroom materials, CD-ROMs, and videos.

TERRAPIN SOFTWARE, INC.
10 Holworthy St, Cambridge, MA 02138 800-972-8200 http://www.terrapin.com
Ask for 16-page catalog of software programs for elementary school students in math, science and computing.

THAYER BIRDING SOFTWARE
P. O. Box 11703, Naples, FL 34101 800-865-2473 http://www.birding.com
Manufacturer Distributor Retail Mail Order (Elementary School to High School)
Ask for brochure. CD-ROM, Birds of North America, contains over 2,700 photos and almost 700 songs.

THE LEARNING TEAM
84 Business Park Drive, Armonk, NY 10504 800-793-TEAM Fax 914-273-2227
http://learningteam.org
Ask for 16-page catalog. Books and multimedia, including CD-ROMs: Investigating Lake Lluka, Exploring the Nardoo, Insects, The Dynamic Rainforest, and many more.

THE MAC ZONE
707 S Grady Way, Renton, WA 98055-3233 800-248-0800
http://www.maczone.com
Ask for 92-page catalog. Retail mail order MacIntosh computer supplies.

THE MONA GROUP
432 Tulpehocken Ave, Elkins Park, PA 19027 215-885-6610 Fax 215-885-6686
http://www.monagroup.com **Manufacturer Distributor (Elementary School)**
Ask for brochure. Interactive, self-paced software, including Cells & Genes; Biology: Molecules, Cells and Genes; Biochemistry; and Mini-Modules.

TIGER DIRECT
8700 W Flager St, 4th Flr, Miami, FL 33174-2428 800-888-4437
http://www.tigerdirect.com
Ask for 120-page catalog. Software, hardware, systems, and accessories.

TOM SNYDER PRODUCTIONS
80 Coolidge Hill Rd, Watertown, MA 02172-2817 800-342-0236 Fax 617-926-6222
http://www.teachtsp.com
Ask for 52-page catalog. Interactive group software including science. Ask for CD Sampler of products.

VERNIER SOFTWARE
Contact Christine Mosier 8565 S W Beaverton-Hillsdale Hwy, Portland, OR 97225-2429 503-297-5317   Fax 503-297-1760   Email cmosier@vernier.com http://www.vernier.com (High School to College)
Ask for 42-page catalog. Software and hardware for the chemistry and physics laboratory. Ask about workshops for teachers.

VIDEODISCOVERY
1700 Westlake Ave, N, Suite 600, Seattle, WA 98109-3012 800-548-3472 206-285-5400 Fax 206-285-9245 http://www.videodiscovery.com
See on-line catalog. CD-ROMs, including Real Science! CD-ROM series.

VIEWS OF THE SOLAR SYSTEM
by Calvin J. Hamilton   Produced and distributed by the National Science Teachers Association 800-722-NSTA 1996 CD-ROM $ 21.95
See the Solar System with up-to-date views, including NSTA journal articles on the subject.

WINDOWS MAGAZINE
Subscriptions, P. O. Box 420215, Palm Coast, FL   32142 800-829-9150 904-445-4662, ext 817 http://www.winmag.com 12 issues per year $ 24.94
Major news and information source about computer operating systems including hardware and software. Approximately 350 pages per issue.

ZTEK CO.
P. O. Box 11768, Lexington, KY 40577-1768 800-247-1603 606-281-1611 Fax 606-281-1521 Email info@ztek.com http://www.ztek.com
Ask for 32-page catalog of educational multimedia on CD-ROM, software, and videodiscs, as well as multimedia equipment.

Chapter

4

Education

Science Education Sources

These specialized information centers and science education sources in the Chicago area, as well as nationwide, provide unique opportunities for science education.

CHALLENGER CENTER FOR SPACE SCIENCE EDUCATION
1029 N Royal St, Suite 300, Alexandria, VA 22314 800-98-STARS 703-683-9740
Fax 703-683-7546 Email cosmic@challenger.org
http://www.challenger.org/cosmic/
Challenger Center is a not-for-profit education organization serving a network of Learning Centers and educational institutions throughout North America. Inquire about a site near you.

CHICAGO CHILDREN'S MUSEUM - EARTH BALLOON PROGRAMS
Navy Pier Chicago, 700 E Grand Ave, Chicago, IL 60611 312-464-7670
http://www.chichildrensmuseum.org
This giant, 20-foot-diameter inflatable globe goes out to schools and special events to create a unique and fun educational experience. Museum staff will explore the where's and whys of geography/earth science with you and your students on a journey inside the Earth Balloon.

CHICAGO CHILDREN'S MUSEUM - SCIENCE WORKSHOPS
Navy Pier Chicago, 700 E Grand Ave, Chicago, IL 60611 312-464-7683
http://www.chichildrensmuseum.org
Inquire about hands-on workshops for students, grades K-5. There are a variety of workshops to choose from including three science-based programs through the Inventing Lab, Waterways and Under Construction exhibits. For educator programs ask about our Exploratours and special workshops/events.

DO-IT
(Disabilities, Opportunities, Internetworking, and Technology) University of Washington, P O Box 354842, Seattle, WA 98195-4842 206-685-DOIT Fax 206-685-4045 Email doit@U.washington.edu
http://weber.u.washington.edu/~doit/
Ask for brochure. Resources include electronic resources, videotapes, presentation materials, and free printed materials.

ERIC CLEARINGHOUSE FOR SCIENCE, MATHEMATICS, AND ENVIRONMENTAL EDUCATION
1929 Kenny Rd, Columbus, OH 43210-1080 800-276-0462 614-292-5680 Fax 614-292-0263 Email ericse@osu.edu http://www.ericse.ohio-state.edu
Established in 1966, ERIC (Educational Resources Information Center) is a national system to provide users with ready access to an extensive body of education-related literature. Ask for A Pocket Guide to ERIC. Funded by the U. S. Department of Education.

EXPLORASOURCE FOR EDUCATORS
MediaSeek Technologies Inc., 2211 Rimland Dr, Suite 224, Bellingham, WA 98226-5662 800-372-3277 http://www.mediaseek.com
Both on CD-ROM and on the Internet, ExplorAsource selects, lists, and displays detailed information about the products that match specified learning topics.

ILLINOIS DEPARTMENT OF COMMERCE AND COMMUNITY AFFAIRS
Contact Carol Osborne 620 E Adams, Springfield, IL 62701 800-252-8955
Inquire about the Illinois Energy Education Development (ILEED) Program including newsletters, free materials, and workshops and in-school programs for students and teachers.

ILLINOIS STATE BOARD OF EDUCATION
Contact Guen Pollack. N-242, Illinois State Board of Education, 100 N First, Springfield, IL 62777 217-782-2826
Ms. Guen Pollack is the Senior Science Consultant for the Illinois State Board of Education.

KIDWORKS TOURING THEATRE CO.
Contact Andrea Salloum, Artistic Director 923 W Gordon Terrace, # 7, Chicago, IL 60613 773-883-9932
This touring theater company presents hands-on workshops and performances in a variety of productions including science.

MIDWEST CONSORTIUM FOR MATHEMATICS AND SCIENCE EDUCATION (MSC)
Operated by North Central Regional Educational Laboratory (NCREL), 1900 Spring Rd, Suite 300, Oak Brook, IL 60523-1480 630-571-4700 800-356-2735 http://www.enc.org/msc/msc.htm
MSC collaborates with other agencies to produce materials and provide technical assistance for schools, teachers, school districts, and administrators in order to improve math and science education.

NATIONAL SCIENCE EDUCATION STANDARDS
National Research Council, 2101 Constitution Ave, NW, HA 486,Washington, DC 20418 202-334-1399 (800-722-NSTA $ 19.95) 1995 280 pages K-12
Ask to be placed on mailing list. Report prepared by the National Committee on Science Education Standards and Assessment, National Research Council.

NATIONAL SCIENCE RESOURCES CENTER (NSRC)
Smithsonian Institution - National Academy of Sciences, Smithsonian Institution, Arts & Industries Building, Room 1201, Washington, DC 20560 202-357-4892 Fax 202-786-2028 Email outreach@nas.edu http://www.si.edu/nsrc
The NSRC works to improve the teaching of science in the nation's schools. NSRC disseminates information about effective science teaching resources, develops curriculum materials, and sponsors outreach and leadership development activities. Ask to be placed on the mailing list for the NSRC Newsletter.

NORTH CENTRAL REGIONAL EDUCATIONAL LABORATORY (NCREL)
1900 Spring Rd, Suite 300, Oak Brook, IL 60523-1480 630-571-4700 800-356-2735 http://www.ncrel.org
One of ten regional laboratories in the United States, NCREL disseminates information to educators and policymakers, develops research-based educational materials, offers opportunities for professional development, and provides policy analysis and evaluation services.

PROJECT KALEIDOSCOPE (PKAL)
Jeanne L Narum, Director 1730 Rhode Island Ave, NW, Suite 803, Washington, DC 20036 202-232-1300 Fax 202-331-1283 Email icopkal@mindspring.com http://www.pkal.org

This organization promotes science education reform across the country in many colleges and universities. PKAL sponsors seminars on facilities planning. Members of the PKAL faculty are selected as leaders who will become creative and productive agents of change.

SCIENCE & TECHNOLOGY INFORMATION SYSTEM (STIS)
National Science Foundation, 4201 Wilson Blvd, Washington, DC 22230 Voice 703-306-0214, Modem 7E1F 703-306-0212 or 703-306-0213
STIS is an electronic dissemination system that provides fast, easy access to NSF publications. There is no cost to you except for possible long-distance phone charges. The service is available 24 hours a day. Science education programs receive funding through the Division of Undergraduate Education, Directorate for Education and Human Resources, National Science Foundation.

U. S. DEPARTMENT OF EDUCATION
Information Resource Center, 600 Independence Ave, S W, Washington, DC 20202-0498 Email webmaster@inet.ed.gov http://www.ed.gov
Resources and programs of the U. S. Department of Education. To subscribe to a free information service that offers 2 or 3 email messages each week: Address an email message to listproc@inet.ed.gov, and type in the body of your message: "subscribe edinfo (your name)".

Chicago Area Schools

Various K-12 schools focusing on science, in or near Chicago, are listed here. Contact your local school board for information about K-12 science schools in your area.

AMUDENSEN HIGH SCHOOL
5110 N Damen Ave, Chicago, IL 60625 773-534-2320 Public High School
This magnet high school has an environmental education program.

BARNARD COMPUTER, MATHEMATICS & SCIENCE CENTER
10354 S Charles, Chicago, IL 60643 773-535-2625 Public Elementary School
A Chicago public school with a strong science emphasis.

BEASLEY ACADEMIC CENTER MAGNET
5255 S State St, Chicago, IL 60609 773-535-1230 Public Elementary School
A Chicago public school with a strong science emphasis.

Children of any age with parents are welcome to enjoy the interactive exhibits and historical artifacts at the Argonne Information Center in Argonne, IL.

Photo Courtesy of Argonne Information Center

BOGAN COMPUTER TECHNICAL HIGH SCHOOL
3939 W 79th St, Chicago, IL 60652 773-535-2180 Public High School
A Chicago public school with a strong science emphasis.

BRENTANO MATH & SCIENCE ACADEMY
2723 N Fairfield Ave, Chicago, IL 60647 773-534-4100 Public Elementary School
A Chicago public school with a strong science emphasis.

CHICAGO ACADEMY FOR MATH, SCIENCE & LANGUAGE
(New Chicago Public School in Region Two of the Chicago Public Schools) Public Elementary School
A Chicago public school with a strong science emphasis.

CHICAGO HIGH SCHOOL FOR AGRICULTURAL SCIENCE
3807 W 111th St, Chicago, IL 60655 773-535-2500 Public High School
A Chicago public school with a strong science emphasis.

DE LA CRUZ MATH & SCIENCE SPECIALTY SCHOOL
2317 W 23rd Pl, Chicago, IL 60608 773-535-4585 Public Elementary School
A Chicago public school with a strong science emphasis.

THOMAS A. EDISON REGIONAL GIFTED CENTER
6220 N Olcott Ave, Chicago, IL 60631 773-534-1209 Public Elementary School
A Chicago public school with a strong science emphasis.

GALILEO SCHOLASTIC ACADEMY OF MATH & SCIENCE
820 S Carpenter, Chicago, IL 60607 773-534-7070 Public Elementary School
A Chicago public school with a strong science emphasis.

NATHANIEL GREENE SCHOOL
3537 S Paulina St, Chicago, IL 60609 773-535-4560 Public Elementary School
A Chicago public school with a strong science emphasis.

FRANK W GUNSAULUS SCHOLASTIC ACADEMY SCHOOL
4420 S Sacramento, Chicago, IL 773-535-7215 Public Elementary School
A Chicago public school with a strong science emphasis.

ROBERT HEALY SCHOOL
3018 S Parnell Ave, Chicago, IL 60616 773-534-9190 Public Elementary School
A Chicago public school with a strong science emphasis.

ILLINOIS MATHEMATICS AND SCIENCE ACADEMY
1500 W Sullivan Rd, Aurora, IL 60506-1000 630-907-5027 Public High School
IMSA is a high school academy in Illinois that offers rigorous courses in mathematics, science, art and humanities while emphasizing interconnections between disciplines. Students live in a pioneering educational community. Illinois residents who have completed nine years of education and are not enrolled in school beyond the ninth grade are invited to apply to the Academy. For further information contact the Academy.

ANNIE KELLER GIFTED MAGNET SCHOOL
3020 W 180th St, Chicago, IL 60655 773-535-2636 Public Elementary School
A Chicago public school with a strong science emphasis.

KATES KELLOGG SCHOOL
9241 S Leavitt, Chicago, IL 60620 773-535-2590 Public Elementary School
A Chicago public school with a strong science emphasis.

KENWOOD ACADEMY HIGH SCHOOL
5015 S Blackstone Ave, Chicago, IL 60615 773-535-1350 Public Elementary School
A Chicago public school with a strong science emphasis.

JOHN H. KINZIE ELEMENTARY SCHOOL
5625 S Mobile Ave, Chicago, IL 60638 773-535-2425 Public Elementary School
A Chicago public school with a strong science emphasis.

LANE TECHNICAL HIGH SCHOOL
2501 W Addison St, Chicago, IL 60618 773-534-5400 Public High School
This magnet high school has a strong science program.

TED LENART REGIONAL GIFTED CENTER
8445 S Kolin, Chicago, IL 60652 773-535-2322 Public Elementary School
A Chicago public school with a strong science emphasis.

LINCOLN PARK HIGH SCHOOL
2001 N Orchard St, Chicago, IL 60614 773-534-8130 Public High School
A Chicago public high school with a strong science emphasis.

NEWBERRY MATHEMATICS AND SCIENCE ACADEMY
700 W Willow St, Chicago, IL 60614 773-534-8000 Public Elementary School
A Chicago public school with a strong science emphasis.

WILLIAM H. RYDER MATH/SCIENCE SPECIALTY SCHOOL
8716 S Wallace, Chicago, IL 60620 773-535-3843 Public Elementary School
A Chicago public school with a strong science emphasis.

MARIA SAUCEDO SCHOLASTIC ACADEMY
2850 W 24th Blvd, Chciago, IL 60623 773-534-1770 Public Elementary School
A Chicago public school with a strong science emphasis.

SAUGANASH ELEMENTARY SCHOOL
6040 N Kilpatrick, Chicago, IL 60646 773-534-3470 Public Elementary School
A Chicago public school with a strong science emphasis.

SCIENCE & ARTS ACADEMY
1825 Miner St, Des Plaines, IL 60016 847-827-7880 Private Elementary School
The Academy admits gifted students ages 3 ½ through 15 years with a minimum IQ of 120. Its curriculum is thematic, interdisciplinary and individual.

SHERIDAN MATH AND SCIENCE ACADEMY
533 W 27th, Chicago, IL 60616 773-534-9120 Public Elementary School
A Chicago public school with a strong science emphasis.

SOUTHSIDE COLLEGE PREPARATORY HIGH SCHOOL
250 E 111th St, Chicago, IL 60628 773-535-9930 Public High School
A Chicago public school with a strong science emphasis.

SUMNER MATH AND SCIENCE ACADEMY
4320 W Fifth Ave, Chicago, IL 60624 773-534-6730 Public Elementary School
A Chicago public school with a strong science emphasis.

ELIZABETH H. SUTHERLAND SCHOOL
10015 S Leavitt St, Chicago, IL 60643 773-535-2580 Public Elementary School
A Chicago public school with a strong science emphasis.

VON STEUBEN METROPOLITAN SCIENCE CENTER
5039 N Kimball Ave, Chicago, IL 60625 773-534-5100 Public High School
A Chicago public school with a strong science emphasis.

WALT DISNEY MAGNET SCHOOL
4140 N Marine Dr, Chicago, IL 60613 773-534-5840 Public Elementary School
A Chicago public school with a strong science emphasis.

WHITNEY YOUNG HIGH SCHOOL
211 S Laflin, Chicago, IL 60607 773-534-7500 Public High School
This magnet high school has a strong science program.

WOODS ACADEMY
6206 S Racine, Chicago, IL 60636 773-535-9250 Public Elementary School
A Chicago public school with a strong science emphasis.

Science Education Opportunities

Opportunities to learn about science and science teaching are listed here. These special opportunities are for children, adults, and teachers in the Chicago area as well as across the country.

ADLER PLANETARIUM - DEPARTMENT OF EDUCATION

Adler Planetarium & Astronomy Museum, 1300 S Lake Shore Drive, Chicago, IL 60605 312-322-0551 http://astro.uchicago.edu/adler/
Contact the Department of Education about current programs and workshops available to the public.

AMERICAN RADIO RELAY LEAGUE
- DEPARTMENT OF EDUCATIONAL ACTIVITIES

Contact Glenn Swanson American Radio Relay League, 225 Main St, Newington, CT 06111 860-594-0267 Fax 860-594-0259 Email gswanson@arrl.org
http://www.arrl.org/
This is the best resource of information about Amateur Radio for all ages. Inquire about educational materials available including video courses, Morse Code and Ham Radio materials, Amateur Radio in the Classroom newsletter, license publications for students, and reference books. Ask for list of School Amateur Radio Clubs and Advisors.

ARGONNE NATIONAL LABORATORY
- DIVISION OF EDUCATIONAL PROGRAMS

Division of Educational Programs, Argonne National Laboratory, 9700 S Cass Ave, Argonne, IL 60439 630-252-4114 http://www.dep.anl.gov
Research participation programs at Argonne are available for college/university faculty and students.

ASTRO-SCIENCE WORKSHOP

Contact Adler Planetarium & Astronomy Museum, 1300 S Lake Shore Drive, Chicago, IL 60605 312-322-0542 Fax 312-322-0323
http://astro.uchicago.edu/adler/
This program is designed to offer students who excel in science opportunities to interact with and learn from professional astronomers.

BROOKFIELD ZOO - SCHOOL RESERVATIONS DEPARTMENT
3300 S Golf Rd, Brookfield, IL 60513 708-485-0263, ext 367
http://www.brookfield-zoo.mus.il.us
Ask for school brochure describing field trips for school groups, educator workshops, and programs to enhance classroom studies.

CAOS CLUB
The Chicago Academy of Sciences, Administrative Headquarters, 2060 N Clark St, Chicago, IL 60614 773-549-0606 Fax 773-549-5199 http://www.caosclub.org
CAoS Club, a distance-learning Internet service, provides teachers and students with relevant, fun science learning. Live science demonstrations and workshops broadcast over the Web, standards-based lesson plans, activities, curricular resources, and more are available to members.

CHANNEL 2 TELEVISION NEWS WEATHER
Contact Steve Baskerville Channel 2 Television, 630 McClurg Ct, Chicago, IL 60611 312-951-3631
If you would like a classroom visit from a member of the Channel 2 Television weather team, call the Channel 2 Newsroom at 312-951-3631. Grades seven or younger, can receive an informal presentation including video presentations about weather topics like Doppler 2000 radar, Earthwatch, Stormwatch, Watches & Warnings, Tornado Warning, and Severe Weather Conditions, including television graphics.

CHICAGO ACADEMY OF SCIENCES - EDUCATION DEPARTMENT
The Chicago Academy of Sciences, 2060 N Clark St, Chicago, IL 60614 773-549-0606 http://www.chias.org
Contact the Education Department about current programs and classes for both teachers and children, like Science in the Park, Nature Exploration Labs, Water Works Lab, and Discovery Tours. Special events include HerPETological Weekend, held annually in September. Ask for a copy of Nature's Notes, a newsletter of news and events for friends of the Academy.

CHICAGO BOTANIC GARDEN - REGISTRAR'S OFFICE
Chicago Botanic Garden, 1000 Lake Cook Road (at Edens Expressway), Glencoe, IL 60022-0400 847-835-8261 http://www.chicago-botanic.org
Call the registrar's office to obtain a Course Guide listing many courses including horticulture, landscape design, nature and botanical crafts classes.

CHICAGO BOTANIC GARDEN
- SCHOOL PROGRAMS FOR CHILDREN AND TEACHERS
Lynne Hubert, Science Education Specialist (847-835-8280) Deb Chapman, Coordinator of Environmental Education (847-835-8239) Linda Patchett, Supervisor of Teacher Services (847-835-8323) http://www.chicago-botanic.org

Chicago Botanic Garden, 1000 Lake Cook Road (at Edens Expressway), Glencoe, IL 60022-0400 Inquire about Hands-On Teacher Workshops for graduate credit, Teacher Overnights and Open Houses, Workshops for Students, the New Explorers Program, the Partners for Growing Science curriculum/field trip program, and the Biodiversity Education Through Action environmental education program.

CHICAGO SYSTEMIC INITIATIVE (CSI)

Clifton Burgess, Codirector Chicago Public Schools, 1819 W Pershing Rd, 6 East (South), Chicago, IL 60609 773-535-8860 http://www.csi.cps.k12.il.us
Major National Science Foundation (NSF) funded initiative to promote system-wide reform and improvement in mathematics, science and technology instruction. Limited to the Chicago Public Schools.

COLLEGE OF DU PAGE - PROGRAMS

Contact Carl Heine, Program Coordinator College of DuPage, 22nd and Lambert Rd, Glen Ellyn, IL 60137 630-942-2208 http://www.cod.edu/
Programs with science opportunities include Kids on Campus grades K-5, Teens on Campus grades 9-12, and Talent Search, for gifted students grades 5-8.

CPS TEACHERS ACADEMY FOR PROFESSIONAL DEVELOPMENT

Judith L. Foster, Executive Director Chicago Teachers Academy 6E (s), Chicago Public Schools, 1819 W Pershing Rd, Chicago, IL 60609 773-535-4240
This unit of the Chicago Public Schools coordinates professional development opportunities for K-12 teachers and administrators. Many services include the areas of science and mathematics. Two citywide events sponsored by the Teachers Academy include the Under the Umbrella Conference that focuses on science, math and reading; and the Science/Mathematics End-of-Year Event that provides a unique opportunity for colleagues to come together for a professional and social experience.

DISCOVERY CENTER MUSEUM

Contact Sarah Wolf 711 N Main St, Rockford, IL 61103 815-963-6769 Fax 815-968-0164 Email discoverycentermuseum@discoverycentermuseum.org http://www.discoverycentermuseum.org
The Museum has over 200 hands-on science exhibits inside the museum and even more in the outdoor science park. Ask for the educator's guide to Discovery Center listing traveling exhibits, special events, and school field trip information.

THE FIELD MUSEUM - PUBLIC PROGRAMS

Education Department, The Field Museum, Roosevelt Road at Lake Shore Drive, Chicago, IL 60605-2497 312-322-8854 http://www.fmnh.org
The Field Museum's Education Department offers a wide range of activities for the public, including adults, families and children. These may include free hall activities, tours, story telling activities, and four annual festivals celebrating biodiversity and

cultures. Paid programs include lectures, seminars, workshops, field trips, and overnight stays at the Museum for groups or families. Call 312-322-8854 for specific information and free seasonal brochure.

THE FIELD MUSEUM - RESOURCE CENTERS
The Field Museum, Roosevelt Road at Lake Shore Drive, Chicago, IL 60605-2497
312-922-9410 http://www.fmnh.org
The Africa Resource Center has books and audiovisuals, telephone 312-922-9410 extension 883, The Webber Resource Center on Indians of the Americas has books, audiovisuals, and hands-on materials, telephone 312-922-9410 extension 497, and the Rice Wildlife Research Station has books, materials and computers on wildlife, telephone 312-922-9410 extension 814.

THE FIELD MUSEUM - SCHOOL AND COMMUNITY SERVICES
The Field Museum, Roosevelt Road at Lake Shore Drive, Chicago, IL 60605-2497
312-322-8852 http://www.fmnh.org
Illinois school and Chicago community groups free admission with registration. School tours & registration information 312-322-8852, Community Outreach 312-922-9410 extension 351, Teacher Services 312-922-9410 extension 365. Only written requests for group visits are accepted. Teacher training fees vary and many programs are free.

THE FIELD MUSEUM
- THE NEW EXPLORERS MATERIALS DEPOSITORY
The Field Museum, Roosevelt Road at Lake Shore Drive, Chicago, IL 60605-2497
312-922-9410, ext 853 http://www.fmnh.org
The popular television series, The New Explorers with Bill Kurtis, is made available to teachers along with educational materials. This collection is found in the Harris Educational Loan Center on the Museum ground floor.

FOREST PRESERVE DISTRICT OF COOK COUNTY
Conservation Department, 536 N Harlem Ave, River Forest, IL 60305
800-870-3666 708-771-1330
Ask for brochure, Getting in Touch with Nature, Classroom Programs for Cook County Schools, including classroom programs, slide programs, and visiting nature centers. Nature centers include Crabtree Nature Center, Barrington, IL 847-381-6592; River Trail Nature Center, Northbrook, IL 708-824-8360; Trailside Museum, River Forest, IL 708-366-6530; Little Red Schoolhouse Nature Center, Willow Springs, IL 708-839-6897; Sand Ridge Nature Center, South Holland, IL 708-868-0606; and Camp Sauawau, Lemont, IL 630-257-2045. Please schedule your program as early as possible, at least three weeks in advance.

FOREST PRESERVE DISTRICT OF DUPAGE COUNTY

P. O. Box 2339, Glen Ellyn, IL 60138 or 185 Spring Ave, Glen Ellyn, Il 60137
630-790-4900 http://www.co.dupage.il.us/forest/fpdhome.html
Ask for Visitor's Guide brochure. Ask for 40-page booklet, Let's Have a Class Outside
Today: A Teacher's Guide to the Forest Preserve District of Dupage County. Nature
centers include Fullersburg Woods Environmental Education Center, Oak Brook, IL;
Willowbrook Wildlife Center, Glen Ellyn, IL; and Kline Creek Farm, West Chicago,
IL.

GEMS, GREAT EXPLORATIONS IN MATH & SCIENCE

**Anne Grall Reichel, Science Coordinator, Lake County Educational Service
Center, 19525 W Washington, Grayslake, IL 60030 847-223-3400, ext 240 Fax
847-223-3415 Email areichel@lake.k12.il.us**
Great Explorations in Math & Science (GEMS) site, Lawrence Hall of Science,
University of California at Berkeley. GEMS is a resource for activity-based science and
mathematics concepts as defined in the National Science Standards. Ask for calendar
of workshops listing several mathematics and science workshops offered throughout the
school year.

GOLDEN APPLE SCIENCE PROGRAM

**Golden Apple Foundation, 8 South Michigan Ave, Suite 700, Chicago, IL
60603-3318 312-407-0006 http://www.goldenapple.org**
Summer workshops for elementary school teachers in city, suburban, public, parochial,
and independent schools that give teachers an opportunity to develop hands-on science
programs. Teachers receive stipends and grants. This program allows teacher
participants to network with and receive ongoing support from colleagues and expert
teachers.

HANDS-ON UNIVERSE

**M/S 50-232, Lawrence Berkeley National Laboratory, Berkeley, CA 94720
510-486-5236 Email houstaff@hou.lbl.gov http://hou.lbl.gov**
Hands-On Universe enables students and teachers to explore the universe, both in the
classroom and online with research astronomers. HOU provides curriculum text and
software, teacher training, image processing software, access to telescopes, and
collaborative communities.

SCHOOL OF HOLOGRAPHY

**Dr. Ted Niemiec, Director of Education School of Holography, 1134 W
Washington Blvd, Chicago, IL 60607 312-226-1007 Fax 312-829-9636
http://museumofholography.com**
Private School The comprehensive curriculum at the School of Holography allows the
student to explore holography as an artist, as a scientist, and as an engineer. Twelve
different courses are offered from introductory to advanced instruction. Tuition fees

vary from $ 175 to $ 375 with laboratory fees and materials extra.

ILLINOIS FUTURE PROBLEM SOLVING PROGRAM
Contact Trevor Steinbach 1320 Anderson, Suite 1000, Batavia, IL 60510
800-544-3772 Fax 630-406-6556 (Elementary School to High School)
The Future Problem Solving Program is a non-profit tax-exempt educational
organization. Discovering rich and varied ways of thinking, students experience the
excitement of creative thinking.

INSTITUTE FOR MATHEMATICS AND SCIENCE EDUCATION
Contact Marty Gartzman, Director of Outreach Institute for Mathematics and
Science Education, Room 2075 SEL, University of Illinois at Chicago, 950 S
Halstead, Chicago, IL 60607-7019 312-996-2448 Fax 312-413-4711
Contact the Institute about current programs, workshops and materials. The Institute
offers staff development workshops for teachers of mathematics and science at the
elementary, middle school, and secondary levels.   The UIC Maneuvers with
Mathematics Project has developed seven modules of fun mathematical explorations
for middle grade students.

INVENTOR'S COUNCIL
Don Moyer, President Inventor's Council, 431 S Dearborn 705, Chicago, IL
60605 312-939-3329 Email patent@donmoyer.com http://donmoyer.com
The Inventor's Council holds inventor's workshops on one Saturday morning each
month at the Harold Washington Library Center, 400 S State St, Chicago, Illinois.
Topics include: How to Evaluate Patents, Patent Success Stories, How to Get the Best
Patent, Finding the Best Way to Get New Products Made, How to Get Manufacturers
to Invest in Inventions. This not-for-profit Council asks for contributions and supplies
write-ups on various topics.

JASON FOUNDATION FOR EDUCATION
395 Totten Pond Road, Waltham, MA 02154 617-487-9995
Email info@jason.org http://www.jasonproject.org
The Jason Project encourages interdisciplinary, hands-on, and inquiry based teaching
and is designed for students grades 4-9. Students are taken on real research projects
where students engage in interactive exchanges with researchers.

JURICA NATURE MUSEUM
Contact Fr. Theodore Suchy. Scholl Science Center, Illinois Benedictine College,
5700 College Rd, Lisle, IL 60532 630-829-6546 Fax 630-829-6551
Email tsuchy@ben.edu http://www.ben.edu/resources/J_Museum/index
Loan program available to teachers. Visitors experience the African savanna, tropical
rain forest, the woodlands, wetlands and prairie of Northern Illinois along with other
smaller animal habitat dioramas. Insects, fish, reptiles and all kinds of birds are

displayed along with many fossil specimens and skeletons.

LAKE COUNTY EDUCATIONAL SERVICE CENTER
Anne Grall Reichel, Science Coordinator, Lake County Educational Service Center, 19525 W Washington, Grayslake, IL 60030 847-223-3400, ext 240 Fax 847-223-3415 Email areichel@lake.k12.il.us
Great Explorations in Math & Science (GEMS) site, Lawrence Hall of Science, University of California at Berkeley. GEMS is a resource for activity-based science and mathematics concepts as defined in the National Science Standards. Ask for calendar of workshops listing several mathematics and science workshops offered throughout the school year.

LAKE COUNTY FOREST PRESERVES
2000 N Milwaukee Ave, Libertyville, IL 60048-1199 847-367-6640
http://www.co.lake.il.us/forest/index.htm
Ask for Group Environmental Education Program Guide including information about educational programs, prices, reservations, locations, dates, self-guided programs, and naturalist-guided programs. Over 20 programs available.

LAP TOP COMPUTER EDUCATION
Contact Mary Charles Loyola University Chicago, 1041 Ridge Rd, Wilmette, IL 60091 847-853-3342 (Elementary School through High School)
Chicago area schools without computers can have lap top computers brought to their classroom for a fun hands-on introduction to computers.

LEARNING LAB
Division of Educational Programs, Argonne National Laboratory, 9700 S Cass Ave, Argonne, IL 60439 630-252-5448
The Learning Lab, located in the Argonne Information Center, is an Argonne Division of Educational Programs operated classroom for distance learning for Chicago area students and teachers.

LEON M. LEDERMAN SCIENCE EDUCATION CENTER - MATH SCIENCE CONSORTIA DEMONSTRATION SITE
Fermi National Accelerator Laboratory, P. O. Box 500 MS 777, Batavia, IL 60510-0500 630-840-8258
At this science education center the visitor may preview the Internet, science education computer bulletin boards, and see multimedia materials. The Teacher Resource Center is a demonstration site for mathematics and science materials in the Math Science Consortia, North Central Regional Educational Laboratory for the Eisenhower National Clearinghouse. Phone for an appointment.

LEON M. LEDERMAN SCIENCE EDUCATION CENTER
- PRECOLLEGE EDUCATION PROGRAMS

Fermi National Accelerator Laboratory, P. O. Box 500 MS 777, Batavia, IL 60510-0500 630-840-8258

Contact this center for current information about programs for high school teachers and students, programs for elementary and mid level schools, programs for students of all ages, and science materials programs - in total over 50 programs of science education opportunities. This Science Education Center is equipped with a technology classroom, classroom laboratory, and hands-on exhibits dedicated to physical science concepts related to Fermilab. Science toys are available in a small retail shop.

LEON M. LEDERMAN SCIENCE EDUCATION CENTER
- TEACHER RESOURCE CENTER

Susan Dahl, Education Specialist, Teacher Resource Center, Fermi National Accelerator Laboratory, Leon M. Lederman Science Education Center, P O Box 500 MS 777, Batavia, IL 60510-0500 630-840-8258

Email SDahl@fnalv.fnal.gov Monday-Friday 8:30-5:00; Saturday 9:00-3:30. Call for an appointment. This extensive teacher resource center is filled with books, periodicals, kits, videotapes, etc. - for teachers, administrators, librarians, scientists, and Science Center program participants.

THE MORTON ARBORETUM - THE EDUCATION PROGRAM

4100 Illinois Route 53 (just north of interstate 88), Lisle, IL 60532-1293 630-719-2400 http://www.mortonarb.org

Quarterly The Education Program is published quarterly and contains a course catalog of classes offered at the Arboretum for students of all age levels and abilities.

MUSEUM OF SCIENCE AND INDUSTRY
- AFTER CLASS EXPLORERS (A.C.E.)

Museum of Science and Industry, 57th St and Lake Shore Drive, Chicago, IL 60637 773-684-1414 http://www.msichicago.org

This after-school program brings together the Museum and nearby Chicago Public Schools to link classroom education with the resources at the Museum.

**Twelve miles of trails and eleven miles of roads make discovering
more than 3,600 different woody plants an exciting adventure at
the Morton Arboretum in Lisle, Illinois.**

Photo Courtesy of the Morton Arboretum

MUSEUM OF SCIENCE AND INDUSTRY - MSI SCHOLARS

Museum of Science and Industry, 57th St and Lake Shore Drive, Chicago, IL 60637 773-684-1414 http://www.msichicago.org
A safe place for children to learn after school, the Museum is free everyday after 2 p.m. to Chicago students.

MUSEUM OF SCIENCE AND INDUSTRY - MSI SUMMER CAMPS

Museum of Science and Industry, 57th St and Lake Shore Drive, Chicago, IL 60637 773-684-1414 http://www.msichicago.org
Science Summer Camp and LEGO Summer Camp are two great summer programs, full of activities for youngsters.

MUSEUM OF SCIENCE AND INDUSTRY
- NASA TEACHER RESOURCE CENTER

Museum of Science and Industry, 57th St and Lake Shore Drive, Chicago, IL 60637 773-684-1414 http://www.msichicago.org
Space-related workshops and curriculum materials for teachers.

MUSEUM OF SCIENCE & INDUSTRY - NEW EXPLORERS

Museum of Science and Industry, 57th St and Lake Shore Drive, Chicago, IL 60637 773-684-1414 http://www.msichicago.org
The popular television series, The New Explorers with Bill Kurtis, is made available to teachers along with educational materials. Workshops and tape support groups also are provided for teachers.

MUSEUM OF SCIENCE AND INDUSTRY
- SCIENCE AND EDUCATION DEPARTMENT

Museum of Science and Industry, 57th St and Lake Shore Drive, Chicago, IL 60637 773-684-1414 Fax 773-684-1591 http://www.msichicago.org
Inquire about the many educational programs and services available at the Museum of Science and Industry. Look in the index of this guide book under Museum of Science and Industry.

MUSEUM PARTNERS PROGRAM - CHICAGO SYSTEMIC
INITIATIVE (TEACHER TRAINING PROGRAM)

Contact Chicago Systemic Initiative Chicago Public Schools, 1819 W Pershing Rd, 6 East (South), Chicago, IL 60609 773-535-8860 http://www.csi.cps.k12.il.us
Program enabling junior high school teachers to brush up on science, while earning college course credit hours. Courses are held at major Chicago-area museums and informal educational institutions, such as Adler Planetarium, Chicago Academy of Sciences, Chicago Botanic Gardens, The Field Museum, Shedd Aquarium, and others.

NATIONAL OCEANIC AND ATMOSPHERIC ADMINISTRATION (NOAA)
Teacher at Sea Program, Public Affairs Correspondence Unit, 1305 East-West Highway, Station 8624, Silver Spring, MD 20910
http://www.wrc.noaa.gov/teacher-at-sea/ and http://www.tas.noaa.gov
Ask for brochure and application. Inquire about science teacher opportunities to go aboard an ocean-going research vessel.

OAK PARK CONSERVATORY
John Seaton, Head Horticulturist 615 Garfield St, Oak Park, IL 60304
708-386-4700 Fax 708-383-5702 http://www.oakparkparks.com
Hours: Monday 2:00-4:00; Tuesday 10:00-4:00; Wednesday, Sunday 10:00-6:00. Admission free.
This conservatory includes a cactus section, tropical plants, as well as seasonal floral shows. Inquire about current educational programs.

ORIENTAL INSTITUTE MUSEUM - EDUCATION DEPARTMENT
Contact Carole Krucoff Oriental Institute Museum, University of Chicago, 1155 E 58th St, Chicago, IL 60637 773-702-9507 Fax 773-702-9853 Email c-krucoff@uchicago.edu
The Museum is a showcase for the history, culture, and archaeology of the Middle East. Contact the Education Department about current programs.

THE POWER HOUSE - EDUCATIONAL PROGRAMS
Commonwealth Edison, 100 Shiloh Blvd, Zion, IL 60099 847-746-7492
http://www.ucm.com/powerhouse
Teachers and schools can request the following educational programs for presentation to students at The Power House: Alternative Energy Sources, The Nature of Energy, The Nature Trail Trek, Nuclear Power Generation, Safety & Electricity, The Wonders of Electricity, Bubbleology and pH and the Environment. (A program that visits schools, Safety and Electricity, is available for K-3.) Ask for brochure on tours and educational programs.

THE POWER HOUSE - ENERGY RESOURCE CENTER
Contact Lori Defiore Commonwealth Edison, 100 Shiloh Blvd, Zion, IL 60099
847-746-7850 Email pwhlh@ccmail.ceco.com http://www.ucm.com/powerhouse
Hours: Tuesday-Saturday 10:00-5:00
This science education resource center is open to both students and teachers for research and study. It contains over 500 books, 28 periodicals, six computers and four video VCR's with monitors.

PROJECT ASTRO-CHICAGO

Contact Bryan Wunar Community Programs, Adler Planetarium & Astronomy Museum, 1300 S Lake Shore Drive, Chicago, IL 60605 312-322-0542 Fax 312-322-2257 Email wunar@adlernet.org http://astro.uchicago.edu/adler/
This program supports student learning, and interest in astronomy and science, by developing and sustaining partnerships between volunteer astronomers and educators. For teachers grades 4-9 and community organizations.

PROJECT WET

(Water Education for Teachers) 201 Culbertson Hall, Montana State University-Bozeman, P O Box 170570, Bozeman, MT 59717-0570 406-994-5392 Fax 406-994-1919 Email rwwmb@montana.edu
http://www.montana.edu/wwwwet
Ask for brochure. Project WET is an international, interdisciplinary, water science and education program for formal and non-formal educators K-12. Curriculum, activity guide, and instruction and delivery network.

REGIONAL MATH/SCIENCE CENTER

The Office of TRIO Programs (M/C 342), The University of Illinois at Chicago, 322 S Green St, Suite 202, Chicago, IL 60607-3502 312-996-5045
Fax 312-413-1271
Ask for brochure. The purpose of the Regional Math/Science Center is to provide an intensified mathematics and science curriculum that will: (1) encourage more low-income participants to enter colleges and major in mathematics and science-related careers; (2) demystify mathematics and science by providing a success-oriented curriculum; (3) provide exposure to careers in math and science; and much more. Inquire about current programs for high school students.

SCIENCE DISCOVERY CENTER

H. R. McCall School, 3215 N McAree, Waukegan, IL 60087 847-360-5480
Fax 847-361-5390
A science resource center for use by local district schools is now available for student fun. Built from a portable classroom this center is equipped with work stations providing hands-on science from real dinosaur eggs to giant swinging bowling ball pendulums. School systems interested in developing a science resource center should contact the school principal. Reservations are required.

SCIENCE LINKAGES IN THE COMMUNITY (SLIC)

Michael Hyatt, Executive Director, CURL-SLIC 820 N Michigan Ave, Suite 1000, Chicago, IL 60611   312-915-7770 Fax 312-915-7770
Email mhyatt@luc.edu
This new program of the AAAS was created to organize science opportunities for students in the urban areas and within community organizations. Contact the SLIC

office for current opportunities in your area.

SCIENCE-BY-MAIL
Contact Melissa Cotter Dempsey Museum of Science, P O Box 6080, Boston, MA
02212-6080 800-729-3300 617-589-0438 Fax 617-589-0474 http://www.mos.org
$ 49.00 per membership group of one to four kids. $ 294 for a classroom.
Kids grades 4-9 complete science packets with fun investigations and mail them to a
pen-pal scientist for encouraging feedback.

PBS SCIENCELINE
1320 Braddock Place, Alexandra, VA 22314 703-739-7538
Email scienceline@pbs.org   http://www.pbs.org/learn/scienceline
Created for K-5 science teachers, this professional development program concentrates
on innovations in science teaching. A collaborative effort of PBS and the National
Science Teachers Association.

SCITECH - EDUCATION PROGRAMS
- THE SCIENCE AND TECHNOLOGY INTERACTIVE CENTER
Contact Cindy Strasser, Education Programs Coordinator SciTech, 18 W Benton,
Aurora, IL 60506 630-859-3434, ext 28 Fax 630-859-8692
Email cstrasser@scitech.com   http://www.scitech.mus.il.us
Programs and workshops available at SciTech include classes and demonstrations,
Summer Science Camp, early childhood programs, and Overnights. Fees vary from $
15 to $ 120. Contact the Education Programs Coordinator for current information.

JOHN G. SHEDD AQUARIUM - PUBLIC PROGRAMS
Contact the Education Department, John G. Shedd Aquarium, 1200 S Lake
Shore Drive, Chicago, IL 60605   312-692-3333   Main phone 312-939-2438
http://www.shedd.org Fee range from $ 12 to $ 240 Age: Preschool to Adult
Special courses are available to the public in classrooms and laboratories. Scheduled
on the evening and weekends these classes cover a multitude of fun topics from baby
belugas to creatures of the deep.

JOHN G. SHEDD AQUARIUM - SCHOOL PROGRAMS
Contact Mike Chamberlain Education Department, John G. Shedd Aquarium,
1200 S Lake Shore Drive, Chicago, IL 60605 312-692-3333 Main phone
312-939-2438 http://www.shedd.org Various times Monday through Friday Free
to Illinois schools ($ 10 lab fee) Age: Kindergarten through college.
Special classes and labs ranging from 45 minutes to 1 ½ hours are available to school
groups. Call 312-692-3333 for reservations. A variety of teachers' workshops are
offered throughout the year. Ask for a school brochure.

THE SMILE PROGRAM

Department of Biology, Chemistry, and Physical Science, Illinois Institute of Technology, Chicago, IL 60616 312-567-5745 Fax 312-567-3494 Email physjohnson@minna.iit.edu http://www.iit.edu/~smile/
SMILE is a long range tuition-free program designed to improve the effectiveness of science and mathematics instruction in Chicago area schools. Program activities consist of a series of in-service courses for teachers from grades K through 12.

SPRING VALLEY ENVIRONMENTAL EDUCATION
OUTREACH PROGRAM

Contact David Brooks Spring Valley Nature Sanctuary, 1111 E Schaumburg Rd, Schaumburg, IL 60194 847-985-2100 Fax 847-985-9692
Teachers, invite a naturalist from Spring Valley Nature Sanctuary to visit your class for a one hour lesson including games and activities.

STAFF DEVELOPMENT CATALOGUE
-CHICAGO TEACHERS ACADEMY

Contact Dee Sampson, Manager Chicago Teachers Academy 6E(s), Chicago Public Schools, 1819 W Pershing Rd, Chicago, IL 60609 773-535-4240
A Staff Development Catalog is published and disseminated to all Chicago Public School teachers. This catalogue, produced by the CPS Teachers Academy, is a collaboration among central service units, schools, outside learning institutions, and local colleges and universities. This resource lists numerous professional development opportunities for K-12 teachers and administrators. Participants may receive stipends, instruction materials, or lane promotional credit for successfully completing each workshop. The catalog is published tri-annually and disseminated to every teacher in the Chicago Public Schools.

STARLAB

Adler Planetarium & Astronomy Museum, 1300 S Lake Shore Drive, Chicago, IL 60605 312-322-0551 Fax 312-322-2257 http://astro.uchicago.edu/adler/
This program is designed to bring a portable planetarium on-site to schools and community organizations to explore the night sky and learn about astronomy.

TEACHER WORKSHOPS - ADLER PLANETARIUM

Contact Maria Mau Adler Planetarium & Astronomy Museum, 1300 S Lake Shore Drive, Chicago, IL 60605 312-322-0551 Fax 312-322-2257 http://astro.uchicago.edu/adler/
These professional development programs enhance teachers knowledge about science as well as how to use technology to link classrooms with informal science education resources at the Adler. For K-12 teachers.

TEACHERS ACADEMY FOR MATHEMATICS AND SCIENCE (TAMS)
3424 S State St, Chicago, IL 60616-3834 (On the campus of Illinois Institute of Technology) 312-808-0100 Fax 312-808-0103
Founded by Leon Lederman, Nobel laureate in physics, TAMS provides many opportunities for teacher training in mathematics and science. Over 70 schools chosen and interested in staff development now receive ongoing teacher training and educational materials assistance. Technology workshops for individual teachers in the Chicago Public Schools are also available through the Academy. TAMS also sponsors conferences on mathematics and science education.

WALTER E. HELLER NATURE CENTER
2821 Ridge Rd, Highland Park, IL 60035 847-433-6901
http://www.als.uiuc.edu/pdhp/ Hours: Monday-Saturday 8:30-5:00; Sunday 10:00-4:00. Park hours: 6:00-9:00 seven days a week. Admission free.
This Center is a 97 acre forest with more than three miles of marked trails, including a building with a community room, a classroom, and a reference library. Request a Park District of Highland Park 80-page catalog listing special events, educational nature classes, programs for school groups preschool through high school, and athletic programs.

WORKING IN THE SCHOOLS (WITS)
Matt Pickering, Executive Director 150 E Huron, Suite 900, Chicago, IL 60611 312-751-WITS Fax 751-7244
Ask for brochure. As a volunteer or a corporate partner local children directly benefit in all subjects. Volunteers devote approximately three hours every week. Corporate partners allow their employees time off every other week to tutor during the work day. WITS provides role models for school children, helps students and teachers achieve their goals, encourages community involvement, creates camaraderie among volunteers, and re-energizes public education.

Chapter

5

Events

Chicago Area Events, Competitions, and Awards

AMERICAN CHEMICAL SOCIETY - CHICAGO SECTION
ANNUAL SCHOLARSHIP EXAMINATION
Contact Ronald J. Sykstus American Chemical Society, Chicago Section, 7173 N
Austin, Niles, IL 60714 847-647-8405 Fax 847-647-8364
Each year in May the Chicago Section of the American Chemical Society sponsors an
Annual Scholarship Examination for Chicagoland high school students. This exam has
been administered annually on the campus of the University of Illinois at Chicago.

ARGONNE NATIONAL LABORATORY
- OFFICE OF PUBLIC AFFAIRS
Argonne National Laboratory, 9700 S Cass Ave, Argonne, IL 60439 630-252-5562
For special events open to the public contact Argonne's Office of Public Affairs for
current information.

BROOKFIELD ZOO - SPECIAL EVENTS
3300 S Golf Rd, Brookfield, IL 60513 708-485-0263, ext 365
http://www.brookfield-zoo.mus.il.us
Ask for brochure describing the many special events held each year at Brookfield Zoo.

CHICAGO CHILDREN'S MUSEUM - EDUCATOR'S PREVIEW
Navy Pier Chicago, 700 E Grand Ave, Chicago, IL 60611 312-464-7683
http://www.chichildrensmuseum.org **Annual event in September.**
This open house is free to all educators and provides an opportunity to explore the museum, attend mini-workshops, sign up for field trips, network with colleagues, and gather educational resources to support the classroom experience.

CHICAGO CHILDREN'S MUSEUM - RUBE GOLDBERG CONTEST
Navy Pier Chicago, 700 E Grand Ave, Chicago, IL 60611 312-527-1000
http://www.anl.gov/OPA/rube/ (or http://www.anl.gov) **Annual event in March.**
This exciting contest, sponsored by Argonne Labs, challenges high school students to create contraptions in the spirit of Rube Goldberg's comic inventions. The public is invited to watch them in action.

THE CHICAGO REGIONAL BRIDGE BUILDING CONTEST
Contact Carlo Segre, 312-567-3498 http://www.iit.edu/~hsbridge/ Department of Physics, Siegel Hall, Illinois Institute of Technology, Chicago, IL 60616 312-567-3375 **Annual event.**
This engineering design contest is annually held in February on the campus of IIT in Herman Union Bldg. Ask for rules and information about availability of bridge building kits. This popular event sends the top two winners to the International Contest and provides awards and scholarships to winning bridge designs.

CHICAGOLAND SKY LINERS KITE CLUB
Contact Tom and Leora McCune Chicagoland Sky Liners Kite Club, 981 Twisted Oak, Buffalo Grove, IL 60089 708-537-7066
The 11th annual Sky Circus was held at Schaumburg, Illinois, in 1994. For current information about kite festivals in the U. S. and internationally see the current KiteLines magazine for Pocket Kite Calendar and Almanac.

DEPAUL CREATIVITY CONTEST
Contact David J. Lang, Program Coordinator Entrepreneurship Program, Department of Management, DePaul University, 1 E Jackson Blvd, Chicago, IL 60604 312-362-8353
High School Students, Undergraduate Students, and a combined category of Graduate Students and the general public may submit projects in different fields, including Sciences & Humanities and Physical & Engineering Sciences. Finalists will be invited to present oral presentations for a start-up business at the Creativity Contest. Contest held in the spring of each year.

DUPAGE AREA ENGINEERS' WEEK PROGRAM
Contact Dr. John S. Kallend, Chair Illinois Institute of Technology, Daniel F. and Ada L. Rice Campus, 201 East Loop Road, Wheaton, IL   60187-8489 630-691-7508 http://www.eweek.org
Held yearly in February to communicate what engineering is and what engineers do, and to attract students to careers in math, science and engineering. Telephone 312-567-3163 to register for activities.

ELLIS P. STEINBERG AWARD
Office of Public Affairs, Argonne National Laboratory, 9700 S Cass Ave, Argonne, IL 60439 630-252-5561 Fax 630-252-5533 Annual award.
This award is given for excellence in science teaching at the junior or senior high school level. This award is jointly administered by the Argonne Chapter of Sigma Xi and Argonne National Laboratory. Inquire about nomination information.

ENGINEERS WEEK - POSTER-ESSAY COMPETITION
Contact Walt Linzing Illinois Engineering Council, 53 W Jackson Blvd, Suite 1730, Chicago, IL 60604 312-831-3023 Fax 312-831-3999 Deborah Zroka 773-935-6376 http://www.eweek.org
In conjunction with National Engineering Week each February, Chicago engineering societies will be hosting a poster-essay competition for area schools.

FUTURE CITY COMPETITION
Illinois Engineering Council, 53 W Jackson Blvd, Suite 1730, Chiccago, IL 60604 800-843-5410 703-684-2852 312-930-9119 http://www.eweek.org
In conjunction with National Engineering Week each February, Chicago engineering societies will be hosting a student design competition for area schools. Future City Competition will require middle grade students to design a future city with the aid of the award-winning computer game, SimCity 2000, and with the assistance of an engineer mentor. Judging is held at the University of Illinois at Chicago.

GETTING EXCITED ABOUT SCIENCE
Contact Steve Belliveau for available dates. 800-890-6244
Steve Belliveau combines his science education with his skill as a magician to present a general science show that captivates students and teachers alike.

GOLDEN APPLE FOUNDATION
8 South Michigan Ave, Suite 700, Chicago, IL 60603-3318 312-407-0006 http://www.goldenapple.org
Nonprofit organization that recognizes excellent teachers K-12 in Cook, Lake, and DuPage Counties. Nomination period is September through November each year. Golden Apple Award-winners become part of the foundation's Academy of educators, creating programs to recruit and renew teachers.

THE IIT 100 SPEEDWAY
Illinois Institute of Technology, Alumni Office - IIT 100, 10 W 35th St, Chicago, IL 60616 312-567-3000 The IIT 100 race is annually held in April.
Students compete with student engineered cars for monetary prizes and a pizza party. Ask for rules and information about this popular event. Divisions include high school, college, and alumni/faculty. Cost of registration is $ 25.00 per team, which will provide a kit to construct the vehicle. This event is sponsored by Snap-On Tools and Ford Motor, Inc.

IIT INDUSTRIAL DESIGN OPEN HOUSE
School of Industrial Design, IIT, 35th & State St, Chicago, IL 60616 312-595-4900 Annually in May.
This one day event allows guests to meet designers and student designers for brief consultations about their invention designs.

THE ILLINOIS SCIENCE OLYMPIAD
Brent Williamson, State Director Homewood-Flossmoor High School, 999 Kedzie Ave, Flossmoor, IL 60422-2299 708-799-3000, ext 315 Evenings 219-838-3429 Fax 708-799-3142 Email jbwilliamson@kiwi.dep.anl.gov
http://webmasterworks.com/olympiad/index.html
Ask to be placed on the mailing list to receive a newsletter. The goal of this organization is to improve the quality of science education and is accomplished through classroom activities and the encouragement of tournaments where student teamwork accomplishes scientific tasks in all areas of applied science, including biology, chemistry, physics, earth sciences and engineering. Divisions include A1 (grades K-3), A2 (grades 3-6), B (grades 5-9), and C (grades 9-12).

MACSHANE LASER ARTS
Contact Jim MacShane, 512 Braeside Drive, Arlington Hts, IL 60004 847-398-4983
Ask for brochure. Presentations, light shows and workshops that demonstrate the possibilities of high technology and arts as educational teammates.

MAD SCIENCE OF NORTHERN ILLINOIS
Contact Donna and Marc Price 1423 Rosewood Avenue, Deerfield, IL 60015 847-374-1212 Fax 847-374-1755 Madscini@aol.com (Elementary School).
In-class science workshops that bring hands-on science to children. Inquire about courses, workshops, science events, and birthday parties.

MAD SCIENCE OF THE WESTERN SUBURBS
Contact Suzanne and Carl Armbruster   2716 Gleneagles Ct, Naperville, IL 60565 630-357-5460 Fax 630-357-0891 (Elementary School).
In-class science workshops that bring hands-on science to children. Inquire about courses, workshops, science events, and birthday parties.

MUSEUM OF SCIENCE AND INDUSTRY
Special Science Programs, Museum of Science and Industry, 57th St and Lake Shore Drive, Chicago, IL 60637 773-684-1414 http://www.msichicago.org
Science programs are held at the Museum around a theme or topic such as Earth Day or Space Day.

SCHOOL TECHNOLOGY FAIR
Contact Jessica Billings Illinois Association of School Boards, 430 E Vine St, Springfield, IL 62703-2236 217-528-6988, ext 1104 Fax 217-753-2485
Held annually, each November in Chicago. Teams of teachers and students demonstrate projects. Ask for information.

SCIENCE/MATHEMATICS END-OF-YEAR EVENT
Contact Jim Cowden Chicago Teachers Academy 6E (s), Chicago Public Schools, 1819 W Pershing Rd, Chicago, IL 60609 773-535-8178 Annual event.
This citywide event provides a unique opportunity for K-12 to meet for a professional and social experience. Activities include an opportunity for networking, a featured keynote presentation, dinner, and distribution of instructional materials donated by vendors. This event is hosted by one of the downtown hotels in Chicago.

SIX FLAGS GREAT AMERICA PHYSICS DAYS
Lisa Scheuring, Special Events Representative Six Flags Great America, P. O. Box 1776, 542 N Route 21, Gurnee, IL 60031 847-249-1952
Each May, Six Flags Great America hosts Physics Days. This successful program brings high school students from all over the Midwest to the amusement park for educational fun in a recreational atmosphere. On the rides students measure their acceleration, horsepower, and centripetal force as they become a moving part of science experiments.

UNDER THE UMBRELLA CONFERENCE
Contact Jim Cowden Chicago Teachers Academy 6E (s), Chicago Public Schools, 1819 W Pershing Rd, Chicago, IL 60609 773-535-8178 Annual event.
The annual Under the Umbrella Conference takes place at the end of January. This one-day conference is open to K-12 teachers, administrators, and support staff. Activities include workshops, a featured keynote presentation, and an extensive exhibit of instruction materials and resources. Workshop topics include exemplary programs, instructional strategies, novel activities, assessment, and standards.

The Science/Mathematics End-of-Year Event provides a unique
and fun opportunity for hundreds of teaching colleagues of the
Chicago Public Schools to come together for a professional and
social event. This event is sponsored by the CPS Teachers
Academy for Professional Development.

Photos Courtesy of the CPS Teachers Academy

WEIRD SCIENCE KIDS

Lee Marek, Instructor. Naperville North High School, 899 N Mill St, Naperville, IL 60563-8998 630-420-6513 Fax 630-420-3246 Email lmarek@aol.com Email lmarek@fnal.gov
The Weird Science Kids make chemistry fun with wild, mad science demonstrations. This group of teachers often go on the road with their show. You may have seen Lee Marek squirt television's David Letterman with a fire extinguisher, cover him with shredded Styrofoam and blind him with burning magnesium. The Weird Science Kids often make presentations to local audiences. Inquire about Weird Science Videos.

WORLDWIDE YOUTH IN SCIENCE AND ENGINEERING (WYSE) ENGINEERING DESIGN COMPETITION

David L Powell, Director, WYSE, University of Illinois at Urbana-Champaign, College of Engineering, 1308 W Green St, Room 207, Urbana, IL 61801-2982 800-843-5410 217-333-2860 Fax 217-244-2488 Email d-powell@uiuc.edu http://www.engr.uiuc.edu/wyse/
Annually WYSE conducts the Academic Challenge, a written exam competition as well as Engineering Design Competition in Chicago. Ask for current information and a copy of the Engineering Library for Pre-College Students and Teachers catalog of brochures, books, and videotapes. Note, two sessions of an engineering camp, Exploring Your Options, are offered in the summer on the Champaign/Urbana U of I campus.

National Events, Competitions, and Awards

THE DUPONT CHALLENGE

Contact Gail Rudd Science Essay Awards Program, General Learning Communications, 900 Skokie Blvd, Suite 200, Northbrook, IL 60062 847-205-3000 Fax 847-564-8197 http://www.glcomm.dupont.com
The DuPont Challenge is an annual national science essay contest, Junior Divison grades 7-9 and Senior Division grades 10-12. Annually nearly $ 8,000 in educational grants for students are awarded. Each essay must be between 700 and 1,000 words and conform to all rules. Inquire about the current rules and deadlines to the Science Essay Awards Program at the above address.

DURACELL/NSTA SCHOLARSHIP COMPETITION

Contact Eric Crossley National Science Teachers Association, 1840 Wilson Blvd, Arlington, VA 22201-3000 888-255-4242 703-312-9258 Fax 703-522-6193 Email ecrossley@nsta.org http://www.nsta.org/programs/duracell.shtml
This competition awards saving bonds to young inventors in grades 7-12. First place winner will receive a $ 20,000 savings bond. Inquire about rules and deadlines.

EARTH SCIENCE WEEK
American Geological Institute, 4220 King St, Alexandria, VA 22302
703-379-2480 Fax 703-379-7563 http://www.earthsciweek.org
Earth Science Week is held annually in October.

EXEMPLARY ELEMENTARY SCIENCE PRINCIPAL AWARD
Sponsored by the Ciba Chemical Corporation and the Council for Elementary
Science International Contact Kathleen B. Horstmeyer, 726 Hillview Rd,
Malvern, PA 19355
The award consists of a $ 1,000 prize and an expense-paid trip to the NSTA National
Convention. Request application packet. No fax or email applications accepted.

INTERNATIONAL SCIENCE AND ENGINEERING FAIR
Contact Sharon Manley Science Service, Inc., 1719 N St, NW, Washington, DC
20036 202-785-2255 Fax 202-785-1243 Email smanley@sciserv.org Email
youth@sciserv.org http://www.sciserv.org and http://www.tss-inc.com/sciserv/
For over forty years Science Service has administered the International Science and
Engineering Fair. More than 1100 students participate from over 30 different
countries. Students in grades 9-12 are eligible and two student finalists and a team of
up to three are selected from each of the 485 regional science fairs. Sponsored by Intel.

NASA/NSTA SPACE SCIENCE STUDENT INVOLVEMENT PROGRAM
(SSIP) National Science Teachers Association, 1840 Wilson Blvd, Arlington, VA
22201-3000 703-243-7100 http://www.nsta.org/programs/
This competition encourages students to work in a team to create and design futuristic
aircraft or spacecraft; investigate the effect of human activity on the Earth's ecosystem;
propose experiments that could be performed at NASA facilities or on space flights;
or design an expedition to Mars. Inquire about rules and deadlines.

NSTA AWARD PROGRAMS
National Science Teachers Association, 1840 Wilson Blvd, Arlington, VA
22201-3000 703-243-7100 http://www.nsta.org.programs
Ask for brochure or see web site for current programs. NSTA administers over 20
award programs for students and teachers of science.

PRESIDENTIAL AWARDS FOR EXCELLENCE IN SCIENCE AND MATHEMATICS TEACHING (PAESMT)

NSF/PAESMT, Room 885, 4201 Wilson Blvd, Arlington, VA 22230 In Illinois 630-406-5730 MATH and 217-782-2826 SCIENCE.

This program was established by The White House and identifies outstanding teachers of science and mathematics, K-12, who will serve as models for their colleagues and who will form a leadership core to help advance the major reform movements in these disciplines. Contact the Illinois Science Teachers Association for local nomination forms and nomination deadlines.

TANDY TECHNOLOGY SCHOLARS

Contact Phyllis Sparks TCU Box 298990, TCU Station, Fort Worth, TX 76129 817-924-4087 Fax 817-927-1942 Email TandyScholar@tcu.edu http://www.tandy.com/scholars/

High schools throughout the United States may nominate outstanding students in math, science or computer science or may nominate an outstanding teacher in these areas to receive scholarships and awards. Application deadline for applications is Mid-October.

TAPESTRY/NSTA

1840 Wilson Blvd, Arlington, VA 22201-3000 800-807-9852
Email pbowers@nsta.org http://www/nsta.org/programs/toyota.htm

Toyota's Appreciation Program for Excellence to Science Teachers Reaching Youth (TAPESTRY). Competition is open to science teachers of grades 6-12. $ 400,000 in grants to teachers is available with up to $ 10,000 for your innovative project. Inquire about rules and deadlines.

TOSHIBA/NSTA EXPLORAVISION AWARDS PROGRAM

National Science Teachers Association, 1840 Wilson Blvd, Arlington, VA 22201-3000 800-EXPLOR-9 703-243-7100 http://toshiba.com

The purpose of the competition is to encourage students to combine their imagination with the tools of science and technology to create and explore a vision of the future. Each contest entry is limited by rules and consists of a project description (ten pages or less), bibliography and ten storyboard frames. Student members of the four first place teams will each receive a $ 10,000 U. S. savings bond. See Toshiba web site for other programs.

WESTINGHOUSE SCIENCE TALENT SEARCH
Science Service, Inc., 1719 N St, NW, Washington, DC 20036 202-785-2255 Fax 202-785-1243 http://www.sciserv.org For public relations information Email John Armstrong at armstrdj@westinghouse.com
Since 1942, Science Service, Inc., has administered this nationwide competition that has included five future Nobel Prize winners. High school seniors complete independent research projects and submit written reports on their findings. Finalists enjoy traveling to Washington, DC, and meet the President of the United States. Sponsored by the Westinghouse Foundation and Science Service.

YOUNG INVENTORS AWARDS PROGRAM
Craftsman/NSTA Young Inventors Awards Program, 1840 Wilson Blvd, Arlington, VA 22201-3000 888-494-4944 Email younginventors@nsta.org http://www.nsta.org/programs/craftsman.htm
Request entry materials for your classroom. Deadline mid March each year. The program offers students in grades 4-6 the opportunity to win $ 5,000 to $ 10,000 savings bonds by inventing a new hand tool or improving an existing one.

Chapter

6

Excursions

Excursion Reference Books

AMUSEMENT PARK PHYSICS: A TEACHER'S GUIDE
by Nathan A. Unterman J. Weston Walch, Publisher, 321 Valley St, P. O. Box
658, Portland, ME 04104-0658 800-341-6094 Fax 207-772-3105
http://www.walch.com 159 pages $ 20.95 (800-722-NSTA $ 20.95)
This guide provides tutorials, practice problems, and lab exercises appropriate for
studying the motion of amusement park rides.

ASTC DIRECTORY
Association of Science-Technology Centers, 1025 Vermont Ave, NW, Suite 500,
Washington, DC 20005   202-783-7200, ext 140   Fax 202-783-7207 Email
pubs@astc.org http://www.astc.org Published Annually Nonmembers $ 40.00
The "yellow pages" of the science-center field.   Science centers, museums, and
institutions of informal science education.

HIKING & BIKING IN LAKE COUNTY, ILLINOIS
by Jim Hochgesang Roots and Wings Publications, P. O. Box 167, Lake Forest,
IL 60045 128 pages $ 10.95
 For direction to nature excursions this book describes 25 different nature trails and
forest preserves.

THE NATURE OF CHICAGO
by Isabel S. Abrams Chicago Review Press, Inc., 814 Franklin St, Chicago, IL 60610 800-888-4741 1997 278 pages $ 14.95
This resource guide is for those who enjoy and study nature in the Chicago area. It is full of resource listings.

TEACH THE MIND, TOUCH THE SPIRIT:
A GUIDE TO FOCUSED FIELD TRIPS
The Field Museum, Education Department, Roosevelt Road at Lake Shore Drive, Chicago, IL 60605-2497 312-922-2497, ext 351 http://www.fmnh.org 80 pages $ 10.00
This book describes museums as educational opportunities, structuring your field trip, The Field Museum opportunities, and a reference bibliography.

TEN-MINUTE FIELD TRIPS
by Helen Ross Russell Produced and distributed by the National Science Teachers Association 800-722-NSTA 1991 176 pages $ 16.95
More than 200 short, close-to-home excursions in science for grades K-8 are described. Each excursion is categorized by science subject area and lists classroom activities with teacher preparation needs. Excursions are described for both rural and urban locations. Fun for both teachers and parents.

TREKS FOR TROOPS: TROOP REFERENCE FOR TRIPS
Girl Scouts of Chicago, 222 S Riverside Plaza, Chicago, IL 60606 1994 38 pages
 This reference lists over 100 places in Metropolitan Chicago where one can take a group.

U. S. SPACE CAMP FOUNDATION
One Tranquility Base, Huntsville, AL 35805-3399 800-63-SPACE
http://www.spacecamp.com
Ask for 20-page program guide describing Space Camp programs.

Chicago Area Excursion Opportunities

ADLER PLANETARIUM & ASTRONOMY MUSEUM
1300 S Lake Shore Drive, Chicago, IL 60605 312-922-7827 312-322-0304
http://astro.uchicago.edu/adler/ Winter Hours: Monday-Thursday 9:30-5:00; Fridays and Weekends 9:00-6:00. Summer Hours: Saturday-Wednesday 9:00-6:00; Thursday and Friday 9:00-9:00. Admission to the Museum: Adults $ 5.00; children 4-17 and senior citizens $ 4.00; children 3 and under free. Star Rider Theater tickets are an additional $ 5.00 for all ages per show. Tuesday is free admission to the Museum.   Continued...

See the Museum's new wing with new exhibits and Star Rider Theater, a virtual-reality experience.

ARGONNE INFORMATION CENTER
Office of Public Affairs, Argonne National Laboratory, 9700 S Cass Ave, Argonne, IL 60439 630-252-5562 http://www.anl.gov/OPA/AIC Open to the public, free of charge, from 10:00 - 3:00 Tuesday - Saturday, except holidays.
No registration is required and children of any age are welcome if accompanied by an adult. The Center offers an excellent introduction to Argonne and is filled with interactive computerized exhibits, displays, and historical artifacts from 50 years of scientific research. Four of the features of the Center are: 1) A user-controllable, table-top electron accelerator that lets you use magnets to bend and control a particle beam's path. 2) An interactive and video tour of Argonne's Advanced Photon Source, source of the nation's most brilliant X-rays for scientific research. 3) Internet access to advanced, remote-controlled microscopes that let scientists perform experiments from hundreds of miles away. 4) Samples of a new room-temperature ceramic that can make quick, long-lasting repairs of roads and potholes, even in freezing weather. Two and one-half hour guided tours of Argonne are also available to Center visitors. Most tours are scheduled on Saturday. Visitors taking the tour must be at least 16 years old.

ANDREW B. BARBER AND CLARENCE D. OBERWORTMANN HORTICULTURAL CENTER
Contact Debbie Greene, Pilcher Park   225 N Gougar Rd, Joliet, IL 815-741-7277 Fax 815-722-5317 debgreene@jolietpark.org http://jolietpark.org/andrewb.htm http://www.jolietpark.org
This new center features a multi-purpose room, resource center, kitchen, gift shop, and covered deck. The multi-purpose room has flower shows, exhibits, and learning opportunities for children and adults.

BROOKFIELD ZOO
3300 S Golf Rd, Brookfield, IL 60513 708-485-0263 http://www.brookfield-zoo.mus.il.us Memorial Day-Labor Day 9:30-5:30 seven days a week; Labor Day-Memorial Day 10:00-4:30. General admission: Adults $ 4.00; children 3-11 and senior citizens $ 1.50; children under 3 years free. Car parking $ 4.00. Attractions additional. Tuesday and Thursday half price admission April-September, Tuesday and Thursday free admission October-March.
Home to over 23,00 animals, Brookfield Zoo attractions include Seven Seas Panorama, Habitat Africa, The Fragile Kingdom, Tropic World, Children's Zoo, Motor Safari, Aquatic Bird House, Reptile House, Pachyderm House, Australia House and Discovery Center.

CAMP SAGAWAU
12545 W 11th St, Lemont, IL 60439 630-257-2045 (Forest Preserve District of Cook County 708-771-1330)
This environmental education center was established to promote the study of nature and is open only for scheduled programs including workshops, college credit courses, outdoor nature photography, birding, naturalist guided walks, field trips for adult groups, college and high school classes, and a winter Nordic ski program.

CERNAN EARTH AND SPACE CENTER
Triton College, 2000 N 5th Ave, River Grove, IL 60171 708-583-3100
http://www.triton.cc.il.us/cernan/cernan_home.html Hours: Monday-Thursday 9:00-5:00; Friday 9:00-11:00pm; Saturday 1:00-11:00pm; Sunday 1:00-5:00 Adults $ 5.00; children and seniors $ 2.50. Laser Shows: Adults $ 6.00; children and seniors $ 3.00
This planetarium has sky shows, exhibits, and educational programs. Inquire about current programs.

CHICAGO BOTANIC GARDEN
1000 Lake Cook Road (at Edens Expressway), Glencoe, IL 60022 847-835-5440 http://www.chicago-botanic.org Garden hours: 8:00 a.m.-Sunset everyday except Christmas Day.   Parking $ 5.00 per car Monday - Friday; $ 6.00 per car Saturdays, Sundays and Holidays; includes admission to Garden. Tram Tickets: Adults $ 4.00; reduced rates for children, seniors and members.
The Chicago Botanic Garden has created display gardens on its 385 acres that have influenced the development of many gardens throughout the world.   Home of the Chicago Horticultural Society.   The Chicago Botanic Garden includes a Plant Information Service, Garden Shop, Food for Thought Cafe, and a Library.

CHICAGO CHILDREN'S MUSEUM
Navy Pier, 700 E Grand Ave, Chicago, IL 60611 312-527-1000
http://www.chichildrensmuseum.org Hours: 10:00-5:00 Tuesday-Sunday (and Mondays when school is not in session). Adults and children $ 6.00 for an all-day pass, seniors $ 5.00. Ask about the benefits of family memberships. Note: Thursday night from 5:00-8:00 is Jewel-Osco Free Family Night.
For children the world is a science experiment. Here your child can explore and learn science through experience in the Inventing Lab, Waterways, Under Construction, and many more exhibits. Ask for a copy of the 'Handprint', a newsletter and calendar of programs, events and workshops.

CLEARBROOK CENTER - LEKOTEK
(Toy Lending Library) Clearbrook Center for the Handicapped, 3705 Pheasant Dr, Rolling Meadows, IL 60008 847-392-2812 Fee $ 65 per year
Ask for descriptive brochure. This toy loan center for children with special needs is open to everyone in the Chicagoland area.

CRABTREE NATURE CENTER
Palatine Road, Barrington, IL 60010 847-381-6592 (Forest Preserve District of Cook County 708-771-1330) Parking lot and trails hours: Daily 8:00-4:30. Exhibit building hours: Daily 9:00-4:00. Hours extended 30 minutes on weekends and during summer. Admission free.
Operated by the Cook County Forest Preserve District, this center includes a glacier-formed landscape with self-guided nature trails and a museum. School groups may phone ahead to schedule a presentation on nature.

DANADA EQUESTRIAN CENTER FOREST PRESERVE
on Naperville Road, 1/2 mile north of I-88, Wheaton, IL 630-688-6012
(Forest Preserve District of DuPage County 630-790-4900)
http://www.co.dupage.il.us/forest/fpdhome.html
Ask for brochure. Opportunities include educational programs, hay rides, Fall Festival, trails, and fishing. Ask for: A Teacher's Guide to the Forest Preserve District of DuPage County.

DISCOVERY CENTER MUSEUM
Contact Sarah Wolf 711 N Main St, Rockford, IL 61103 815-963-6769 Fax 815-968-0164 Email discoverycentermuseum@discoverycentermuseum.org http://www.discoverycentermuseum.org Hours: Tuesday-Saturday 10:00-5:00; Sunday 12:00-5:00; closed Monday; open Monday on school holidays. Adults $ 4.00; children $ 3.00; members and children under 2 years free admission.
The Museum has over 200 hands-on science and arts exhibits inside the museum and even more in the outdoor science park. Themes range from electricity to weather to puzzles to aviation, with something for every child between 1 and 101. Ask for a copy of the Discovery Center's special events flyer listing traveling exhibits, special events, and more.

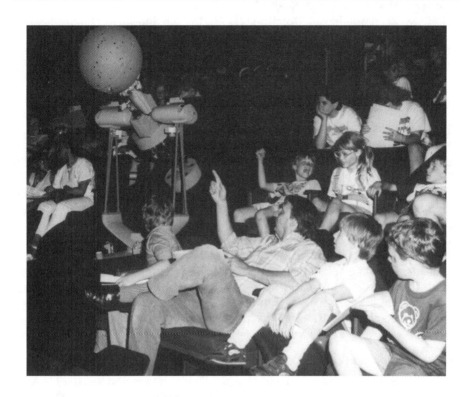

The Cernan Earth & Space Center at Triton College has planetarium sky shows, exhibits, and educational programs.

Photo Courtesy of Cernan Earth & Space Center

DUPAGE CHILDREN'S MUSEUM
Wheaton Park District Community Center, 1777 S Blanchard Rd, Wheaton, IL 60187 630-260-9960 Group Visits 630-260-9907 Fax 630-260-1656 http://www.dcmrats.org   Tuesday-Saturday 9:30-5:00; Wednesday Evenings 5:00-8:00;   Sunday 12:00-5:00;   Member Mondays 9:00-Noon.   Adults and Children $ 4.50; members and children under 1 admission free.

Ask for calendar of adventures showing special activities almost every day of the month. Learning Lab topics offered at the museum or in your classroom include Magnet Experimentation, What's Inside, Estimation Lab, No Numbers Math, Windows, GeoSpace, Kid's Design Engineering Lab.

104 Science Fun in Chicagoland

EDWARD L. RYERSON CONSERVATION AREA
21950 N Riverwoods Rd, Deerfield, IL 60015 Nan Buckardt, Environmental Education Manager 847-948-7750 Fax 847-948-7712 Email ryersonwoods@co.lake.il.us Conservation Area hours: 9:00-5:00 seven days a week; Visitors Center closed Thanksgiving, Christmas and New Years Day. Admission free.
Inquire about educational programs available.

ELGIN PUBLIC MUSEUM
225 Grand Blvd, Elgin, IL 60120 847-741-6655 Summer hours (April 15 - October 15): Tuesday-Sunday 12:00-4:00. Winter hours (October 15 - April 15): Saturday-Sunday 12:00-4:00 Adults $ 1.00; children 50 cents.
This natural history museum has exhibits on life science and geology. Ask for newsletter describing special events. School groups may be scheduled Monday-Friday during the winter.

EVANSTON ECOLOGY CENTER
Evanston Environmental Association, Evanston Ecology Center, 2024 McCormick Blvd, Evanston, IL 60201 847-864-5181 Ladd Arboretum open at all times. Ecology Center hours: Tuesday-Saturday 9:00-4:30.
Ask for a copy of The Evanston Ecology Center Newsletter that describes current programs and events at the Center.

FABYAN MUSEUM
1511 S Batavia Ave, Geneva, IL 60134 630-232-4811 Open first weekend in May through second weekend in October. Hours: Tuesday, Wednesday, Thursday 11:00-3:00; Saturday and Sunday 1:00-5:00. Admission free.
This museum is the home of the late Col. George Fabyan, pioneer in acoustics and inventor of the tuning fork. Also on this site is the Riverbank Accoustical Laboratories operated by IIT (630-232-0104) and the Riverbank Laboratory, Tuning Fork Section (630-232-2207).

FERMILAB - GUIDED TOURS
Fermilab, Education Office, P O Box 500, Batavia, IL 60510-0500 630-840-5588
Contact Fermilab Education Office for guided tours by appointment. A minimum of 10 people is needed to book a tour, with 40 being the maximum.

FERMILAB - SELF-GUIDED TOURS

Fermilab, Batavia, IL 60510-0500 Wilson Hall at Fermilab may be reached on Pine Street off Kirk Road between Butterfield Road (Route 56) and Wilson Street, Batavia. Accessible from Interstate 88 (East-West Tollway) via Farnsworth Avenue North exit. Self-guided tour hours: 8:30-5:00 seven days a week.

Pick up a self-guided tour brochure at the reception desk in Wilson Hall. Be sure to stop at the Lederman Science Center on Pine Street, open to the public Monday-Friday 8:30-5:00 and the first and third Saturday from 9:00-3:00.

THE FIELD MUSEUM

Roosevelt Road at Lake Shore Drive, Chicago, IL 60605-2497 312-922-9410 http://www.fmnh.org Hours: 9:00-5:00 seven days a week. Closed Christmas and New Years Day. Adults $ 7.00; children, senior citizens $ 4.00; teachers and military personnel with ID free. Wednesday free.

This great Museum of Chicago is a world class showplace of the natural science of the Earth and of the diverse cultural history of humanity. Living Together, Eskimos and North West Coast Indians, Life Over Time, Plants of the World, Africa, Traveling the Pacific, What is an Animal, Precious Gems, and Inside Ancient Egypt are examples of exhibits. Check the Harris Loan Center for exhibit pamphlets to supplement your visit, or ask the Education Department for a self-guided tour sheet. Always plan to make a return visit to see what you missed.

THE FIELD MUSEUM - PUBLIC PROGRAMS

The Field Museum, Roosevelt Road at Lake Shore Drive, Chicago, IL 60605-2497 312-922-9410 http://www.fmnh.org

Weekend Programs and Activities 312-922-9410. Natural History Field Trips 312-922-9410 extension 362, Children's Workshops 312-922-9410 extension 854, Adult Courses, Performances, Lectures 312-922-9410 extension 575. Contact these divisions for current activities brochure.

FOREST PRESERVE DISTRICT OF COOK COUNTY

Conservation Department, 536 N Harlem Ave, River Forest, IL 60305 800-870-3666 708-771-1330

Ask for brochure, Getting in Touch with Nature, Classroom Programs for Cook County Schools, including classroom programs, slide programs, and visiting nature centers. Nature centers include Crabtree Nature Center, Barrington, IL 847-381-6592; River Trail Nature Center, Northbrook, IL 708-824-8360; Trailside Museum, River Forest, IL 708-366-6530; Little Red Schoolhouse Nature Center, Willow Springs, IL 708-839-6897; Sand Ridge Nature Center, South Holland, IL 708-868-0606; and Camp Sauawau, Lemont, IL 630-257-2045. Please schedule your program as early as possible, at least three weeks in advance.

FULLERSBURG WOODS ENVIRONMENTAL EDUCATION CENTER
Contact Tom Pray 3609 Spring Rd, Oak Brook, IL 60521 630-850-8110 Fax 630-850-7701 (Forest Preserve District of DuPage County 630-790-4900) http://www.co.dupage.il.us/forest/fpdhome.html Hours: 9:00-5:00 seven days a week. Admission free
Programs include field trip opportunities, Learn to Be a Nature Detective, Trees Please!, From Grass to Hawks, Migration Headache, Dig Dem Bones, Maple Syrup Program, Animals in Danger, Wildlife and You. Ask for: A Teacher's Guide to the Forest Preserve District of DuPage County.

GARFIELD PARK CONSERVATORY
Lisa Roberts, Director 300 N Central Park Ave, Chicago, IL 60624 312-746-5100 Fax 773-638-1777 http://www.garfield-conservatory.org Hours: 9:00-5:00 seven day a week. Admission free.
One of the most beautiful botanical gardens under glass in the world. Its four acres include the Palm House, the Aroid House, the Fernery, Horticultural Hall and Show House, and the Cactus House. Phone ahead for free school class tours.   GROVE, THE   Contact Lorin Ottlinger   1421 Milwaukee Ave, Glenview, IL 60025 708-299-6096 Hours: Monday-Friday 8:00-4:30; Saturday and Sunday 9:00-5:00. Kennicott House: Sunday 1:00-4:00.   Admission free. This national landmark administered by the Glenview Park District is the 1836 homestead of the the Kennicott family. The Grove is a public museum and nature preserve. Ask for brochures about festivals and fairs held each year, animal programs that visit schools, as well as educational programs, including the Kindergarten Program, Animal Habits and Habitats, Earth Science, Pioneer Skills, Insects, Archaeology, and Pond Life.

MUSEUM OF HOLOGRAPHY /CHICAGO
Contact Loren Billings   1134 W Washington Blvd, Chicago, IL 60607 312-226-1007 Fax 312-829-9636 Email museum@concentric.net http://museumof holography.com Hours: Wednesday-Sunday 12:30-5:00.   Tour groups by appointment seven days a week. Weekdays: Adults $ 3.00; school groups $ 2.50 each. Weekends and evenings: Adults $ 3.50; school groups $ 3.00 each.
This institution is dedicated to display, promote and encourage the advancement of holography as an art form. The museum displays holographic three dimensional images in various exhibition rooms. This holographic art is often the result of new research and technology produced at the Museum. A school of holography is also associated with the museum.

INTERNATIONAL MUSEUM OF SURGICAL SCIENCE

International College of Surgeons, 1524 N Lake Shore Drive, Chicago, IL 60610 312-642-6502 Tuesday-Saturday 10:00-4:00; Closed Sunday, Monday, and Holidays. Suggested donation for admission.

This museum exhibits the methods and the history of surgery from various cultures world wide. Phone ahead for class visits to the museum. Inquire about The MED Project, a summer program for Chicago high school students.

JFK HEALTH WORLD

1301 S Grove Ave, Barrington, IL 60010 847-842-9100 Fax 847-842-9101 Monday-Thursday 12:00-3:00 Children $ 3, chaperones $ 1, and teachers free.

Museum for young children on health. Workshops, courses, library.

JURICA NATURE MUSEUM

Contact Fr. Theodore Suchy. Scholl Science Center, Illinois Benedictine College, 5700 College Rd, Lisle, IL 60532 630-825-6545 Fax 630-829-6551 Email tsuchy@ben.edu http://www.ben.edu/resources/J_Museum/index Hours: May 16-July 31: Wednesday 1:00-3:00; Sunday 2:00-4:00. September 1-May 15: Monday- Thursday 1:00-5:00; Friday 1:00-4:00; Sunday 2:00-4:00. Closed August. Open other times by appointment. Admission free, donation accepted.

Visitors experience the African savanna, tropical rain forest, the woodlands, wetlands and prairie of Northern Illinois along with other smaller animal habitat dioramas. Insects, fish, reptiles and all kinds of birds are displayed along with many fossil specimens and skeletons. Loan program available to teachers.

KLINE CREEK FARM

County Farm Road (One-half mile south of North Ave), Winfield, IL 630-876-5900 Fax 630-293-9421 Mailing address: Kline Creek Farm, P. O. Box 2339, Glen Ellyn, IL 60138-2339 (Forest Preserve District of DuPage County 630-790-4900) http://www.co.dupage.il.us/forest/fpdhome.html

Seasonal program offerings include Fall Harvest, Maple Sugaring, Spring Planting, and The Kitchen Garden. Ask for a teacher's guide.

KOHL CHILDREN'S MUSEUM

165 Green Bay Rd, Wilmette, IL 60091 888-KOHL-KID 847-256-6056 Hotline 847-251-7781 http://www.kohlchildrensmuseum.org Hours: Tuesday-Saturday 10:00-5:00; Sunday 12:00-5:00; Closed Mondays. Adults and children $ 5.00; senior citizens $ 4.00; children under 1 free; Members free.

For the young, the world is a science experiment. Here your child can explore and investigate hands-on exhibits including H20, a dynamic water play environment; StarMax Technology Center by Motorola, featuring creative learning software selected by the Museum's education staff; and Construction Zone, a house under construction and filled with simple and complex machines. Ask for calendar of special events.

LAKE COUNTY FOREST PRESERVES

2000 N Milwaukee Ave, Libertyville, IL 60048-1199 847-367-6640
http://www.co.lake.il.us/forest/index.htm
Ask for Group Environmental Education Program Guide including information about educational programs, prices, reservations, locations, dates, self-guided programs, and naturalist-guided programs. Over 20 programs available.

LEON M. LEDERMAN SCIENCE EDUCATION CENTER
- PRECOLLEGE EDUCATION PROGRAMS

Fermi National Accelerator Laboratory, P. O. Box 500 MS 777, Batavia, IL 60510-0500 630-840-8258
Contact this center for current information about programs for high school teachers and students, programs for elementary and mid level schools, programs for students of all ages, and science materials programs - in total over 50 programs of science education opportunities. This Science Education Center is equipped with a technology classroom, classroom laboratory, and hands-on exhibits dedicated to physical science concepts related to Fermilab. Science toys are available in a small retail shop.

LILACIA PARK

Lombard Park District, 150 S Park (Maple and Park), Lombard, IL 60148 630-953-6000, ext 411 Park hours: 9:00-9:00 seven days a week. Park District hours: Monday-Friday 8:30-5:00. Park admission free, except first two weeks in May at Lilac Time. Lilac Time admission: Adults $ 2.00; senior citizens and children $ 1.00.
This botanical garden contains eight acres of lilacs.

LINCOLN PARK CONSERVATORY

2400 N Stockton Drive at Fullerton Parkway, Chicago, IL 60614 312-742-7736 Hours: 9:00-5:00 seven days a week. Admission free.
Ask for brochure that includes information about the Palm House, the Fernery, the Cactus House, outdoor gardens, and flower shows held each year.

LINCOLN PARK ZOOLOGICAL GARDENS

2200 N Cannon Drive, Chicago, IL 60614 312-742-2000 http://www.lpzoo.com Hours: 9:00-5:00 every day. Admission free. Parking $ 7.00.
The Lincoln Park Zoo is home to more than 1,600 animals, birds and reptiles from every corner of the globe. See the Great Ape House, the Bird House, the Mammal Area, the Lion House, the Penguin & Seabird House, the Primate House, the Antelope & Zebra Area, Koala Plaza, Farm-in-the-Zoo, and the Children's Zoo with baby animals. Over 25 different programs are presented for visitors each day at various times throughout the Zoo.

LITTLE RED SCHOOL HOUSE NATURE CENTER

9800 S 104th Ave, (Willow Springs Road), Willow Springs, IL 60480 708-839-6897
(Forest Preserve District of Cook County 708-771-1330)   Summer Hours:
Monday-Thursday 9:00-4:30; Saturday and Sunday 9:00-5:00; closed Friday.
Winter Hours: Saturday-Thursday 9:00-4:00; closed Friday. Admission free.
Ask for brochure describing programs and events held throughout each month. Topics
include birdwatching, nature walks, astronomy, and archeology.

LIZZADRO MUSEUM OF LAPIDARY ART

220 Cottage Hill Ave, Elmhurst, IL 60126 630-833-1616   Fax 630-833-1225
http://www.elmhurst.org Hours: Tuesday-Saturday 10:00-5:00; Sunday 1:00-
5:00; closed Monday and major holidays. Adults $ 2.50; seniors $ 1.50; children
under 13 free admission.
This museum exhibits art forms made from minerals and rocks. Lapidary art is an
example of how art and the science of geology combine to reveal nature's beauty.

METROPOLITAN WATER RECLAMATION DISTRICT
OF GREATER CHICAGO

Contact Mr. Hugh H. McMillan 100 E Erie St, Chicago, IL 60611 312-751-6634
Ask for brochure. Tours are free of charge. Inquire about the nine different, possible
tour sites. Visitors should call 312-751-6634 prior to mailing their request letter to clear
an available date and time. All tours are arranged through the Public Information
Office. Speakers can also be arranged for group presentations.

THE MORTON ARBORETUM

4100 Illinois Route 53 (just north of interstate 88), Lisle, IL 60532-1293
630-719-2400 http://www.mortonarb.org Hours: 7:00 a.m.- 7:00 p.m. during
daylight savings time, 7:00 a.m. - 5:00 p.m. the rest of the year. Admission $ 7.00
per car, $ 3.00 on Wednesdays.
Open every day of the year, the Arboretum features more than 3,600 different kinds of
woody plants from around the world over 1,700 acres. Twelve miles of trails, 11 miles
of roads, as well as an hour-long tram tour ($ 2.00 per person) make discovering the
Arboretum fun and easy. The Arboretum includes an information building, restaurant
and coffee shop, and gift shop.

MOTOROLA MUSEUM

Sharon Darling, Director Motorola, Inc., 1297 E Algonquin Rd, Schaumburg, IL
60196 847-576-6400 847-576-6559 http://www.mot.com Hours: Monday-Friday
9:00-4:30; Closed on holidays observed by Motorola, Inc., and the first two weeks
in January.
The museum is open to the public by appointment by telephoning 847-576-6400.
Admission free. This museum provides interactive exhibits which chronicle the
revolution in electronics technology over the 20th Century. More than 3,000 samples

of Motorola products, marketing materials, and memorabilia are housed at the museum.

THE MUSEUM OF SCIENCE AND INDUSTRY
57th St and Lake Shore Drive, Chicago, IL 60637 773-684-1414
http://www.msichicago.org Open every day except Christmas Day. Hours:
Memorial Day through Labor Day: 9:30-5:30 daily.   Labor Day through
Memorial Day: 9:30-4:00 weekdays and 9:30-5:30 weekends and most holidays.
General Admission: Adults $ 7.00; Children 3-11 $ 3.50; Senior Citizens $ 6.00;
and children under 3, Illinois school groups, and park district camps free.
Museum admission is free on Thursdays. Admission with Omnimax Theater
included: Adults $ 12.00; Children 3-11 $ 7.50; Senior Citizens $ 10.00. Parking
$ 5.00. Additional fees apply for additional Omnimax features and LEGO
MindStorms workshops.
This world-famous hands-on Museum is internationally famous. Dedicated to the
science and technology of the past, present and future, the Museum of Science and
Industry truly has something for everyone. In addition to popular long-standing
exhibits, there is an ever-changing array of new exhibitions, events and attractions.
Major attractions include the Pioneer Zephyr (A 1930's sleek, silver train.), U-505
Submarine (Captured off the coast of Africa during World War II.), Coal Mine (With
new equipment, this original exhibit is contemporary with its old charm firmly in
place.), MSI Presents: Lego MindStorms (This workshop features the most advanced
computer programming modules. Reservations are necessary.), Virtual Reality
Experiences (Visitors can experience virtual reality in different locations throughout the
Museum.), Take Flight (Climb aboard a real 727 Boeing jet.), Idea Factory (A
learning-through-play environment for infants through 10-year-olds. Children must be
accompanied by a parent, or care giver.), and the Henry Crown Space Center (See some
of the famous artifacts from the U. S. Space Program.).

THE MUSEUM OF SCIENCE AND INDUSTRY - IDEA FACTORY
Museum of Science and Industry, 57th St and Lake Shore Drive, Chicago, IL
60637 773-684-1414 http://www.msichicago.org
The Idea Factory is for infants through 10-year-olds and allows them to have their own
special experience with interactive exhibits designed just for them. Parents must
accompany their children and appointments may be necessary at busy times. There is
no additional charge for the Idea Factory.

This student enjoys the lightning exhibit from the Illinois Wild
Weather Exhibit. It is one of the many interactive hands-on
opportunities at SciTech in Aurora.

Photo Courtesy of SciTech

NATIONAL LEKOTEK CENTER
(Toy Lending Library) National Lekotek Center, 2100 Ridge Ave, Evanston, IL 60201 847-328-0001 Fee $180 per year
Ask for descriptive brochure of the National Lekotek Center, a not-for-profit charitable organization. Also ask for a current list of over 20 Illinois Lekotek sites including Chicago, Chicago Heights, Flossmoor, Franklin Park, Libertyville, Lombard, Rolling Meadows, South Holland, and Tinley Park. Some centers have no fee and focus on special community needs.

NATURE MUSEUM OF THE CHICAGO ACADEMY OF SCIENCES
Administrative Headquarters, 2060 N Clark St, Chicago, IL 60614 773-549-0606 Fax 773-549-5199 Email cas@chias.org http://www.chias.org Hotline information 773-871-2668.
The Nature Museum of the Chicago Academy of Sciences, a place to explore science through nature and the environment, will open in Chicago's Lincoln Park on the corner of Fullerton Ave and Cannon Drive in the spring of 1999.

NORTH PARK VILLAGE NATURE CENTER
Contact Any Conrad 5801 N Pulaski Rd, Chicago, IL 60646 312-744-5472 Fax 312-744-1134 Email environment@ci.chi.il.us http://www.ci.chi.il.us Hours: 10:00-4:00 seven days a week; closed Thanksgiving Day, Christmas, New Years Day. Admission free.
The only Nature Center in the City of Chicago. Ask for calendar of events that includes activities almost every day of the month, pre-school registration information, school field trip descriptions and deadlines, teacher training program information, and a request for volunteers to work at the Center.

NORTHERN ILLINOIS UNIVERSITY ANTHROPOLOGY MUSEUM
Contact M. Demmer Stevens Building, Northern Illinois University, DeKalb, IL 60115-2854 815-753-0230 Fax 815-753-6302 Email mdemmer@niu.edu http://www.niu.edu/anthro_museum Hours: Monday-Friday 9:00-5:00; closed weekends and holidays. Admission free.
This museum contains over 5,000 ethnographic objects, and specializes in cultures in Southeast Asia, New Guinea, and the Southwest and Plains Native Americans. Other collections are from Africa, modern Greece, Mesoamerica, and South America, totaling over 50,000 skeletal specimens. The Museum maintains a research library of 1,000 books and journals.

OAK PARK CONSERVATORY
John Seaton, Head Horticulturist   615 Garfield St, Oak Park, IL 60304
708-386-4700 Fax 708-383-5702 http://www.oakparkparks.com Hours: Monday
2:00-4:00; Tuesday 10:00-4:00; Wednesday, Sunday 10:00-6:00. Admission free.
This conservatory includes a cactus section, tropical plants, as well as seasonal floral
shows. Inquire about current educational programs.

ORIENTAL INSTITUTE MUSEUM
University of Chicago, 1155 E 58th St, Chicago, IL 60637 773-702-9521 Tuesday,
Thursday, Friday, Saturday 10:00-4:00; Wednesday 10:00-8:30; Sunday
12:00-4:00. Admission free.
The Museum is a showcase for the history, culture, and archaeology of the Middle East.

PILCHER PARK - JOLIET PARK DISTRICT
Contact Debbie Greene, Pilcher Park, Route 30 near I-80, Joliet, IL 815-741-7277
Fax 815-722-5317 debgreene@jolietpark.org http://jolietpark.org Hours: March
to October 9:00-6:00 Daily; November to February 9:00-4:30 Daily.
This nature center includes trails for hiking and biking, a greenhouse, and an artesian
well. Ask for Field Trip Information brochure.

THE POWER HOUSE / ComEd
Commonwealth Edison, 100 Shiloh Blvd, Zion, IL 60099 847-746-7080
http://www.ucm.com/powerhouse Hours: Monday-Saturday 10:00-5:00. Closed
Sunday. Admission free.
This interactive, hands-on science museum is a fun, educational experience where one
learns about energy. The exhibits focus on The Nature of Energy, The Sources and
Forms of Energy, Energy Use Through Time, and Energy in Transition. It includes a
theater and educational resource center.

PREHISTORIC LIFE MUSEUM
Privately owned. Within Dave's Rock Shop, 704 Main St, Evanston, IL 60202
847-866-7374 Hours: Monday, Tuesday, Thursday, and Friday 10:30-5:30;
Saturday 10:00-5:00; closed Wednesday and Sunday. Admission free.
This private collection of fossils date back 1.5 billion years for algae samples and 600
millions years for fossils and has been collected over a 35 year period. Housed in one
room, this collection of Earth's life history includes dinosaur eggs and nests.

RIVER TRAIL NATURE CENTER

Contact John M. Elliott   3120 W Milwaukee Ave, Northbrook, IL 60062
847-824-8360 Email johnrtnc@flash.net http://www.flashnet/~jeffrtnc/ (Forest
Preserve District of Cook County 708-771-1330)   November-February hours:
8:00-4:30 seven days a week; museum open 9:00-4:00 Saturday-Thursday; Closed
Friday. March-October hours: Monday-Friday 8:00-5:00; Saturday and Sunday
8:00-5:30; museum open Monday-Thursday 9:00-4:30, Saturday and Sunday
9:00-5:00, closed Friday. Admission free.

At the Center naturalists present 15 minute presentations on nature topics. Center
exhibits include native mammals, fish, amphibians, and reptiles. There are three
self-guiding nature trails. November through March nature programs go out to any
school in Cook County. A sugar maple festival is held each spring in March and a
honey festival is held each fall in October.

SAND RIDGE NATURE CENTER

Contact Robert Munz Paxton Avenue, two blocks north of 159th St, South
Holland, IL 60473 708-868-0606 (Forest Preserve District of Cook County
708-771-1330)

This Center includes four nature trails, a vegetable garden with unusual vegetables and
herbs, and an exhibit building.

SCI-TECH CAMP FOR ELEMENTARY CHILDREN

Beth A. Wiegmann, Department of Curriculum and Instruction, Northern Illinois
University, DeKalb, IL 60115 815-753-9025

Summer science camp for children grades 3-6 and workshops for inservice teachers.

SCITECH
- THE SCIENCE AND TECHNOLOGY INTERACTIVE CENTER

18 W Benton, Aurora, IL 60506   630-859-3434   http://www.scitech.mus.il.us
Hours: Wednesday, Friday, Sunday noon-5:00; Thursday noon-8:00; Saturday
10:00-5:00. Adults $ 5.00; children under 18 $ 3.00; students with ID $ 3.00;
family $ 10.00; Age: preschool through adult.

This interactive science center has more than 200 hands-on exhibits on two floors
demonstrating physics concepts from science and technology. At SciTech you will have
an opportunity to satisfy your curiosity by enjoying scientific exploration and
experimentation. SciTech's Discovery Shop has many fun science toys and materials.
"Nobody flunks museum." -Frank Oppenheimer.

THE JOHN G. SHEDD AQUARIUM

1200 S Lake Shore Drive, Chicago, IL 60605 312-939-2438 http://www.shedd.org
Hours: 9:00-6:00 seven days a week. Closed Christmas Day and New Year's Day.
Adults 12-64 $ 11.00; children 3-11 $ 9.00; senior citizens over 65 $ 9.00; and
children under 3 free. Admission includes Oceanarium. Admission discounted

on Thursday.

As the largest indoor aquarium in the world the John G. Shedd Aquarium has more than 8,000 aquatic animals in natural habitat exhibits. Do not miss the Oceanarium that has its own indoor nature trails.

THE JOHN G. SHEDD AQUARIUM - TRIPS, EVENTS & TRAVEL
John G. Shedd Aquarium, 1200 S Lake Shore Drive, Chicago, IL 60605 312-692-3153 Main phone 312-939-2426 http://www.shedd.org
Special events, travel and college credit courses are available, including diving trips, animal encounters and research trips. Inquire about current programs.

SIX FLAGS GREAT AMERICA PHYSICS DAYS
Lisa Ignoffo, Special Events Representative Six Flags Great America, P. O. Box 1776, 542 N Route 21, Gurnee, IL 60031 847-249-2133 ext. 6439 Each spring in May, Six Flags Great America hosts Physics Days.
This successful program brings high school students from all over Chicagoland to the amusement park for educational fun in a recreational atmosphere. On the rides students measure their acceleration, horsepower, and centripetal force as they become a moving part of science experiments.

SPRING VALLEY NATURE SANCTUARY
Contact David Brooks   1111 E Schaumburg Rd, Schaumburg, IL 60194 847-985-2100 Fax 847-985-9692 Hours: 9:00-5:00 seven days a week; closed Thanksgiving, Christmas and New Year's Day. Admission free.
Field trips are popular at the Sanctuary. A museum contains dioramas depicting sanctuary ecosystems as well as a small pond, nature library, and orientation mini-theater. Sanctuary highlights include Volkening Heritage Farm, Merkle Cabin Historical Museum, Bob Link Arboretum, Illinois Heritage Grove, Spring Wildflower Display Area, Illinois Habitat Self-guided Interpretive Trail. Inquire about the Autumn Harvest Festival, the Sugar Bush Festival, the Spring Valley Environmental Education Outreach Program, and Group Venture Program.

THE TIME MUSEUM
Clock Tower Inn, 7801 E State St, (Interstate 90 and business highway 20), P O Box 5285, Rockford, IL 61125-0285   815-398-6000 Hours: Tuesday-Sunday 10:00-5:00; closed Monday. Adults $ 3.00; students $ 1.50.
This museum is an extraordinary museum of timekeeping, from Stonehenge to the Atomic clock.

TRAILSIDE MUSEUM
738 Thatcher Ave, at Chicago Ave, River Forest, IL 60305 708-366-6530 (Forest Preserve District of Cook County 708-771-1330) Hours: 10:00-4:00 every day; except closed on Thursdays. Open 8:00-4:00 for injured animals. Admission free.

This natural history museum has wild birds and mammals on display and is a wildlife rehabilitation center. Trailside Museum has no nature trails. Group reservations must be made by calling the Museum.

WALTER E. HELLER NATURE CENTER

2821 Ridge Rd, Highland Park, IL 60035 847-433-6901
http://www.als.uiuc.edu/pdhp/ Hours: Monday-Saturday 8:30-5:00; Sunday 10:00-4:00. Park hours: 6:00-9:00 seven days a week. Admission free.
This Center is a 97 acre forest with more than three miles of marked trails, including a building with a community room, a classroom, and a reference library. Request a Park District of Highland Park 80-page catalog listing special events, educational nature classes, programs for school groups preschool through high school, and athletic programs.

WILDLIFE PRAIRIE PARK

3826 N Taylor, R.R. # 2, Box 50, Peoria, IL 61615 309-676-0998 Adults & teens $ 4.00; Senior citizens $ 3.00; Ages 4-12 $ 2.00; Ages 3 & under Free.
This park is a sister park to Brookfield Zoo. This 2,000 acre zoological park is home to wolves, bison, waterfowl, black bear, elk, cougar, otter and much more. Includes a Pioneer Farmstead, one-room school house, long cabin, and renovated cabooses.

WILLOWBROOK WILDLIFE CENTER

Willowbrook Forest Preserve, Park Blvd between Roosevelt and Butterfield Roads, Glen Ellyn, IL 60137 630-942-6200 Fax 630-469-0034 (Forest Preserve District of DuPage County 630-790-4900)
http://www.co.dupage. il.us/forest/fpdhome.html   Hours: 9:00-5:00 seven days a week; except Thanksgiving, Christmas Eve, Christmas and New Year Day. Admission $ 1.00.
Educational programs include Young Explorers, Willowbrook Safari, Tracking, Wildlife Habitat and Survival, Sensory Awareness, Birds of Prey, Half-day Programs, and Outreach Programs. Ask for 40-page booklet, Let's Have a Class Outside Today: A Teacher's Guide to the Forest Preserve District of DuPage County.

WOOD LIBRARY - MUSEUM OF ANESTHESIOLOGY

Dr. George Bause, Curator Patrick Sim, Librarian   520 N Northwest Hwy, Park Ridge, IL 60068 847-825-5586 Fax 847-825-1692 Email wlm@asahq.org http://www.asahq.org/wlm Monday-Friday 9:00-4:45. Admission free.
The American Society of Anesthesiologists' Wood Library includes a museum of equipment from the interesting medical history of anesthesiology.

Chapter

7

Groups

Reference Books on Science Groups

Find science groups across the country in these resource guides.

IDEAAAS: SOURCEBOOK FOR SCIENCE, MATHEMATICS, AND TECHNOLOGY EDUCATION

Directorate for Education and Human Resources Programs, American Association for the Advancement of Science, 1200 New York Ave, NW, Washington, DC 20005-3920 800-222-7809 http://www.aaas.org/ehr 1995 256 pages $ 24.95

Listings of more than 1,000 organizations and their 10,000 resources and programs.

NSTA HANDBOOK

Published and distributed by the National Science Teachers Association 800-722-NSTA 1997-98 260 pages $ 6.50 Published annually.

This handbook publishes the names and addresses of board members, officers of affiliate organizations across the country, NSTA information, and more.

TRIANGLE COALITION FOR SCIENCE AND TECHNOLOGY EDUCATION - MEMBER CONTACT DIRECTORY

Walter L Purdy, Executive Director   Triangle Coalition for Science   and Technology Education, 5112 Berwyn Rd, College Park, MD 20740-4129 301-220-0870 Fax 301-474-4381 Email tricoal@aol.com
http://www. triange-coalition.org

Over 100 associations, societies, academies, councils, corporations and alliances are described under the categories of Science and Engineering; Business, Industry and Labor; Education; and Affiliated Local Alliances.

Chicago Area Science Groups

AMERICAN CHEMICAL SOCIETY - CHICAGO SECTION

7173 N Austin, Niles, IL 60714 847-647-8405 Fax 847-647-8364

This group supports the Chicagoland members of the American Chemical Society and provides information about publications and schedules programs in chemical education. Each year this group sponsors the American Chemical Society Scholarship Examination for Chicagoland high school students, the Undergraduate Research Symposium, and Kids & Chemistry programs.

BIO WEST

For information contact: Fermi National Accelerator Laboratory, Lederman Science Center, P. O. Box 500 MS 777, Batavia, IL 60510-0500 630-840-8258

Network of high school biology teachers with monthly meetings and newsletter.

CHEM WEST

For information contact: Fermi National Accelerator Laboratory, Lederman Science Center, P. O. Box 500 MS 777, Batavia, IL 60510-0500 630-840-8258

Network of high school chemistry teachers with monthly meetings and newsletter.

CHICAGO ALLIANCE FOR MINORITY PARTICIPATION (AMP) PROGRAM

Chicago AMP Office, Chicago State University, 9501 S King Dr, Chicago, IL 60628-1528 773-995-3296 Fax 773-995-2966

Chicago AMP is a consortium of Chicago Colleges, Universities, and research organizations to provide programs that improve the quality of science, mathematics, engineering and technology education for minority students.

CHICAGO ASTRONOMICAL SOCIETY

P. O. Box 30287, Chicago, IL 60630-0287

Founded in 1862, this group is America's oldest astronomical society. Anyone interested in astronomy and telescopes may enjoy this group that meets each month at the Adler Planetarium. Free telescope viewing is available each month at various locations around Chicagoland. Ask for a copy of the society's newsletter, Cosmic Quarterly, that includes a membership application.

CHICAGO AUDUBON SOCIETY
5801-C N Pulaski Rd, Chicago, IL 60646 312-539-6793 http://www.audubon.org
Society dedicated to wildlife preservation.

CHICAGO SPIE/OSC OPTICAL GROUP
Contact Rudolph Guzik, Executive Director P O Box 725, Frankfort, IL 60423
815-469-7104   Fax   815-469-7105   Email   chgospie@charlie.cns.iit.edu
http://www.spie.org/chicago.html
Contact this group about their educational programs and materials related to light, lasers, optics, and optical engineering. This is the local chapter office for the Society of Photo-Optical Instrumentation Engineers (SPIE) and the Optical Society of America (OSA).

EARTH SCIENCE CLUB OF NORTHERN ILLINOIS
Contact Karl Everett, President P. O. Box 321, Downers Grove, IL   60515
630-416-7456
One of 32 Illinois mineralogical and geological societies. Meetings at various times for different study groups and topics, College of DuPage, Building K, 22nd & Lambert Rd, Glen Ellyn, IL. Ask for a copy of The Earth Science News, Earth Science Club of Northern Illinois.

EDGEWATER, UPTOWN, ROGERS PARK SCIENCE CLUBS
Contact Mary Charles Loyola University Chicago, 1041 Ridge Rd, Wilmette, IL 60091 847-853-3342 (Elementary School through High School)
Over twenty science clubs in schools and public housing provide students and young people fun with science.

ENVIRONMENTAL EDUCATION ASSOCIATION OF ILLINOIS
Science Education Center, Department of Elementary Education - Reading, Western Illinois University, 1   University Circle, Macomb, IL 61455-1390
708-481-2330 Fax 708-481-1454 Membership fees Student $ 10.00, Regular $ 15.00
This group sponsors environmental education conferences, workshops, and promotes educational curricula like Project Wild, Project Learning Tree, and CLASS Project.

ILLINOIS ASSOCIATION OF BIOLOGY TEACHERS (IABT)

Phil McCrea, Regional Membership Coordinator   New Trier High School, 385 Winnetka Ave, Winnetka, IL 60093 847-446-7000 Fax 847-501-6400 Email mccreap@nttc.org $ 5.00 dues per year.

One of the largest state affiliates of the National Association of Biology Teachers, this group has quarterly meetings and a newsletter.

ILLINOIS ASSOCIATION OF CHEMISTRY TEACHERS

Contact M. Wolff Natural Science Department, Joliet Junior College, 1215 Houbolt, Joliet, IL 60436

Membership includes newsletter of news and opportunities for Illinois chemistry teachers.

ILLINOIS COMPUTING EDUCATORS (ICE)

Affiliate of International Society for Technology in Education, c/o Frada Boxer, 650 Appletree Lane, Deerfield, IL 60015 847-940-7132 Email frada@iceberg.org http://www.iceberg.org General membership $ 35.00 per year.

Membership includes programs, meetings, newsletter, network for resources, and Public Domain software.   Various chapters of this organization meet in the Chicagoland area. Request a membership application.

THE ILLINOIS SCIENCE OLYMPIAD

Brent Williamson, State Director Homewood-Flossmoor High School, 999 Kedzie Ave, Flossmoor, IL 60422-2299 708-799-3000, ext 315 Evenings 219-838-3429 Fax 708-799-3142 Email jbwilliamson@kiwi.dep.anl.gov http://webmasterworks.com/olympiad/index.html

Ask to be placed on the mailing list to receive a newsletter.   The goal of this organization is to improve the quality of science education and is accomplished through classroom activities and the encouragement of tournaments where student teamwork accomplishes scientific tasks in all areas of applied science,   including biology, chemistry, physics, earth sciences and engineering.   Divisions include A1 (grades K-3), A2 (grades 3-6), B (grades 5-9), and C (grades 9-12).

ILLINOIS SCIENCE TEACHERS ASSOCIATION (ISTA)

Diana Dummitt, Executive Secretary ISTA, College of Education, University of Illinois, 1310 S Sixth Street, Champaign, IL 61820 Regular membership $ 25.00 per year.

This association of Illinois science teachers K-12 includes SPECTRUM, Journal of the Illinois Science Teachers Association (Quarterly) and in the fall the annual ISTA Convention has major speakers, group sessions, workshops, and extensive commercial exhibits.

ILLINOIS SECTION - AMERICAN ASSOCIATION OF PHYSICS TEACHERS (ISAAPT)
http://www.phy.ilstu.edu/isaapt.html
This group of physics teachers holds an annual spring conference.

ILLINOIS STATE ACADEMY OF SCIENCE
Contact Pat Zimmerman   Illinois State   Museum, Spring & Edwards Sts, Springfield, IL 62706 217-782-6436 Fax 217-782-1254
Email zimmerma@museum.state.il.us   http://www.museum.state.il.us/isas/
Articles about new developments in science written by members of the academy and published in Transactions of the Illinois State Academy of Science. Inquire about membership. Annual meetings of the Academy are held at a college or university or industrial institution. Since 1907.

ILLINOIS STATE PHYSICS PROJECT (ISPP)
Physics Department, Illinois Institute of Technology, Chicago, IL 60616-3793 312-567-3375; Contact Gerry Lietz, DePaul University, Physics Department, 2219 N Kenmore Ave, Chicago, IL 60614 312-325-7333
http://www.npcts.edu/acad/physics/org
This friendly group of high school and college physics teachers meets each month of the school year at various school sites in the Chicago area to share new teaching ideas and questions about the subject of physics. All teachers and students of physics are welcome to attend. A newsletter is mailed each month summarizing the last meeting, announcing the next meeting, and including news items for physics teachers.

INVENTOR'S COUNCIL
Don Moyer, President Inventor's Council, 431 S Dearborn 705, Chicago, IL 60605 312-939-3329 Email patent@donmoyer.com http://www.donmoyer.com
The Inventor's Council holds inventor's workshops on one Saturday morning each month at the Harold Washington Library Center, 400 S State St, Chicago, Illinois. Topics include: How to Evaluate Patents, Patent Sucess Stories, How to Get the Best Patent, Finding the Best Way to Get New Products Made, How to Get Manufacturers to Invest in Inventions. This not-for-profit Council asks for contributions and supplies write-ups on various topics.

THE LINCOLN PARK ZOOLOGICAL SOCIETY
2200 N Cannon Drive, Chicago, IL 60614 312-742-2000 http://www.lpzoo.com
Membership in the Society includes the Zoo Guidebook, Zoo Review magazine, discounts on educational programs, invitations to picnics, parties, and previews as well as free parking.

MIDDLE LEVEL SCIENCE-MATH-TECHNOLOGY NETWORK

For information contact: Fermi National Accelerator Laboratory, Lederman Science Center, P O Box 500, MS 777, Batavia, IL 60510-0500 630-840-8258
Network of middle and junior high school science and math teachers integrating and learning to use technology. Network has monthly meetings and a newsletter.

MUSEUM OF SCIENCE AND INDUSTRY - SCIENCE CLUB NETWORK

Museum of Science and Industry, 57th St and Lake Shore Drive, Chicago, IL 60637 773-684-1414 http://www.msichicago.org
Working with Chicagoland public schools and community organizations, the Museum provides science programs for youth.

NORTHERN ILLINOIS ROCKETRY ASSOCIATION (NIRA)

For information call Bob Kaplow 847-428-1181 or Bob Wiersbe 630-690-6353 http://ourworld.compuserve.com/homepages/Mark_Bundick Membership $ 3.00
This club located in DuPage County is affiliated with the National Association of Rocketry (NAR). Monthly club meetings first Friday of every month 7:30-9:00 pm, Glen Ellyn Civic Center, 535 Duane, Glen Ellyn, IL. Monthly club launches usually the third Sunday of each month, March-November, 2:00-5:00 pm at various locations. Membership includes six issues of The Leading Edge.

NUCLEAR ENERGY INFORMATION SERVICE

P. O. Box 1637, Evanston, IL 60204-1637 847-869-7650 Fax 847-869-7658 Since 1981
A safe-energy educational resource, as well as an advocacy group.

OPTICAL SOCIETY OF CHICAGO

Contact George Magerl 640 Pearson St., Suite 200, Des Plaines, IL 60016 800-783-2321 847-298-6692 Fax 847-298-1423 Email info@bea-co.com http://www.osa.org
Ask for information about Optics Classroom Kits from the Optical Society of America.

PHYSICS NORTHWEST

Contact Larry Martin Email martin@npcts.edu or Contact David Thiessen 847-374-7811, ext 610 Email dthiessen@d113.lake.k12.il.us
http://www.npcts.edu/acad/physics/org/physicsnw.html
Network of high school physics teachers with monthly meetings and newsletter. Ask to be placed on the mailing list.

PHYSICS WEST

For information contact: Fermi National Accerator Laboratory, Lederman Science Center, P. O. Box 500 MS 777, Batavia, IL 60510-0500 630-840-8258; http://www.npcts.edu/acad/physics/org
Network of high school physics teachers with monthly meetings.

Rockford's Discovery Center Museum is home to over 200 exhibits, including Tot Spot, a special hands-on area just for children under six.

Photo Courtesy of Discovery Center

WORLDWIDE YOUTH IN SCIENCE AND ENGINEERING (WYSE)

(formerly Illinois Jets) David L Powell, Director University of Illinois at Urbana-Champaign, College of Engineering, Room 207, 1308 W Green St, Urbana, IL 61801-2982 800-843-5410 217-333-2860 Fax 217-244-2488 Email d-powell@uiuc.edu http://www.engr.uiuc.edu/wyse/

Annually, WYSE conducts written exam competitions as well as engineering design competitions in Chicago. Two sessions of an engineering camp, Exploring Your Options, are offered in the summer on the Champaign/Urbana U of I campus. Please contact WYSE for further information.

National Science Groups

AMERICAN ASSOCIATION FOR THE ADVANCEMENT OF SCIENCE

(AAAS) 1200 New York Ave, NW, Washington, DC 20005-3920 800-222-7809 202-326-6400 http://www.aaas.org   http://www.sciencenetlinks.com

This distinguished organization continues to promote science education through its programs and publications. Ask for 20-page catalog, Guide to Publications and Resources.

AMERICAN ASSOCIATION OF PHYSICS TEACHERS

One Physics Ellipse, College Park, MD 20740-3845 301-345-4200 Fax 301-209-0845 Email aapt-memb@aapt.org http://www.aapt.org

This group is composed of over 10,000 physics teachers from both the high school and college level. AAPT publishes The Physics Teacher magazine. Ask for the AAPT Products Catalog.

AMERICAN CHEMICAL SOCIETY

Education Division, 1155 16th St, NW, Washington, DC 20036 202-452-2113 800-209-0423 Fax 800-209-0064 304-728-2170 http://www.acs.org/edugen2/education/conted/conted.htm

Ask for 46-page Science Teaching Resources Catalog that includes posters, videotapes, magazines, educational materials, curriculum supplements, National Chemistry Examinations, and the annual Chemistry Calendar.

AMERICAN GEOLOGICAL INSTITUTE

4220 King St, Alexandria, VA 22302 703-379-2480 AGI Publications Center, P. O. Box 205, Annapolis Junction, MD 20701 301-953-1744 Email agi@agiweb.org http://www.agiweb.org/

This federation of professional associations serves geoscientists. Ask for 6-page brochure listing publications available, including Earth Science Guidelines Grades K-12, Earth-Science Education Resource Directory, and Careers in the Geosciences.

AMERICAN METEOROLOGICAL SOCIETY

1200 New York Ave, NW, Suite 410, Washington, DC 20005 202-682-9337 Fax 202-682-9341 Email amsedu@dc.ametsoc.org http://www.ametsoc.org
The AMS offers many programs for teachers and schools. For example, Project ATMOSPHERE promotes studies in the atmospheric sciences at elementary and secondary schools.

AMERICAN RADIO RELAY LEAGUE
- DEPARTMENT OF EDUCATIONAL ACTIVITIES

Contact Glenn Swanson American Radio Relay League, 225 Main St, Newington, CT 06111 860-594-0267 Fax 860-594-0259 Email gswanson@arrl.org http://www.arrl.org/
This is the best resource of information about Amateur Radio for all ages. Inquire about educational materials available including video courses, Morse Code and Ham Radio materials, Amateur Radio in the Classroom newsletter, license publications for students, and reference books. Ask for list of School Amateur Radio Clubs and Advisors.

AMERICAN SOCIETY OF PLANT PHYSIOLOGISTS

15501 Monona Dr, Rockville, MD 20855-2768 301-251-0560 Fax 301-279-2996 Email asppef@aspp.org http://aspp.org
Ask for brochure. See web site for Education Foundation description of programs.

ASTRONOMICAL SOCIETY OF THE PACIFIC

Membership Department, 390 Ashton Ave, San Francisco, CA 94112-1787 415-337-1100 Email membership@aspsky.org http://www.aspsky.org $ 35.00 per year.
This is the organization you need to belong to if you are involved with astronomy education. The newsletter, The Universe in the Classroom, features articles, resource lists, news bulletins, new photographs on astronomy for readers not trained in science.

CHEMICAL EDUCATIONAL FOUNDATION

1525 Wilson Blvd, Suite 750, Arlington, VA 22209 703-527-6223 Fax 703-527-7747 http://www.chemed.org
Distributes information about chemical products through web site, videos, publications, and training.

THE EISENHOWER NATIONAL CLEARINGHOUSE
FOR MATHEMATICS AND SCIENCE EDUCATION

Ohio State University, 1929 Kenny Rd, Columbus, OH 43210-1079 800-621-5785 614-292-7784 Fax 614-292-2066 Email editor@enc.org http://www.enc.org
Request to be placed on mailing list for newsletter, ENC Update.

EXCALIBUR NATIONAL HONOR SOCIETY
FOR EXCELLENCE IN SCIENCE

Peter J Valiente, President, 201 Pasadena Ave, Metairie, LA 70001 504-835-2545
Fax 504-837-1864

Ask for brochure. Any high school which includes grades 9-12 shall be eligible to apply for a chapter of the Honor Society.

FUTURE SCIENTISTS AND ENGINEERS OF AMERICA (FSEA)

George Westrom, Executive Director Contact Keith Brush P. O. Box 9577, Anaheim, CA 92812 714-229-2224 Fax 714-229-2228 Email fsea@fsea.org http://www.fsea.org/FSEA/

FSEA chapters are for students in grades 4-12 and chapter meetings after school hours allow students to work on challenging science and engineering projects. Each FSEA project is conducted by a teacher and Mentor team. Chapters are sponsored by business, professional societies, and community organizations. Ask for FSEA Handbook and newsletter, FSEA Blueprint.

HISTORY OF SCIENCE SOCIETY, INC.

Contact Dr. Keith Benson, History of Science Society, Inc., University of Washington, Box 351330, Seattle, WA 98195 206-543-9366 Fax 206-685-9544 Email hssexec@u.washington.edu http://weber.u.washington/~hssexec/

Dedicated to the study of the history of science, this society publishes ISIS, OSIRIS, The HSS Newsletter, and Guide to the History of Science. Founded in 1924, the Society advances research and teaching in the history of science.

INSTITUTE OF ENVIRONMENTAL SCIENCES AND TECHNOLOGY

940 E Northwest Hwy, Mt. Prospect, IL 60056 847-255-1561
Membership $ 80.00 per year.

The purpose of this professional society of engineers, scientists, and educators is to understand the effects of environmental factors as they relate to the production and safe operation of manufactured products. Areas of interest include knowledge pertaining to environmental sciences, design, contamination control, encourage courses in the environmental sciences, and to recognize related achievement. Publishes The Journal of the IEST.

INTERNATIONAL COUNCIL OF ASSOCIATIONS
FOR SCIENCE EDUCATION

Jack Holbrook, Executive Secretary ICASE, P O Box 6138, Limassol, Cyprus
Fax (+357 5) 633007 Email icase@zenon.logos.cy.net
http://sunsite.anu.edu.au/icase/

ICASE was established in 1973 to extend and improve science education for children and young people throughout the world. This association has 132 member organizations.

INTERNATIONAL SOCIETY FOR TECHNOLOGY IN EDUCATION
Contact Maia Howes 1787 Agate St, Eugene, OR 97403-1923 800-336-5191
541-346-4414 Fax 514-346-5890 Email ISTE@oregon.uoregon.edu
http://www.iste.org
This professional organization is dedicated to the improvement of all levels of
education through the use of computer-based technology. Ask for a copy of ISTE's
50-page publications catalog offering special journals, books on computers in
education, and educational software for educators and the classroom.

INTERNATIONAL TECHNOLOGY EDUCATION ASSOCIATION
1914 Association Dr, Suite 201, Reston, VA 20191-1539 703-860-2100 Fax
703-860-0353 Email itea@iris.org http://www.iteawww.org
This association is dedicated to promoting technological literacy. Ask for 35-page
catalog of publications and classroom materials.

JUNIOR ENGINEERING TECHNOLOGY SOCIETY, INC. (JETS)
1420 King St, Suite 405, Alexandria, VA 22314-2715 703-548-5378 Fax
703-548-0769 Email jets1@nae.edu http://www.asee.org/jets
This nationwide organization is for precollege students (grades 9-12) interested in
engineering, technology, mathematics and science. JETS activities include testing for
the National Engineering Aptitude Search and the National Engineering Design
Challenge. Ask for listing of career-related and other publications available from
JETS-Guidance at the above address. JETS has offered programs since 1949.

NATIONAL ACTION COUNCIL
FOR MINORITIES IN ENGINEERING, INC.
3 W 35th St, 3rd Floor, New York, NY 10001 212-279-2626
Email mmasullo@ncme.org http://www.ncme.org
This nonprofit organization is dedicated to bringing the talents of African Americans,
Hispanics, and American Indians to the nation's workforce.

NATIONAL ANTI-VIVISECTION SOCIETY
53 W Jackson Blvd, Chicago, IL 60604 800-888-6287 312-427-6065 Fax
312-427-6524 Email navs@navs.org http://www.navs.org
The Dissection Alternatives Loan Program provides materials to students and teachers
on a free-of-charge basis. Ask for brochure.

NATIONAL ASSOCIATION FOR RESEARCH IN SCIENCE TEACHING (NARST)
Dr. Arthur L White, Executive Secretary, The Ohio State University, 1929 Kenny
Road, Rm 200E, Columbus, OH 43210 614-292-3339 Fax 614-292-1595 Email
White.32@osu.edu http://science.coe.uwf.edu/narst/narst.html
Inquire about membership, publications and activities.

NATIONAL ASSOCIATION OF BIOLOGY TEACHERS (NABT)
Contact Kathy Frame 11250 Roger Bacon Dr, #19, Reston, VA 20190-5202
800-406-0775   703-471-1134   Fax   703-318-0380   Email NABTer@aol.com
http://www.nabt.org $ 48.00 dues per year.
This is the only national association specifically organized to assist teachers in the
improvement of biology education. Ask for publications and membership brochures.

NATIONAL ASSOCIATION OF GEOSCIENCE TEACHERS, INC.
Contact Robert Christman   P. O. Box 5443, Bellingham, WA 98227-5443
360-650-3587 Fax 360-650-7302 Email xman@cc.wwu.edu $ 35.00 per year
includes subscription to Journal of Geoscience Education.
This association seeks to foster improvement in teaching earth sciences at all levels and
to disseminate knowledge in this field to the general public. Ask for information about
materials available.

NATIONAL AUDUBON SOCIETY
700 Broadway, New York, NY 10003 212-979-3000 http://www.audubon.org
http://www.audubon.org/bird/watch/kids/index.html
The National Audubon Society is dedicated to wildlife, wilderness and environmental
preservation and education. Ask for list of Audubon Books available from various
publishers.

NATIONAL EARTH SCIENCE TEACHERS ASSOCIATION
P. O. Box 53213, Washington, DC 20009-3213 $ 15.00 per year.
Membership includes quarterly journal, The Earth Scientist. Ask for brochure.

NATIONAL ENERGY FOUNDATION
Contact Gary Swan 5225 Wiley Post Way, Suite 170, Salt Lake City, UT 84116
801-539-1406 Fax 801-539-1451 Email info@nef1.org http://www.nef1.org
This nonprofit organization provides programs and materials to help promote an
awareness of energy-related issues. Ask for 15-page catalog of publications and
science kits. Materials include Out of the Rock, a mineral resource and mining
education program for K-8 produced in conjunction with the U. S. Bureau of Mines.

NATIONAL SCIENCE EDUCATION LEADERSHIP ASSOCIATION (NSELA)
P. O. Box 99381, Raleigh, NC 27624-9381 http://science.coe.uwf.edu/NSELA
/NSELA.html
The professional organization serves a membership of science supervisors and
department heads. Inquire about membership, publications, and activities.

NATIONAL SCIENCE RESOURCES CENTER (NSRC)

Smithsonian Institution - National Academy of Sciences, Smithsonian Institution, Arts & Industries Building, Room 1201, Washington, DC 20560 202-357-4892 Fax 202-786-2028 Email outreach@nas.edu http://www.si.edu/nsrc

The NSRC works to improve the teaching of science in the nation's schools. NSRC disseminates information about effective science teaching resources, develops curriculum materials, and sponsors outreach and leadership development activities. Ask to be placed on the mailing list for the NSRC Newsletter.

NATIONAL SCIENCE TEACHERS ASSOCIATION

1840 Wilson Blvd, Arlington, VA 22201-3000 800-722-NSTA 703-243-7100 Fax 703-243-7177 http://www.nsta.org

This association plays a major role in improving science teaching at all levels, preschool through college. Its membership is composed of 50,000 science teachers, science supervisors, administrators, scientists, and others involved directly and indirectly with science education.

NORTH AMERICAN ASSOCIATION FOR ENVIRONMENTAL EDUCATION

P. O. Box 400, Troy, OH 45373 937-676-2514 Email jthoreen@igc.apc.org http://www.naaee.org $ 45.00 per year.

Ask for brochure about membership and benefits. NAAEE is the world's largest association of environmental educators.

OPTICAL SOCIETY OF AMERICA

2010 Massachusetts Ave, NW, Washington, DC 20036 800-762-6960 202-416-1430 Fax 202-416-6140 http://www.osa.org

Ask for information about Optics Classroom Kits from the Optical Society of America.

THE PLANETARY SOCIETY

65 North Catalina Ave, Pasadena, CA 91106-2301 626-793-5100 Fax 626-793-5528 Email tps@mars.planetary.org http://planetary.org $ 25.00 per year.

Dedicated to exploration, creative research, test programs, astronomical observations, student activities, conferences and workshops. Membership includes newsletter. Ask for Educator Resources Catalog of materials.

SCHOOL SCIENCE AND MATHEMATICS ASSOCIATION

Contact Donald L. Pratt Dept of Curriculum & Foundations, Bloomsburg University, 400 E 2nd St, Bloomsburg, PA 17815-1301 717-389-4915 Fax 717-389-3615 Email pratt@bloomu.edu http://hubble.bloomu.edu/ssma/

Founded in 1901, the purpose of this association is to disseminate research findings and its implications for school practice. Inquire about membership, journals, and benefits.

SCIENCE EDUCATION FOR STUDENTS WITH DISABILITIES
Contact Edward C. Keller   236 Grand St, Morgantown, WV   26505-7509
304-293-5201 ext 2513   Fax 304-293-6363
Email ekeller@wvu.edu   http://www.as.wvu.edu/~scidis/
This groups exists to promote and advance the teaching of science with any manner of disability in the learning process. The SESD Goodnewsletter is published twice a year.

THE SCIENCE OLYMPIAD
5955 Little Pine Lane, Rochester, MI 48306   313-651-4013   Fax 810-651-7835
Email scipio@spioneers.com http://www.spinoneers.com
The goal of this international organization is to improve the quality of science education and is accomplished through classroom activities and the encouragement of tournaments, including at the district level, 100 regional, 41 state, and one national tournament.

SCIENCE SERVICE, INC.
1719 N St, NW, Washington, DC 20036   202-785-2255   Fax 202-785-1243
http://www.sciserv.org
The Science Youth Program of Science Service, Inc. includes the following activities: Westinghouse Science Talent Search, and the International Science and Engineering Fair. Science Service, Inc. publishes Science News, The Weekly Newsmagazine of Science.

THE SEISMOLOGICAL SOCIETY OF AMERICA
201 Plaza Professional Bldg, El Cerrito, CA 94530-4003 510-525-5474 Fax 510-525-7204 Email info@seismosoc.org http://www.sesmosoc.org
Ask for brochure describing seismology resources for teachers.

THE SOCIETY FOR COLLEGE SCIENCE TEACHERS (SCST)
Dr. Brian Shmaefsky, Membership Chairman, Biotechnology/Biology, Kingwood College, 20000 Kingwood Dr, Kingwood, TX 77339-3801 281-359-1609
Ask for brochure. SCST is an affiliate of the National Science Teachers Association and the American Association for the Advancement of Science. This organizations provides a forum for interdisciplinary interaction among teachers of science at all institutions of higher education. Established in 1979. Membership includes newsletter.

SOCIETY OF PHOTO-OPTICAL INSTRUMENTATION ENGINEERS
(SPIE) P. O. Box 10, Bellingham, WA 98227-0010 360-676-3290
Email education@spie.org http://www.spie.org
Ask for 75-page catalog, SPIE's Continuing Education Catalog, including programs, videotapes, broadcasts, and short courses, and SPIE's Publications Catalog. Optical technology for engineering.

SOCIETY OF WOMEN ENGINEERS

120 Wall St, 11th Floor, New York, NY 10005-3902 212-509-9577
Fax 212-509-0224 http://www.swe.org
This center of information on women in engineering informs young women, their parents and counselors and the public of the qualifications and achievements of women engineers.

U. S. DEPARTMENT OF ENERGY

1000 Independance Ave, SW, Room 3F-077, Washington, DC 20585 202-586-5447 Fax 202-586-3119 Email toni.joseph@oer.doe.gov
The Department of Energy has six national laboratories designated as Laboratory Science Education Centers, including Argonne, IL. These centers provide a range of college and precollege education programs. Contact Education Programs, Argonne National Laboratory, 9700 S Cass Ave, Argonne, IL 60439 at 312-972-3373 for current information about programs.

YOUNG ENTOMOLOGIST'S SOCIETY, INC.

Contact Gary A. Dunn 1915 Peggy Place, Lansing, MI 48910-2553 517-887-0499
Fax 517-887-0499 Email YESbugs@aol.com http://www.tesser.com/minibeast/
and http://insects.ummc/sa.umich.edu/yes/yes.htm/ Retail Non-profit
One-year educator membership includes various resources and a one-year subscription to Insect World, $ 48.00. Ask for the 70-page Minibeast Merchandise Catalog including programs and services, products and materials, and tips for selecting materials. Resource materials include books, educational games, models, audiovisual materials, and toys.

Chapter

8

Instruments

Scientific Measurement Instruments

Tools are a part of any field of knowledge. Good science comes from knowing the tools for scientific measurement and how they are used. The following instruments provide a beginning for the person who wants to conduct quality experiments in science. See Chapter 10, Materials, for sources where you can purchase these instruments.

ALTIMETER
Measures atmospheric pressure and height in units of feet.
The aneroid barometer is adapted for use in aircraft as an altimeter allowing measurement of height above the ground.

ANEMOMETER
Measures wind speed in units of miles per hour.
This instrument is also called a cup anemometer.

ANEROID BAROMETER
Measures atmospheric pressure in units of inches or millimeters of mercury.
Aneroid barometers use a partially evacuated metal chamber connected to a spring and a dial that directly displays atmospheric pressure on the dial without need for liquid

mercury as in the mercury barometer.

BALANCE
Measures mass in units of grams (g).
A balance measures how much Earth's gravity pulls down on an object compared to standard mass sizes. This comparison is a measure of the object's inertia, or resistance to motion. By definition, one kilogram of water has a volume of one liter and one gram of water has a volume of one milliliter.

BAROGRAPH
Measures atmospheric pressure over time.
The barograph adapts the aneroid barometer for continuously recorded pressure changes on a moving sheet of recording paper.

ECHO SOUNDER
Measures ocean depth in units of feet and meters.
A sounding instrument, used in sea water, for automatically determining the depth of the sea floor or of an object beneath a ship.

GRADUATED CYLINDER
Measures volume in units of milliliters (ml).
Read liquid volume in a graduated cylinder in milliliters at the bottom of the liquid's curved surface, called the meniscus.

HYDROMETER
Measures density in units of grams per milliliter (g/ml).
The hydrometer floats in a liquid to measure its density. The higher the hydrometer floats, the more dense the liquid. The hydrometer is often confused with the hygrometer.

HYGROMETER
Measures relative humidity in units of percent.
The hygrometer operates on the principle that a synthetic fiber will curl with increasing air moisture or humidity. Humidity is read from a circular dial on the hygrometer. The hygrometer is often confused with the hydrometer.

MERCURY BAROMETER
Measures atmospheric pressure in units of inches or millimeters of mercury.
The mercury barometer is a long glass tube of liquid mercury inverted into an open dish of liquid mercury. The atmospheric pushes on the mercury surface in the dish forcing the mercury in the tube to a height corresponding to atmospheric pressure.

METER STICK
Measures length in units of meters (m), centimeters (cm), millimeters (mm).
The meter stick measures one meter long which is equivalent to 100 cm, 1000 mm, and 39.37 inches. The meter was originally defined so that 10 million meters would exactly measure the distance from the equator to the north pole of the Earth.

MICROMETER
Measures length in units of .01 of a millimeter.
Dimensions of small objects can be measured with this instrument. A thimble is turned on a graduated barrel to close a spindle and a stationary anvil onto an object. The micrometer can measure the diameter of a copper wire or a human hair.

MOHS HARDNESS SCALE
Measures mineral & rock hardness on a scale from 1 - 10.
The Mohs hardness scale measures relative hardness on a scale from 1 (talc) to 10 (diamond). For example, if a mineral of hardness 4 will scratch a sample mineral, but a hardness 3 mineral will not, then your sample has a hardness of 3-4.

PH SCALE
Measures acidity (or alkalinity) on a scale from 0 - 14.
The pH scale is a logarithmic scale. A value of 7 denotes a neutral solution, values below 7 indicate greater acidity, and values above 7 indicate greater alkalinity.

PIPETTE
Measures liquid volume in units of milliliters (ml).
A calibrated glass tube for measuring small liquid volumes where the liquid is drawn into the tube by suction.

PROTRACTOR
Measures angular distance in units of degrees.
An instrument used for measuring angles on paper or in the laboratory.

RICHTER SCALE
Measures earthquake intensity on a scale from 0 - 10.
A scale of earthquake intensity based on the motion of a seismometer. An earthquake of magnitude 10 would shake the entire Earth.

SCALE OR BATH SCALE
Measures weight in units of pounds or kilograms.
A scale measures weight, the pull or force of gravity, with a spring mechanism. On the Earth's surface weight in pounds has a direct correspondence to mass in kilograms. One kilogram equals 2.2 pounds. On other planets the correspondence is different. In the

metric system force or weight is measured in newtons; in the English system force or weight is measured in pounds.

SEISMOMETER
Measures earthquake vibrations.
Seismographs measure vibrational waves moving through the Earth from earthquake sources. In a seismograph a heavy weight freely suspended from a support does not move with Earth movement. The seismometer records vibrational intensity of the seismometer's surroundings, which is the Earth's vibrational movement.

SLING PSYCHROMETER
Measures relative humidity in units of percent.
The sling psychrometer is made of two thermometers with one wet and one dry bulb. The drop in temperature on a wet bulb thermometer allows the measurement of relative humidity by using a humidity data table. A larger drop in temperature would correspond to a lower humidity.

THERMOGRAPH
Measures temperature over time.
A thermograph is made from a thermometer which continuously records temperature on a moving sheet of recording paper.

THERMOMETER
Measures temperature in units of degrees centigrade (Celsius) or Fahrenheit.
The thermometer measures temperature by observing a liquid which expands with increasing molecular motion due to heat addition. The thermometer measures temperature as the amount of average molecular motion. Heat is thermal energy. The Kelvin scale is defined by gas laws and absolute zero.

VERNIER CALIPER
Measures length in units of .1 of a millimeter.
The vernier caliper is a caliper with a vernier scale which allows the measurement of length to the nearest .1 of a millimeter. The alignment of marks on the vernier scale accurately measures one more figure of length. This instrument can measure the diameter of a child's marble or a pencil.

WIND VANE
Measures wind direction in units of angular degrees.
An instrument used to determine wind direction. A design like an arrow, mounted on a vertical axis, is forced to point in the direction of the wind's motion. A north wind blows from the north to the south.

Chapter

9

Libraries

Library Directories

DIRECTORY OF SPECIAL LIBRARIES AND INFORMATION CENTERS
Edited by Brigitte T. Darnay Gale Research Company, Detroit, MI 48226 Vols 1-2, Bound in 3 parts. Available at major libraries.
This extensive reference lists North American libraries, describes their collections, and indexes them by geographic regions and by science categories. This reference has it all for the information addict.

INQUIRY IN THE LIBRARY
American Association for the Advancement of Science, 1200 New York Ave, NW, Washington, DC 20005-3920 800-222-7809 http://www.aaas.org/ehr 1996 92 pages $ 14.95
From the AAAS Science Library Institute, this manual provides sample activities which can be conducted in the library, including an extensive bibliography of books.

SCIENCE & TECHNOLOGY LIBRARIES
The Haworth Press, Inc., 10 Alice St, Binghamton, NY 13904-1580 607-722-5857 Quarterly $ 40.00 per year.
This periodical publishes articles written for librarians of science and technology libraries. A list of books for sale at the end of each issue, however, includes various reference books listing science and technology libraries.

Chicago Area Libraries with Science Collections

This list contains libraries which have good to fine science book collections. Many libraries specialize in various topics. Some are general collection libraries with good science collections.

Some of the libraries listed below have limited circulation privileges or they are not open to the public. (Libraries not open to the public are listed below in an attempt to make this list as complete as possible.) Please contact each library for the current library policies and computer modem access numbers to their catalogs if available.

Local public libraries are not included in the following list with the exception of Chicago's three major public libraries. Your local public library will have many good children's science books and books about science fair project ideas.

ABBOTT LABORATORIES - LIBRARY INFORMATION SERVICES
Abbott Laboratories, 100 Abbott Park Rd, Abbott Park, IL 60064-3500 847-937-4600
Not open to the public. This library is available, however, through interlibrary loan. The collection contains 25,000 volumes and 1300 journals.

ADLER PLANETARIUM - LIBRARY
Dr. Evelyn D. Natividad, Library Administrator Adler Planetarium & Astronomy Museum, 1300 S Lake Shore Drive, Chicago, IL 60605 312-322-0593 http://astro.uchicago.edu/adler/
This reference library is open to the public by appointment, but does not extend circulation privileges. The collection contains over 5,000 volumes related to astronomy.

AMERICAN NUCLEAR SOCIETY - LIBRARY
American Nuclear Society, 555 N Kensington Ave, La Grange Park, IL 60525 708-352-6611
This library is open to the public with restrictions. The collection contains approximately 3000 volumes and 150 periodicals on nuclear energy, science and business management.

AMOCO CORPORATION - CENTRAL RESEARCH LIBRARY
Technical Information Center, 150 W Warrenville, Naperville, IL 60563-8469 630-420-4818
This library is not open to the public, but is available through interlibrary loan. The collection contains approximately 45,000 volumes and 2500 journals on science and technology.

AMOCO CORPORATION - LIBRARY/INFORMATION CENTER
Amoco Corporation, 200 E Randolph St, P O Box 87703, Chicago, IL 60680-0703
312-856-5961
This library is open by appointment to individuals for specific research and contains 70,000 books and documents as well as 1000 journals related to petrochemicals, business and law.

BROOKFIELD ZOO - LIBRARY
Contact Mary Rabb 3300 S Golf Rd, Brookfield, IL 60513 708-485-0263, ext 580
Fax 708-485-3532 http://www.brookfield-zoo.mus.il.us
This library can be contacted for reference information.

CENTER FOR RESEARCH LIBRARIES
6050 S Kenwood Ave, Chicago, IL 60637-2804 773-955-4545 By appointment.
Donald Simpson, President. Founded 1949.
This information center is an extensive storage center for hard to find research dissertations, especially foreign dissertations. The reading room is open to the public at no cost when given 48 hours notice of specific reading need. If you know what you want and it is hard to find, this might be the place to go.

CHICAGO BOTANIC GARDEN - LIBRARY
Nancy H. McCray, Librarian Chicago Botanic Garden, 1000 Lake Cook Road (at Edens Expressway), Glencoe, IL 60022-0400 847-835-8200 Fax 847-835-4484
Email cbglib@nslsilus.org http://www.chicago-botanic.org
This library is open to the public and requires a parking fee for nonmembers. The collection contains about 16,000 volumes and 400 periodicals on horticulture, botany and natural history.

CHICAGO PUBLIC LIBRARY
- CARTER G. WOODSON REGIONAL LIBRARY
Emily Guss, Director Carter G. Woodson Regional Library, 9525 S Halsted St, Chicago, IL 60628 312-747-6900 http://www.chipublib.org
One of two major regional libraries in Chicago.

CHICAGO PUBLIC LIBRARY
- CONRAD SULZER REGIONAL LIBRARY
Leah J. Steele, Director Conrad Sulzer Regional Library, 4455 N Lincoln Ave, Chicago, IL 60625 312-744-7616 http://www.chipublib.org
One of two major regional libraries in Chicago.

CHICAGO PUBLIC LIBRARY
- THOMAS HUGHES CHILDREN'S LIBRARY
Laura B. Culberg, Head Harold Washington Library Center, 400 S State St, Chicago, IL 60605 312-747-4200 Fax 312-747-4646 Email lculberg@chipublic.org
http://www.chipublib.org
The Hughes Children's Library contains 100,000 volumes of books for children. A majority of these books are non fiction. Look under Q within the Library of Congress system for children's science books.

CHICAGO PUBLIC LIBRARY CENTRAL LIBRARY
- SCIENCE/TECHNOLOGY INFORMATION CENTER
Diane A. Richmond, Head Harold Washington Library Center, 4th Floor, 400 S State St, Chicago, IL 60605 Science Reference 312-747-4450
http://www.chi.publib.org   Founded 1977.
The Central Library of the Chicago Public Library contains approximately 50,000 different book titles on pure science subjects.

CHICAGO STATE UNIVERSITY
- THE PAUL AND EMILY DOUGLAS LIBRARY
The Paul and Emily Douglas Library, Chicago State University, E 95th St & King Dr, Chicago, IL 60628 Reference desk 773-995-2251
This university library is open to the public, but library privileges are restricted. The Douglas Library contains 360 science periodicals.

CHICAGO ZOOLOGICAL SOCIETY - LIBRARY
Mary S. Rabb, Librarian Chicago Zoological Society, 8400 W 31st St, Brookfield, IL 60513 708-485-0263, ext 580
This library is not open to the public, but extends interlibrary loan privileges. The collection contains 10,000 volumes related to zoology.

CLEARBROOK CENTER - LEKOTEK
(Toy Lending Library) Clearbrook Center for the Handicapped, 3705 Pheasant Dr, Rolling Meadows, IL 60008 847-392-2812 Fee $ 65 per year
Ask for descriptive brochure. This toy loan center for children with special needs is open to everyone in the Chicagoland area.

COMMONWEALTH EDISON COMPANY - LIBRARY
Commonwealth Edison Company, First National Plaza, 35th Floor, P. O. Box 767, Chicago, IL 60690-0767 312-394-3066 Fax 312-394-7336
This collection contains information on energy, the environment, electrical engineering, and management including 300 different journal titles. It is open to the public and requires admission through security.

DE PAUL UNIVERSITY - LINCOLN PARK CAMPUS LIBRARY
Contact Doris Brown DePaul University, 2350 N Kenmore Ave, Chicago, IL 60614 773-325-7800 Fax 773-325-7869 Email dbrown@wppost.depaul.edu http://www.lib.depaul.edu
This university library is open to the public, but circulation privileges are restricted. The general collection of this library contains 620,000 volumes and 4,200 periodicals.

DE VRY INSTITUTE OF TECHNOLOGY
- LEARNING RESOURCE CENTER
De Vry Institute of Technology, 3300 N Campbell Ave, Chicago, IL 60618 773-929-8500
This library is open to the public, but circulation privileges are restricted. This library contains 10,000 volumes and 50 periodicals.

THE FIELD MUSEUM - LIBRARY
Benjamin Williams, Head Librarian The Field Museum, Roosevelt Road & Lake Shore Drive, Chicago, IL 60605 312-922-9410, ext 282 http://www.fmnh.org
The reference library of the Field Museum of Natural History is open to the public, but the library does not circulate its collection. Enter via the west side of the museum's north entrance. This collection contains over 250,000 volumes.

GAS RESEARCH INSTITUTE - LIBRARY SERVICES
Gas Research Institute, 8600 W Bryn Mawr Ave, Chicago, IL 60631 773-399-8386 Fax 773-399-8111
Not open to the public.

GOVERNORS STATE UNIVERSITY - LIBRARY
Governors State University, University Park, IL 60466-0975 708-534-4111 Fax 708-534-4564
This university library is open to the public, but circulation privileges are restricted. This library's general collection contains 300,000 volumes.

ILLINOIS INSTITUTE OF TECHNOLOGY
- PAUL V. GALVIN LIBRARY
35 W 33rd St, Chicago, IL 60616-3793 312-567-6844 Fax 312-567-5318 Founded 1892.
This extensive collection of over 500,000 volumes from science and technology is open to the public, however, circulation privileges are restricted.

ILLINOIS INSTITUTE OF TECHNOLOGY RESEARCH INSTITUTE
- MANUFACTURING TECHNOLOGY INFORMATION ANALYSIS
CENTER

Research Institute, 10 W 35th St, Chicago, IL 60616 800-421-0586

This center is open to the public for literature searches and contains approximately 300 volumes and 300 journals related to manufacturing technology.

INSTITUTE OF GAS TECHNOLOGY
- TECHNICAL INFORMATION CENTER

Institute of Gas Technology, 1700 S Mt Prospect Rd, Des Plaines, IL 60018-1804 847-768-0664 Fax 847-768-0669

This library is open to the public and contains 33,000 volumes, 100,000 technical reports, and 500 periodicals on gas, energy and biomass.

LEON M. LEDERMAN SCIENCE EDUCATION CENTER
- TEACHER RESOURCE CENTER

Susan Dahl, Education Specialist, Teacher Resource Center, Fermi National Accelerator Laboratory, Leon M. Lederman Science Education Center, P O Box 500 MS 777, Batavia, IL 60510-0500 630-840-8258 Email SDahl@fnalv.fnal.gov Monday-Friday 8:30-5:00; Saturday 9:00-3:30. Call for an appointment.

This extensive teacher resource center is filled with books, periodicals, kits, videotapes, etc. -- for teachers, administrators, librarians, scientists, and Science Center program participants.

LINCOLN PARK ZOOLOGICAL GARDENS - LIBRARY

Lincoln Park Zoological Gardens, 2200 N Cannon Dr, Chicago, IL 60614-3895 312-742-2000   http://www.lpzoo.com

This small library is open to the public, but has no circulation privileges.

LOYOLA UNIVERSITY CHICAGO - SCIENCE LIBRARY

Loyola University Chicago, 6525 N Sheridan Rd, Chicago, IL 60626 773-508-2641 Fax 773-508-2993

This university library is open to the public, but public visitation is limited to two hours per week. Circulation privileges are restricted.

LUCENT TECHNOLOGIES (A T & T BELL LABORATORIES)

200 N Naperville Rd, Naperville, IL 60566 630-979-2551

This library is open to the public, but building security restrictions require telephoning for an appointment. The collection contains 30,000 volumes and 325 periodicals on computers, telecommunications, business and electronics.

METROPOLITAN WATER RECLAMATION DISTRICT OF GREATER CHICAGO - TECHNICAL LIBRARY

Andrew King, Librarian Metropolitan Water Reclamation District of Greater Chicago, 100 E Erie St, Chicago, IL 60611 312-751-6658
This small library is open to the public for research purposes only, and has no circulation privileges. The collection is limited to works supporting scientists and engineers at the District.

MORTON ARBORETUM - STERLING MORTON LIBRARY

Michael T. Stieber, Reference Librarian Morton Arboretum, 4100 Illinois Route 53, Lisle, IL 60532-1293 630-719-2427 Fax 630-719-2433
Email mstieber@mortonarb.org   http://www.mortonarb.org
This library is open to the public and circulation privileges are extended to members and through interlibrary loan. The collection contains 25,000 volumes, over 800 periodical titles, and 200 current subscriptions.

MOTOROLA, INC. - CIG/GSS LIBRARY

Jennifer Mielke, Technical Librarian Motorola, Inc., 1501 W Shure Dr, Arlington Heights, IL 60004 847-632-4133
This technical library basically contains technical research journals and is not open to the public.

MOTOROLA, INC. - COMMUNICATION SECTOR LIBRARY

Marion Mason, Library Manager Motorola, Inc., 1301 E Algonquin Rd, Room 1914, Schaumburg, IL 60196 847-576-5940 http://www.mot.com
This industry library is not open to the public. An information pass will be extended, however, to researchers needing information not available elsewhere. This collection contains 8,000 volumes and 500 periodicals on electrical engineering.

MUSEUM OF SCIENCE AND INDUSTRY - NASA TEACHER RESOURCE CENTER

Museum of Science and Industry, 57th St and Lake Shore Drive, Chicago, IL 60637 773-684-1414 http://www.msichicago.org
Space-related workshops and curriculum materials for teachers.

NATIONAL LEKOTEK CENTER

(Toy Lending Library) National Lekotek Center, 2100 Ridge Ave, Evanston, IL 60201 847-328-0001 Fee $180 per year
Ask for descriptive brochure of the National Lekotek Center, a not-for-profit charitable organization. Also ask for a current list of over 20 Illinois Lekotek sites including Chicago, Chicago Heights, Flossmoor, Franklin Park, Libertyville, Lombard, Rolling Meadows, South Holland, and Tinley Park. Some centers have no fee and focus on special community needs.

NATIONAL SAFETY COUNCIL - LIBRARY
Robert J. Marecek, Manager   Contact the Reference Desk   National Safety Council, 1121 Spring Lake Dr, Itasca, IL 60143-3201   630-775-2199   Fax 630-285-0765   Email bob-nsc@dupagels.lib.il.us http://www.nsc.org
This library is open to the public and contains a comprehensive collection of 140,000 documents on health and safety.   Fees apply to researchers requiring extensive assistance.   It is best to telephone ahead for an appointment.

CHICAGO PUBLIC LIBRARY'S NATURECONNECTIONS PROJECT - HAROLD WASHINGTON LIBRARY CENTER
Jane Sorensen, Project Director   Thomas Hughes Room, Harold Washington Library Center, 400 S State St, Chicago, IL 60605   312-747-4633   (Elementary School)
NatureConnections is The Chicago Public Library's unique collection of natural history materials for children, including books, magazines, pamphlets, videos, and discovery objects for "touching."   It also sponsors exciting programs for children and adults. Located at the Thomas Hughes Children's Library and at 42 neighborhood libraries.

NORTHEASTERN ILLINOIS UNIVERSITY - RONALD WILLIAMS LIBRARY
Northeastern Illinois University, 5500 N St Louis Ave, Chicago, IL 60625-4699 773-794-2615 Fax 773-794-2715
This university library is open to the public, but circulation privileges are restricted. Books are available, however, through interlibrary loan.   The total general collection is broad and contains 380,000 volumes and 3,500 periodicals.

NORTHWESTERN UNIVERSITY - SEELEY G. MUDD LIBRARY FOR SCIENCE AND ENGINEERING
Robert Michaelson, Head Librarian   Northwestern University, 2233 N Campus Drive, Evanston, IL 60208   847-491-3362   Fax 847-491-4655
This library is open to the public, but circulation privileges are restricted. For guest circulation information telephone 708-491-7617.   The collection contains 230,000 volumes and 1800 periodicals on science and engineering.

THE POWER HOUSE - ENERGY RESOURCE CENTER
Contact Lori Defiore   Commonwealth Edison, 100 Shiloh Blvd, Zion, IL 60099 847-746-7850   Email pwhlh@ccmail.ceco.com   http://www.ucm.com/powerhouse Hours: Tuesday-Saturday 10:00-5:00
This science education resource center is open to both students and teachers for research and study.   It contains over 500 books, 28 periodicals, six computers and four video VCR's with monitors.

QUAKER OATS COMPANY
- JOHN STUART RESEARCH LABORATORIES - RESEARCH LIBRARY
Quaker Oats Company, 617 W Main St, Barrington, IL 60010-4199 847-304-2058
Fax 847-304-2062
This collection contains 7,000 volumes on food and food processing and is open to the
public by appointment.

ROOSEVELT UNIVERSITY - MURRAY-GREEN LIBRARY
Roosevelt University, 430 S Michigan Ave, Chicago, IL 60605 312-341-3640 Fax
312-341-2425
This library is open to the public, but circulation privileges are restricted. The collection
contains 300,000 volumes of which 12,000 are on science topics.

SEARLE LIBRARY
4901 Searle Pkwy, Skokie, IL 60077 847-982-8285
Not open to the public.

JOHN G. SHEDD AQUARIUM - A RESOURCE FOR THE CURIOUS
Elizabeth J. Ban, Supervisor of Public Information Services John G. Shedd
Aquarium, 1200 S Lake Shore Drive, Chicago, IL 60605 312-692-3224 Email
eban@sheddaquarium.org http://www.shedd.org
A Resource for the Curious is open Thursday through Sunday 1:00 until 4:00 for guests
with Oceanarium tickets. Guests can access print and on-line sources of information,
and speak with Shedd Aquarium experts on a range of topics.

U. S. ENVIRONMENTAL PROTECTION AGENCY
- REGION 5 LIBRARY
Patricia Krause, Library Manager U. S. Environmental Protection Agency, 77 W
Jackson Blvd, 12th Floor, Chicago, IL 60604 312-353-2022 312-886-9506
Fax 312-353-2001 Email krause.patricia@epamail.epa.gov
http://www.epa.gov/region5/library/
This library is open to the public and its collection is primarily EPA reports as well as
many periodicals related to the environment.

UNIVERSITY OF CHICAGO - JOHN CRERAR LIBRARY
5730 S Ellis, Chicago, IL 60637-1434 773-702-7715 Fax 773-702-3022 Founded
1892.
This distinguished collection of science, technology and medicine contains approximately one million (1,000,000) volumes. Although this library is open to the public,
library circulation privileges are not available to the public.

Children at the Water Works Lab, exploring science through nature at the new Nature Museum of The Chicago Academy of Sciences (CaoS)

Photo Courtesy of The Chicago Academy of Sciences

UNIVERSITY OF CHICAGO - SPECIAL COLLECTIONS

Alice Schreyer, Curator Joseph Regenstein Library, 1100 E 57th St, Chicago, IL 60637 773-702-8705 Fax 73-702-3728 Email SpecialCollections@lib.uchicago.edu http://www.lib.uchicago.edu/LibInfo/Libraries/SpCl/ Founded 1891.

This collection of 250,000 volumes and 19,000 linear feet of manuscripts includes works relating to the history of science. Since many of the holdings are rare or unique, readers are expected to be very careful to avoid loss of or damage to any materials and to follow the department's policies for use of the collections. The collections are open to high school juniors or seniors who have a letter from their teacher indicating that the student is responsible and prepared to use original research materials. Visitors should contact the department in advance.

UNIVERSITY OF ILLINOIS AT CHICAGO - SCIENCE LIBRARY
University of Illinois at Chicago, Science & Engineering South Bldg, 845 W Taylor, Chicago, IL 60607 312-996-2716 Fax 312-413-0424
This library is open to the public, but circulation privileges are restricted. The collection contains approximately 60,000 volumes and 1000 periodicals on biology, chemistry, geology and physics.

WASTE MANAGEMENT AND RESEARCH CENTER - LIBRARY
Hazardous Waste Research and Information Center, 1 E Hazelwood Dr, Champaign, IL 61820 217-244-8989 217-333-8957
This library contains 10,000 books and 150 journals and is open to the public with no circulation privileges. Circulation through interlibrary loan is available.

WOOD LIBRARY
Patrick Sim, Librarian   520 N Northwest Hwy, Park Ridge, IL 60068 847-825-5586 Fax 847-825-1692 Email wlm@asahq.org
http://www.asahq.org/wlm
The American Society of Anesthesiologists' Wood Library includes a museum of equipment from the interesting medical history of anesthesiology.

ZENITH ELECTRONICS CORPORATION - TECHNICAL LIBRARY
Zenith Electronics Corporation, 1000 N Milwaukee Ave, Glenview, IL 60025 847-391-8452 Fax 847-391-8555
This library is not open to the public.

Chapter

10

Materials

Reference Books Listing Hands-On Materials

Here are numerous sources of free and inexpensive hands-on materials for fun science activities.

EDUCATORS GUIDE TO FREE SCIENCE MATERIALS
- 38TH EDITION
Edited by Mary H. Saterstrom Contact Kathy Nehmer Educators Progress Service, Inc., 214 Center St, Randolph, WI 53956-1497   920-326-3126 888-951-4469 Fax 920-326-3127 1997 256 pages $ 29.95
This book lists and describes free science materials, including films, filmstrips, slides, videotapes, and printed materials by category of science subject area. Revised annually.

ENERGY EDUCATION RESOURCES
- KINDERGARTEN THROUGH 12TH GRADE
National Energy Information Center, EI-231, Energy Information Administration, Room 1F-048, Forrestal Building, 1000 Independence Ave, SW, Washington, DC 20585 202-586-8800 1992
Ask for a copy of this 31-page booklet listing 86 different sources of educational materials from both public and private institutions and companies. Each source usually offers a catalog listing free materials.

NSTA SCIENCE EDUCATION SUPPLIERS
A Supplement to: Science & Children, Science Scope, and The Science Teacher, National Science Teachers Association, 1840 Wilson Blvd, Arlington, VA 22201-3000 800-722-NSTA http://www.nsta.org Published annually. 165 pages $ 5.00 per copy.
List of science educational materials manufacturers and distributors. The most current and comprehensive list of manufacturers, publishers and distributors of science education materials. See Equipment/Supplies. In 1998, 271 sources of hands-on equipment and supplies were listed.

THE PLASTICS AND THE ENVIRONMENT SOURCEBOOK
The Polystyrene Packaging Council, 1025 Connecticut Ave, NW, Suite 515, Washington, DC 20036 202-822-6424 1993 32 pages Free
Ask for this free catalog listing free and inexpensive curriculum materials and classroom activities using plastics.

Chicago Area Stores Selling
Hands-On Materials and Science Equipment

The following list of retail stores is from recommendations by Chicago area science teachers.

THE ADLER PLANETARIUM STORE
Adler Planetarium & Astronomy Museum, 1300 S Lake Shore Drive, Chicago, IL 60605 312-322-0312 http://astro.uchicago.edu/adler/
This store within the Adler Planetarium carries a good selection of books and educational materials on astronomy, astrophysics and space science.

AMERICAN SCIENCE & SURPLUS
Stores: 5316 N Milwaukee, Chicago, IL 60646 773-763-0313, 15142 S LaGrange Road, Orland Park, IL 708-873-9270, and 1/4 mile east of Kirk Road, on Route 38, Geneva, IL 60185 630-232-2882. Mail order warehouse: American Science & Surplus, 3605 Howard St, Skokie, IL 60076 847-982-0870 Fax 800-934-0722 http://www.sciplus.com
These retail stores sell inexpensive, surplus science equipment. They are a favorite of science students, science teachers and do-it-yourself inventors. Ask for a mail order catalog.

ARVEY PAPER & OFFICE PRODUCTS
(See your telephone directory for store locations.)
These retail stores sell office supplies.

MSI Presents LEGO MindStorms™, a facilitated workshop featuring programmable LEGO® bricks that control robotic creatures in unique environments including a Mars landscape or a haunted house.

Photo Courtesy of the Museum of Science and Industry
Photography by Edward G. Lines, Jr.

CHICAGO BOTANIC GARDEN - THE GARDEN SHOP
Chicago Botanic Garden, 1000 Lake Cook Road (at Edens Expressway), Glencoe, IL 60022-0400 847-835-8205 http://www.chicago-botanic.org
This retail shop carries a wide variety of items related to botany, wildlife and geology.

CHICAGO BOTANIC GARDEN
- THE WHEELBARROW RESOURCE AND GIFT SHOP
Chicago Botanic Garden, 1000 Lake Cook Road (at Edens Expressway), Glencoe, IL 60022-0400 847-835-8384 http://www.chicago-botanic.org
A retail shop in the Fruit & Vegetable Garden with gifts and resources related exclusively to the Midwest's best fruit and vegetables.

CHICAGO CHILDREN'S MUSEUM SHOP
Navy Pier, 700 E. Grand Ave, Chicago, IL 60611 312-595-0600
This shop has many fun science items for children including a large book selection.

CLASS MATE
3925 W 103rd St, Chicago, IL 60655 773-239-8053
http://www.edumart.com/classmate
School supplies including science materials.

CREATIVE REUSE WAREHOUSE
721 W O'Brien, 312-421-3640 Hours: Tuesdays, Thursdays & Saturdays 9:00-5:00; Sundays Noon-4:00. One block south of Roosevelt between 12th Place and 13th Street, just east of Halstead.
Supplies for Peanuts! Industry and business discards are made available for art classes, craft projects, learning games, and many other expressions of creativity. Telephone to register for workshops.

DAVE'S ROCK SHOP
704 Main St, Evanston, IL 60202 847-866-7374
This lapidary store specializes in minerals, rocks and fossils. Ask to see private museum collection of fossils dating back 1.5 billion years for algae samples and 600 millions years for fossils that has been collected over a 35 year period. Housed in one room, this collection of Earth's life history includes dinosaur eggs and nests.

DOOLIN AMUSEMENT SUPPLY CO.
511 N Halsted, Chicago, IL 60622 312-243-9424 Party supplies
A retail source of balloons and novelties for science experiments.

GRAY'S DISTRIBUTING CO., INC. - THE LEARNING TREE
4419 Ravenswood Ave, Chicago, IL 60640 773-769-3737
http://www.edumart.com/thelearningtree
School supplies including science materials.

HARRISON SUPPLY
345 N Wolf Rd, 3 blks N of Dundee, Wheeling, IL 847-537-0255
This retail store sells raw materials by the pound, including brass, aluminum and plastic. This fun place for the inventor or science teacher also sells motors and much more.

KAY BEE TOYS
(See your telephone directory for store locations.)
This toy retailer carries toys that use science principles as well as basic science toys.

KITE HARBOR
435 E Illinois St, Chicago, IL 60611 312-321-5483 Fax 847-674-3539 Email kitehbr@interaccess.com http://interaccess.com/~kitehbr/ and 109 N Marion, Oak Park, IL 60301 708-848-4907
This retail store specializes in kites. It also has science toys like hot air balloons, helicopters, boomerangs, the swinging wonder, model planes, and juggling equipment.

KOHL LEARNING STORE
165 Green Bay Rd, Wilmette, IL 888-KOHL-KID 847-251-7168
http://www.kohlchildrensmuseum.org
This retail store within the Kohl Children's Museum is open to the public and sells many quality educational science toys for the preschool and elementary school child.

KRASNY & COMPANY INC.
2829 N Clybourn, Chicago, IL 60618 773-477-5504 Restaurant and party supplies
Retail source of clear straws and balloons for science experiments.

LEON M. LEDERMAN SCIENCE EDUCATION CENTER - INSTRUCTIONAL MATERIALS
Fermi National Accelerator Laboratory, P. O. Box 500 MS 777, Batavia, IL 60510-0500 630-840-8258 Email sdahl@fnal.gov
A variety of Education Office developed educational materials such as kits, teachers guides, and multimedia material are available for purchase at this center. Cost varies. Contact the center for an order form.

LIZZADRO MUSEUM OF LAPIDARY ART - SHOP
220 Cottage Hill Ave, Elmhurst, IL 60126 630-833-1616 Fax 630-833-1225
http://www.elmhurst.org
This excellent museum exhibits art forms made from minerals. It is an example of how art and the science of geology combine to reveal nature's beauty. The shop at the Museum sells many fine examples of minerals, meteorites, petrified wood, and lapidary art.

MIDWEST MODEL SUPPLY CO.
12040 S Aero Dr, Plainfield, IL 60544 800-573-7029   815-254-2151   Fax 815-254-2445 Email mwmodelsup@aol.com Distributor Wholesale Quantity School Orders
Ask for literature. Source for Estes Rockets & accessories, bridge building kits, aero-space models, plane programs, mousetrap racers, and model making materials.

MUSEUM OF SCIENCE AND INDUSTRY STORE, "THE BIG IDEA^{SM}"
Museum of Science and Industry, 57th St and Lake Shore Drive, Chicago, IL 60637 773-684-1414 http://www.msichicago.org
This store sells science books, toys and novelties.

NATURAL WONDERS
(See your telephone directory for store locations.) Retail stores of science toys and gifts.
Ask for brochure, Our Discount for Teachers, that provides a savings of 15% on purchases for the classroom.

NOODLE KIDOODLE
**(See your telephone directory for store locations.)
http://noodlekidoodle.com**
Toy stores that include many fun science toys.

PRECIOUS POSSESSIONS
Downtown, 28 N Michigan Ave, Chicago, IL 60602 312-726-8118; Harlem Iring Plaza, 4126-E N Harlem Ave, Norridge, IL 60634 708-452-0333
Retail source of crystals, minerals, precious stones.

STANTON HOBBY SHOP INC.
Contact Jeff Ruby 4718 N Milwaukee Ave (near Lawrence Ave), Chicago, IL 60630 773-283-6446 Fax 773-283-6842 Email stantonhob@aol.com
This very large hobby store has everything for the young scientist: Estes rockets, dinosaur models, chemistry lab kits, Smithsonian kits, human anatomy models, remote control units, wood, metal & plastic building supplies.

STOREHOUSE OF KNOWLEDGE
Contact Kevin Sewart 2822 N Sheffield, Chicago, IL 60657   773-929-3932 (Preschool and Elementary School)
This retail store for school supplies has an extensive section of books and materials on science for the preschool and elementary school age child. As a parent/teacher store, it has many science gift ideas.

THE DRUM
5216 N Clark, Chicago, IL 60640 773-769-5551
This store specializes in artist supplies and theatrical makeup and costumes. Lots of fun. Wigs and lab coats for the mad scientist.

THE SCOPE SHOPPE INC.
Contact Mike Schlinder P. O. Box 1208, 113 Read St, Elburn, IL 60119
800-577-2673 630-365-9499 Fax 630-365-9519 Email SCOPECAM@aol.com
Ask for catalog/reference manual. This store sells microscopes for the classroom at all levels of instruction. Educational microscope care, repair and sales.

TOM THUMB HOBBY & CRAFTS
1026 Davis St, Evanston, IL 60201 847-869-9575 Open seven days a week.
This large store has a good selection of hobby materials including a section of educational science toys.

TOY STATION
270 Market Square, Lake Forest, IL 60045 708-234-0180
This store sells many different science kits, Educational Insights Science Kits, microscopes, telescopes and astronomy materials.

TOYS R US
(See your telephone directory for store locations.)
This major toy retailer often carries toys that use science principles.

TOYSCAPE
2911 N Broadway, Chicago, IL 60657 773-665-7400
Email toyscape@earthlink.net
Retail store of fine toys and books.

TROST HOBBY SHOP
3111 W 63rd St, Chicago, IL 60629 773-925-1000
This store carries basic hobby needs as well as science model kits, chemistry sets and kites.

UNCLE FUN
1338 W Belmont, Chicago, IL 60657 773-477-8223
A unique toy store with hard to find inexpensive toys. They have many toys demonstrating science concepts and processes. The name of this store says it all.

USTOY CONSTRUCTIVE PLAYTHINGS
5314 W Lincoln Ave, Skokie, IL 60076 847-675-5900 http://www.ustoyco.com
This parent/teacher retail store is filled with educational fun for young children.

Mail Order Suppliers
of Hands-On Materials and Science Equipment

These sources were selected by the author or recommended by science teachers.

A G INDUSTRIES
Contact Aaron Tibbs 15335 N E 95th St, Redmond, WA 98052 800-233-7174 425-885-4599 Fax 425-885-4672 Email atibbs@whitewings.com http://www.whitewings.com Manufacturer Retail and Wholesale (Elementary School to High School)
Ask for 12-page catalog. Educational kits for constructing paper airplane gliders, boats and origami. Whitewings series includes the History of Passenger Planes, Future of Flight, History of Jet Fighters, Racers, Space Shuttle, Science of Flight. Display cases for home and retail stores.

ACCULAB
8 Pheasant Run, Newtown, PA 18940 800-656-4400 Fax 800-356-0338 Email scales@acculab.com http://www.acculab.com Manufacturer Distributor (High School to College)
Ask for catalog. Manufacturer of weighing products, ie. electronic balances.

ACTIVITIES INTEGRATING MATHEMATICS AND SCIENCE (AIMS)
AIMS Education Foundation, P. O. Box 8120, Fresno, CA 93747-8120 888-SEE-AIMS 209-255-4094 Fax 209-255-6396 Email aimsed@fresno.edu http://www.AIMSedu.org Non-Profit (Elementary School)
Ask for 56-page Programs and Products Catalog. The goal of the AIMS program is to enrich the education of students in K-9 using a hands-on approach that is consistent with Science for All Americans (AAAS) and Curriculum and Evaluation Standards for School Mathematics (National Council of Teachers of Mathematics).

THE ADMEN, INC.
Contact Ed Veissi 6400 Chestnut St, Morton Grove, IL 60053-2644 847-581-1010 Fax 847-581-1020 Email Chemeasy@admen.com Distributor (High School)
Ask for brochure. Distributor of ChemEasy, a small plastic wheel that dials information from the periodic table.

AMERICAN ASSOCIATION OF PHYSICS TEACHERS
- AAPT PRODUCTS CATALOG
American Association of Physics Teachers, One Physics Ellipse, College Park, MD 20740-3845   301-209-3300   Fax 301-209-0845   Email aapt-memb@aapt.org

http://www.aapt.org (High School to College)
Ask for this 28-page catalog. The 1997-98 catalog lists 85 books on physics and physics education. It also offers Physics of Technology Modules, computer software, videodiscs, videotapes, materials for teachers, gift items, workshop materials, and posters.

AMERICAN CHEMICAL SOCIETY
- SCIENCE TEACHING RESOURCES CATALOG
American Chemical Society, Education Division, 1155 16th St, NW, Washington, DC 20036 800-209-0423 Fax 800-209-0064 304-728-2170
http://www.acs.org/edugen2/education/conted/conted.htm Retail (High School)
Ask for 46-page Teaching Resources Catalog that includes posters, videotapes, magazines, educational materials, curriculum supplements, National Chemistry Examinations, and the annual Chemistry Calendar.

ANDY VODA OPTICAL TOYS
RR 5, #387, Brattleboro, VT 05301 Tel/Fax 802-254-6115
Email avoda@together.net http://www.together.net/~avoda/optical.htm/
Manufacturer Retail (All ages)
Ask for brochure. Phenakistascope with six magic wheels, Thaumatrope, Couples spinning pictures, Flipbooks, Greeting Flipbooks, Make-it-yourself Zoetrope.

APOGEE COMPONENTS
1431 Territory Trail, Colorado Springs, CO 80919-3323 719-548-5075 Email tvm@apogeerockets.com http://www.ApogeeRockets.com Distributor (Middle School to High School)
Ask for catalog of rocketry products.

AQUATIC ECO-SYSTEMS, INC.
1767 Benbow Court, Apopka, FL 32703 407-886-3939 Fax 407-886-6787 Email aes@aquatic-eco.com http://www.aquatic-eco.com Manufacturer Distributor (High School to College)
Ask for 496-page catalog. Aquaculture Equipment, Lake & Pond Equipment, Aeration Specialists.

ARBOR SCIENTIFIC
P. O. Box 2750, Ann Arbor, MI 48106-2750 800-367-6695
http://www.arborsci.com Retail (Elementary School and High School)
Ask for 48-page catalog of physics teaching materials for the classroom, including many books and innovations in science education.

ASTRONOMICAL SOCIETY OF THE PACIFIC
390 Ashton Ave, San Francisco, CA 94112-1787 415-337-1100

Email membership@aspsky.org http://www.aspsky.org (High School to College)
Ask for 32-page catalog. Quality materials for astronomy teachers. This is the
organization you need to belong to if you are involved with astronomy education.

BECKLEY CARDY
Beckley Cardy Group, 100 Paragon Parkway, Mansfield, OH 44903 888-222-1332
Fax 888-454-1417 http://www.beckleycardy.com Distributor Retail (Elementary
School)
Ask for 950-page catalog. Major supplier of equipment, supplies, and furniture for
schools, including all science areas.

BELEW SPRUCE SOFTWARE
806 Buchanan Blvd, # 115-164, Boulder City, NV 89005 702-565-8614
Email stargazer@belewspruce.com http://www.belewspruce.com Manufacturer
Distributor (High School)
Ask for brochure. Star Gazer interactive educational astronomy software lets you
discover your universe.

BEN MEADOWS COMPANY, INC.
3589 Broad Street, Atlanta, GA 30341-2272 800-241-6401 Fax 800-628-2068
Email mail@benmeadows.com http://www.benmeadows.com   Manufacturer
(High School to College)
Ask for 472-page catalog. Supplier of forestry, engineering, environmental,
landscaping, safety and science education supplies and equipment.

BRAINSTORM PUBLICATIONS
Educational Games & Books, P. O. Box 200-154, Lake Oswego, OR 97034
503-636-8668 Email LSPREYER@aol.com Manufacturer Retail Mail Order
(High School)
Products include Einstein: A Question & Answer Game for the Whole Class and
Teaching is an Art.

CAMBRIDGE PHYSICS OUTLET
10 Green St, Bldg E, Woburn, MA 01801 800-932-5227 617-932-8427 Fax
617-932-9295 Manufacturer Distributor (High School to College)
Ask for 16-page catalog. Unique materials for teaching chemistry and physics,
including Gears and Levers, Gravity Drop Experiment, Roller Coaster, Sound and
Waves Experiment, The Periodic Puzzle, The Atom Building Game, and more.

Kids doing science at the Teachers Academy for Mathematics and Science (TAMS).   TAMS provides many different opportunities for teacher training.

Photo Courtesy of TAMS
© 1998 Jean Clough

CAPTIVATION, INC.
101 Connecticut Ave, Nashua, NH 03060-5129 603-889-1156 Fax 603-880-5334 Email capinc@tchg.com http://www.tchg.com Manufacturer Distributor Retail Mail Order (Elementary School to High School)
Ask for brochure. Manufacturer of The Teaching Tank, a see-through system that provides opportunity for numerous visual experiments in most science subjects, including experiments on acids, color, density and solubility, dew point, diffusion, volcanic action, centripetal force, horticulture, and many more. Use The Teaching Tank Discovery Book, Volumes 1 and 2, for experiment descriptions, each over 100 pages.

CAROLINA BIOLOGICAL SUPPLY CO.
2700 York Rd, Burlington, NC 27215-3398 800-334-5551 Fax 800-222-7112 Email carolina@carolina.com http://www.carosci.com Retail (Elementary School to High School)
Ask for 1200-page science and math catalog. Major source of science education equipment and supplies.

CASIO, INC.
570 Mt. Pleasant Ave, Dover, NJ 07801 800-582-2763 http://www.casio.com Manufacturer Distributor (Elementary School to High School)
Ask for 32-page catalog. Calculators, Digital Cameras, Handheld Computers, and Label Printers.

CELESTRON INTERNATIONAL
Contact Linda Waible 2835 Columbia St, Torrance, CA 90503 310-328-9560 Fax 310-212-5835 Email l_waible@celestron.com http://www.celestron.com Manufacturer Distributor (High School to Adult)
Ask for catalogs: Telescopes for Astronomy, Celestron Telescopes, Celestron Binoculars & Spotting Scopes, Lab Grade Microscopes, and Celestron Accessories. Major manufacturer of telescopes.

CENCO
3300 CENCO Parkway, Franklin Park, IL 60131-1364 800-262-3626 Fax 800-814-0607 http://www.cenconet.com Retail (Elementary School to High School)
Ask for catalog. Major supplier of science education equipment and supplies.

CHILDWOOD
Contact Karen Beierle 8873 Woodbank Dr, Bainbridge Island, WA 98110 800-362-9825 206-842-9290 Fax 206-842-5107 Email childwood@aol.com Manufacturer Retail Mail Order (Preschool and Elementary School)
Ask for 14-page catalog. Six science themes are packaged with sturdy, full-color, wooden magnetic figures. All hands-on science sets include stories, activities and reproducible mini-books. Sets include Life Cycles: The Butterfly, The Hen and The Frog; The Farm; Sealife; The Bear Cave; Dinosaurs; and Weather.

COLE-PARMER INSTRUMENT CO.
625 E Bunker Court, Vernon Hills, IL 60061-1844 800-323-4340 Fax 847-247-2929 Email info@coleparmer.com http://www.coleparmer.com Wholesale and Retail (High School to Adult)
Major supplier of scientific equipment and supplies to industry and education.

CONNECTICUT VALLEY BIOLOGICAL

82 Valley Road, P. O. Box 326, Southhampton, MA 01073 800-628-7748 Fax 800-355-6813 413-527-4030 Manufacturer Distributor Retail (Elementary School to College)

Ask for 450-page catalog. Major source of science materials including living botanical and zoological material, microscope slides, biological displays, books, video tapes, and much more.

COPERNICUS

Contact Harris Tobias 100 E Main Street, Charlottesville, VA 22902 800-424-3950 804-296-6800 Fax 804-296-2154 Email Copernicus@1q.com http://www.1q.com/Copernicus Distributor Wholesale Retail Mail Order on Web Site (Elementary School to Adult)

Ask for 12-page wholesale catalog. Member of Museum Store Association. Geodome, Volcano, Starglow, Rootbeer Kit, Bubblegum Kit, boomerangs, fly back plane, balloon car, Make a Clock Kit, Rattle Back, large Swinging Wonder, Echo Mike, Radiometer, Drinking Bird, Tornado Tube, magnifying glasses, astronaut ice cream, hand boiler, Magic Garden, abacus, Large Dome Making Kit, glow paint, glow bugs, spiral timer, auto compass, luminous star finder, swinging wonders.

CORD COMMUNICATIONS

Customer Relations, P. O. Box 21206, Waco, TX 76702-1206 800-231-3015 Fax 254-776-3906 Email cust_rel@cord.org http://www.cord.org Manufacturer Distributor (High School)

Ask for catalog. Tech Prep materials include curricular materials, technology workshops, innovative teaching strategies, Internet training tools, and resource books.

CREATIVE PUBLICATIONS

5040 W 111th St, Oak Lawn, IL 60453-5008 800-624-0822 Email creativepublications@tribune.com Retail (Elementary School)

Ask for the 115-page catalog filled with educational materials for math, geometry, science, science measurement, and educational curricula. Also science posters.

CUISENAIRE - DALE SEYMOUR PUBLICATIONS

10 Bank St, P. O. Box 5026, White Plains, NY 10602-5026 800-237-0338 Email info@awl.com http://cuisenaire.com http://awl.com/dsp/ Distributor Retail (Elementary School)

Major supplier of resources for the classroom and home learning environment. The 224-page K-6 Catalog, 113-page Middle School Catalog, and 112-page Seconday Math & Science Catalog includes math, manipulatives, science, and teacher resources.

DAEDALON
35 Congress St, P O Box 2028, Salem, MA   01970-6228   800-233-2490
978-744-5310   Fax 978-745-3065   Email daedalon@cove.com   (High School to College)
Ask for 82-page catalog. Physics experiments and apparatus.

DAIRY COUNCIL OF WISCONSIN
999 Oakmont Plaza Drive, Suite 510, Westmont, IL 60559 800-933-2479
Fax 800-213-6455 http://www.DCWnet.org
Ask for 14-page catalog of educational materials about nutrition.

DATA HARVEST EDUCATIONAL
363 Lang Blvd, Grand Island, NY 14072 800-436-3062
Fax 905-607-3469(Canadian Office) http://www.data-harvest.co.uk
 Manufacturer Distributor (Elementary School to High School)
Ask for 20-page catalog. Exploration kits for data collection in most areas of science.

DAVIS INSTRUMENTS
3465 Diablo Ave, Hayward, CA 94545-2778 800-678-3669 Fax 510-670-0589
Email info@davisnet.com http://www.davisnet.com Manufacturer Distributor
(High School to College)
Ask for 22-page catalog. Manufacturer of high-precision weather stations and instrumentation.

DELTA EDUCATION, INC.
P. O. Box 3000, Nashua, NH   03061-3000   800-442-5444 Fax 800-282-9560
603-886-4632   http://www.delta-ed.com   Manufacturer   Retail Mail Order
(Elementary School)
Ask for 60-page Hands-On Science catalog. This catalog is filled with science kits, toys and educational materials. Also ask for information about Delta Science Modules, SCIS3, and ESS. These three hands-on programs are available through Delta Education.

DENOYER-GEPPERT
5225 Ravenswood Ave, Chicago, IL 60640-2028 800-621-1014 Fax 773-561-4160
Email denoyer@aol.com Retail (Middle School to High School)
Chicago area distributor of science education equipment, life models, and supplies for biology and chemistry.

DEXTER EDUCATIONAL TOYS, INC.
P. O. Box 630861, Miami, FL   33163   305-931-7426 Fax 305-931-0552
Manufacturer Wholesale (Preschool to Elementary School)
Ask for brochure. Manufacturer of creative career role playing costumes and puppets, including The Scientist, The Teacher, The Police Officer, and many more. Ask about local distributor or purchase on school letterhead.

DIDAX INC. EDUCATIONAL RESOURCES
Contact Martin Kennedy   395 Main St, Rowley, MA 01969   800-458-0024
978-948-2340 Fax 978-948-2813 Email catalog@didaxinc.com
http://www.didaxinc.com Retail (Elementary School)
Ask for 128-page catalog of hands-on materials in elementary school mathematics and science.

DIMENSIONS IN LEARNING, INC.
P O Box 639, Forest Park, IL 60130 888-366-6628 708-366-6117
Fax 708-366-8348 Email nkokat@sprintmail.com Distributor (Elementary School to High School)
Ask for 24-page catalog. Distributor of Valiant Technology Ltd. educational materials from Great Britain. Products include Roamer, robot that teaches mathematics; Inventa, system of invention and design; Tronix, system of science and technology using electronics; and more.

DOWLING MAGNETS
Contact JoAnn Chew   P O Box 1829, Sonoma, CA 95476 800-624-6381
707-935-0352 Fax 707-935-1231 Email dowling@DowlingMagnets.com
Manufacturer Wholesale (High School to Adult)
Magnets and magnetic materials of numerous shapes and dimensions for educational use. Ask for catalog.

EDMUND SCIENTIFIC COMPANY
101 E Gloucester Pike, Barrington, NJ 08007-1380 800-728-6999 609-573-3488
Fax 609-573-6272 http://www.edsci.com Retail (All ages)
Ask for 112-page science reference catalog for educators. Since 1942 this well known scientific optical supplier also sells many other items including lasers, microscopes, camera/monitor systems, science classroom anatomy models, nature kits, laboratory safety equipment, balances, weather instruments, timers, magnets, small motors & pumps, robot kits, earth science kits, telescopes, museum animal replicas, and unique classroom materials for teachers.

EDUCATIONAL INNOVATIONS, INC
151 River Rd, Cos Cob, CT 06807 888-912-7474 203-629-6049 Fax 203-629-2739
Email edinnov@aol.com http://www.teachersource.com
Ask for 50-catalog. Science teaching supplies, including ultraviolet detecting beads, Gro-Beast Alligators, Fossil Shark Teeth, Magnets, Owl Pellets, Tornado Tubes, and many more.

EDUCATIONAL TEACHING AIDS
620 Lakeview Parkway, Vernon Hills, IL 60061 800-445-5985 Fax 800-ETA-9326
Email info@etauniverse.com http://www.etauniverse.com Retail Mail Order
(Elementary School and Middle School)
Ask for 111-page K-12 science catalog filled with educational science materials and toys.

EDUCATORS OUTLET
P. O. Box 397, Timnath, CO 80547 800-315-2212 http://www.edoutlet.com
Manufacturer Distributor (Elementary School to High School)
Ask for 16-page science catalog. Materials kits on astronomy, geology, globes & maps, human body, environment, ecology, electricity, light, and more.

ENCYCLOPEDIA BRITANNICA EDUCATIONAL CORPORATION
Instructional Materials, 310 S Michigan Ave, Chicago, IL 60604-9839
800-554-9862 http://www.eb.com Manufacturer (Elementary School)
Ask for 36-page catalog of FOSS modules developed at the Lawrence Hall of Science, University of California, Berkeley, CA 94720 510-642-8941. FOSS, Fully Operational Science System, is a fresh approach to science with a carefully planned and coordinated science curriculum.

ESTES INDUSTRIES
Contact Ann Grimm 1295 H Street, Penrose, CO 81240 800-820-0202 Fax
800-820-0203 719-372-3217 Manufacturer Retail to teachers. (High School to Adult)
Ask for Estes Educator Catalog on school letterhead. Supplies model rockets, engines, accessories, and curricula.

ETA
620 Lakeview Pkwy, Vernon Hills, IL 60061-1838 800-445-5985 Fax
800-ETA-9326 847-816-5050 Fax 847-816-5066 http://www.etauniverse.com
Retail Mail Order (Elementary School)
Major supplier of educational toys and materials. Ask for 124-page ETA Science Catalog and 172-page ETA Math Catalog with supplies for the science classroom.

EXPLORATORIUM STORE
3601 Lyon St, San Francisco, CA 94123 415-561-0393
http://www.exploratorium.edu Retail Mail Order (All ages)
See web page that is filled with quality science toys and books, including the following
toys: Megabubbles Kit, The Kaleidoscope Book and Kit, Zoetrope, Wild Wood,
Magnetron, Gyros, Curiosity Box, Eagle Microscope, Mirage Maker, Micro-Bank,
Erector Sets, Paradox 3-D Jigsaw Puzzle, and Ellipto.

THE FIELD MUSEUM - HARRIS EDUCATIONAL LOAN PROGRAM
**The Field Museum, Roosevelt Road and Lake Shore Drive, Chicago, IL
60605-2497 312-322-8853 http://www.fmnh.org Free for Chicago schools and
community groups. Registration fee $ 30 for groups outside of Chicago. Fees and
admission subject to change. (Preschool to High School)**
Any Chicago-area educator may borrow from an extensive list of Exhibit Cases,
Experience Boxes, and Audiovisual Materials. This center is located on the ground
floor level of the Museum. Check the Museum web site and on-line catalog at
http://www.fmnh.org/stpgrms/Harris_Loan/hhome.htm.

FISHER-EMD (EDUCATIONAL MATERIALS DIVISION)
**4901 W LeMoyne St, Chicago, IL 60651   800-955-1177   Fax 800-955-0740
http://www.fisheredu.com Retail (Elementary School to College)**
Ask for a catalog. Major supplier of science education equipment and supplies
conveniently located in the Chicago area.

FLINN CHEMICAL CATALOG REFERENCE MANUAL
**Flinn Scientific Inc., P. O. Box 219, Batavia, IL 60510 800-452-1261 688 pages
Retail (High School to Adult)**
This catalog, for science teachers only, lists new products, chemicals, chemical solution
preparation, Apparatus & Laboratory Equipment, Books, Computer Software, Safety
Storage Cabinets & Fume Hoods, Safety Supplies & Equipment, Right to Know Laws,
Mystery Substance Identification, Chemical Inventory & Storage, and Chemical
Disposal Procedures.

FORESTRY SUPPLIERS, INC.
**P. O. Box 8397, Jackson, MS 39284-8397 or 205 W Rankin St, Jackson, MS
39201   800-647-5368   Fax 800-543-4203   601-354-3565   Fax 601-355-5126
http://www.forestry-suppliers.com (Elementary School to Adult)**
Ask for 550-page catalog. Materials for forestry, agriculture, horticulture, landscape,
environmental science, aquaculture, wildlife, and laboratory equipment.

FOSS
Full Operating Science System, Center for Multisensory Learning, Lawrence hall of Science, University of California, Berkeley, CA 94720 800-258-1302 510-642-8941 http://www.uslink4.berkeley.edu/foss/ Retail (Elementary School to Middle School)
Ask for catalog of products including books, curriculum materials, videos and science kits. The Center for Multisensory Learning specializes in science curriculum development for all elementary and junior high school students. FOSS materials are for regular education classes.

FOTODYNE, INC.
950 Walnut Ridge Drive, Hartland, WI 53029 800-362-4657 Fax 800-362-3642 414-369-7000 Fax 414-369-7013 http://www.fotodyne.com Manufacturer (High School to College)
Ask for 70-page catalog. High quality photodocumentation products for molecular biology education and research.

FRANKLIN LEARNING RESOURCES
One Franklin Plaza, Burlington, NJ 08016-4907 800-266-5626 Fax 609-239-5943 http://www.franklin.com Manufacturer Distributor (Elementary School to High School)
Ask for educational catalog. Manufacturer of hand-held electronic dictionaries and thesauruses in various languages.

FREY SCIENTIFIC
Beckley Cardy Group, 100 Paragon Parkway, Mansfield, OH 44903 888-222-1332 Fax 888-454-1417 Distributor Retail http://www.beckleycardy.com (Elementary School to College)
Ask for 790-page catalog. Major supplier of hands-on science education equipment and supplies for all science subject areas.

GEOCENTRAL
Contact Cindy Vader 1721 Action Ave, Napa, CA 94559 800-231-6083 707-224-7500 Fax 707-224-7400 Email cindy@geocentral.com Manufacturer Wholesale (Elementary School to High School)
Quantity sets of rocks and minerals for retail sale. Flat boxes of mineral and fossil assortments. Sea shell glow night lights. Agate bookends. Twenty four-page catalog.

GEOTHERMAL EDUCATION OFFICE
664 Hilary Drive, Tiburon, CA 94920 800-866-4GEO 415-435-4574 Fax 415-435-7737 Email mnemzer@aol.com http://ensemble.com/geo (Elementary School to High School)
Ask for brochure. Newsletter, fact sheets, booklets, posters, and curricula.

The Adler Planetarium and Astronomy Museum delights this
young boy with one of the Museum's exhibits. See the new Star
Rider Theatre and newly remodeled Museum.

Photo Courtesy of the Adler Planetarium and Astronomy Museum

GUIDECRAFT USA

P. O. Box 324/Industrial Center, Garnerville, NY 10923-0324 800-544-6526
914-947-3500   Fax 914-947-3770   Email Gdcraft324@aol.com Manufacturer
Distributor Retail Mail Order (Preschool to Elementary School)
Ask for 16-page catalog. Fine wooden toys that teach, including Clock Puzzle House,
Fax Machine, Mini-Animal Puzzles, Time Sequencing, Wooden Educational Games,
3-D Fruit & Vegetable Puzzles, Career Sets, and Alligator Pull Toy.

HACH COMPANY

P. O. Box 389, Loveland, CO 80539-0389 800-227-4224 Fax 970-669-2932
Manufacturer Distributor (High School to College)
Ask for 464-page catalog. Unique systems to water quality testing.

HARRISON COONEY, INC.
Early Childhood Specialists, 9827 W Farragut, Chicago, IL 60018 773-992-0940 Fax 773-992-0944 Distributor (Preschool and Elementary School)
Ask for 130-page catalog. Products include furniture to manipulatives for preschool and primary school.

HARVARD-SMITHSONIAN CENTER FOR ASTROPHYSICS
Science Education Department, 60 Garden St, Cambridge, MA 02138 617-495-9798 Fax 617-496-7670 http://cfa-www.harvard.edu/cfa/sed (Elementary School)
Ask for brochure. Project Aries, astronomy resources for intercurricular elementary science.

HEALTH EDCO
P. O. Box 21207, Waco, TX 76702-1207 800-299-3366, ext 295 Fax 888-977-7653 Email sales@wrsgroup.com http://www.wrsgroup.com (Elementary School to College)
Ask for 224-page catalog. Classroom materials for anatomy, professional education, lifestyle health, elementary health, and women's health.

HEWLETT-PACKARD
Test & Measurement Organization, Hewlett-Packard, P. O. Box 50637, Palo Alto, CA 94303-9511 800-452-4844 Email made2_measure@hp.com http://www.hp.com http://www.hp.com/info/bi16 http://www.hp.com/info/mixsig16 Manufacturer (High School to College)
See web sites. Products described include oscilloscopes and accessories.

HORTICULTURAL SALES PRODUCTS
505C Grand Caribe Isle, Coronado, CA 92118 888-ROOTVUE 619-423-9399 Fax 619-423-9398 Email rootvue@aol.com http://members.aol.com/rootvue Manufacturer (Elementary School to High School)
Manufacturer of Root-Vue-Farm: Watch carrots, radishes and onions take form underground through a glass window. Other products include Worm-Vue Wonders, Wonderfinders, Powersphere, and Naturestation.

HUBBARD SCIENTIFIC
Division of American Educational Products, 1120 Halbleib Road, P O Box 760, Chippewa Falls, WI 54729 800-289-9299 715-723-4427 Fax 715-527-3235 http://amep.com Manufacturer Distributor (Elementary School to High School)
Ask for catalog. Supplier of science materials for the classroom.

I.C.E.
Institute for Chemical Education, Department of Chemistry, University of Wisconsin-Madison, 1101 University Ave, Madison, WI 53706-1396 800-991-5534 608-262-3033 Fax 608-265-8094 Email ice@chem.wisc.edu http://ice.chem.wisc.edu/ice
The Institute of Chemical Education has books and tools to help you communicate the relevance and fun of doing chemistry. Ask for 7-page catalog: Publications, Kits and More.

IDEAL SCHOOL SUPPLY COMPANY
11000 S Lavergne Ave, Oak Lawn, IL 60453 800-845-8149 http://www.ifair.com
Distributor Retail Mail Order (Preschool to Elementary School)
Ask for the 50-page teacher catalog. Science measurement materials, chemistry experiment beakers and test tubes, equilateral prisms, physics pulleys, thermometers, classroom science kits, magnetic toys, natural science materials.

INTERCULTURAL CENTER FOR RESEARCH IN EDUCATION (INCRE)
366 Massachusetts Ave, Arlington, MA 02174 888-INCRE-SI Fax 781-643-1315
Email icre@igc.apc.org http://www.incre.org Manufacturer (Elementary School)
Ask for brochure. Spanish/English hands-on science curriculum for elementary school.

KADON ENTERPRISES, INC.
Contact Kate Jones 1227 Lorene Dr, Suite 16, Pasadena, MD 21122 410-437-2163
Email kadon@gamepuzzles.com http://www.gamepuzzles.com Manufacturer Retail (Elementary School to Adult)
Ask for 15-page catalog of Gamepuzzles: for the Joy of Thinking. This company specializes in sophisticated games and puzzles for the creative thinker

KELVIN
10 Hub Drive, Melville, NY 11747 800-535-8469 Fax 800-756-1025 516-756-1750
Email kelvin@kelvin.com http://www.kelvin.com Manufacturer Distributor Retail Mail Order (Elementary School to High School)
Ask for 50-page catalog. Products and materials for students' inventive work in science, technology, electronics and engineering.

KLINGER EDUCATIONAL PRODUCTS CORP.
112-19 14th Road, College Point, New York, NY 11356-1453 800-522-6252
Fax 718-321-7756   Email klinger_ed@prodigy.com http://leybold-didactic.de
Distributor (High School to College)
Ask for CD-ROM (501-page) catalog. Distributor of Leybold laboratory equipment for the science, mostly physics, classroom, including 36 experiments.

KOLBE CONCEPTS, INC.
P. O. Box 15667, Phoenix, AZ 85060   602-840-9770   Fax 602-952-2706
http://www.kolbe.com Manufacturer Retail (All ages)
Ask for brochure. Think-ercises, Glop Shop - inventor's assortment, Go Power - science experiments, Using Your Senses, Solar Power Winners - experiment book, Decide & Design - inventor's book.

LAB SAFETY SUPPLY INC.
P. O. Box 1368, Janesville, WI 53547-1368 800-356-0783 Info 800-356-2501 Fax 800-543-9910 http://www.labsafety.com Retail (High School)
Ask for 900-page catalog of laboratory equipment and supplies dedicated to personal environmental safety for industry, hazardous waste, and school science laboratories.

LAB-AIDS, INC.
17 Colt Court, Ronkonkoma, NY 11779 516-737-1133 Fax 516-737-1286
http://www.lab-aids.com Manufacturer Distributor (Elementary School to High School)
Ask for 130-page catalog. Manufacturer of economic, educational kits for biology, environmental science, physical science, and elementary science.

LAKESHORE LEARNING MATERIALS
2695 E Dominguez St, Carson, CA 90749 800-428-4414 Fax 310-537-5403
http://www.lakeshorelearning.com Manufacturer Distributor Retail Mail Order (Elementary School)
Ask for 200-page catalog. The catalog of this major distributor of learning materials has eight pages of science materials.

LAMOTTE
P. O. Box 329, Chestertown, MD 21620 800-344-3100 410-778-3100
Fax 410-778-6394 Email ese@lamotte.com http://www.lamotte.com/ese
Manufacturer (High School)
Ask for 36-page Environmental Science Education Catalog. Quality equipment and guidance for water analysis and soil science.

LAWRENCE HALL OF SCIENCE
University of California, Berkeley, CA 94720-5200 510-642-1016 Fax 510-642-1055 Email lhsstore@uclink4.berkeley.edu http://www.lhs.berkeley.edu
See web site filled with books, teachers' and parents' guides, science kits, videos, and ordering instructions. Known as Eureka!: Teaching Tools from the Lawrence Hall of Science.

LEARNING RESOURCES, INC.

Contact Lisa Hoffmann   380 N Fairway Drive, Vernon Hills, IL   60061
800-222-3909 847-573-8400 Fax 847-573-8425 http://www.learningresources.com
Manufacturer Wholesale (Preschool and Elementary School)
Exceptional range of award-winning educational toys. Ask for 72-page catalog. Pretend
& Play Calculator Cash Register, math and science measurement materials, geometry
shapes, base ten products, thermometers, Power of Science line of science accessories,
Idea Factory Science Kits, the Investigator Slide Viewer with slide strip sets, the
Quantum Big Screen Microscope.

LIVING CLASSROOMS

American Forests, P. O. Box 2000, Washington, DC 20013 800-368-5748
202-955-4500 http://www.amfor.org Retail (Elementary School to High School)
Living Classrooms includes 20 famous and historic trees plus three years' worth of
educational curricula.

MATH AND SCIENCE HANDS-ON (M.A.S.H.)

Contact Denise Plunk Southern Illinois University at Edwardsville, P. O. Box
2226, Edwardsville, IL   62026   618-692-2149   Email dplunk@siue.edu
http://www.siue.edu/OSME/ Retail (Elementary School)
Ask for brochure listing science kits and materials.

MAYFLOWER DEVELOPMENT AND TRADING CORP.

P. O. Box 705, Bellevue, WA   98009 425-747-7766   Fax 425-957-9384 Email
switchon@concentric.net http://www.concentric.net/~switchon   Manufacturer
Wholesale Retail Mail Order (Elementary School to High School)
Manufacturer of Switch On!: Innovative Electronic Building Blocks. Have fun setting
up easy-to-connect, safe circuit blocks to switch on: a light bulb, a fire engine, a
flashing door bell, an electric fan, or create your own circuit. An excellent, fun way to
teach electrical circuits to children.

MC MASTER-CARR SUPPLY CO.

P. O. Box 4355, Chicago, IL 60680-4355 630-833-0300 Fax 630-834-9427 Email
sales@mcmaster.com http://www.mcmaster.com (High School to Adult)
Ask for 3000-page catalog. Over 190,000 products for industry, including supplies and
equipment for your physical plant, tools and fasteners, and raw and semi-finished
materials.

MEADE INSTRUMENTS CORP.

6001 Oak Canyon, Irvine, CA 92620-4205 949-451-1450 Fax 949-451-1460
http://www.meade.com Manufacturer Distributor (Elementary School to
College)
Ask for 102-page catalog. Quality optical telescopes, binoculars, and spotting scopes.

METROLOGIC INSTRUMENTS, INC

90 Coles Rd, Blackwood, NJ 08012 800-667-8400 609-228-8100 Fax 609-228-6673
http://www.metrologic.com (High School to College)
Ask for catalog. Manufacturer of lasers and electronic instruments.

MICRO MOLE SCIENTIFIC

P. O. Box 847, Pasco, WA 99301 509-545-4904 Fax 509-545-1-4904
Email Mauch1312@aol.com http://www.cbvcp.com/micromole Manufacturer
Distributor Retail Mail Order (Elementary School to High School)
Ask for 20-page catalog. Microchemistry supplies, demonstration materials, tie-dye
supplies, plastic ware, resource books, and teacher training.

MIDWEST MODEL SUPPLY CO.

12040 S Aero Dr, Plainfield, IL 60544 800-573-7029 815-254-2151 Fax
815-254-2445 Email mwmodelsup@aol.com Distributor Wholesale Quantity
School Orders
Ask for literature. Source for Estes Rockets & accessories, bridge building kits,
aero-space models, plane programs, mousetrap racers, and model making materials.

MIDWEST PRODUCTS CO., INC.

400 S Indiana St, P. O. Box 564, Hobart, IN 46342 800-348-3497 219-942-1134
Fax 219-942-5703 Email tom@midwestproducts.com
http://www.midwestproducts.com
Retail Mail Order (Elementary School to High School)
Ask for 15-page catalog. Source of materials for model aviation, model bridge building,
and kites.

MINDWARE

2720 Patton Rd, Roseville, MN 55113-1138 800-999-0398 Fax 888-299-9273
Retail Mail Order (All Ages)
Ask for 40-page catalog. Products include many science toys, puzzles, and games.

MODERN SCHOOL SUPPLIES, INC.

P. O. Box 958, Hartford, CT 06143 800-243-2329 Fax 800-934-7206 860-243-9565
Email modern@tiac.net http://www.tiac.net/users/modern Distributor (High
School)
Ask for 42-page catalog Science Education Catalog and 114-page Technology
Education Catalog. Products include science furniture, and supplies for biology,
ecology, biochemistry, chemistry, physics, aerospace, and electronics.

MORITEX

6440 Lusk Blvd, Suite D-105, San Diego, CA 92121 800-548-7039
http://www.moritexusa.com Retail (High School to Adult)
This company sells video microscopes that connect to television monitors.

MRS. GROSSMAN'S PAPER CO.

Contact Jeff Shaw 3810 Cypress Drive, Petaluma, CA 94954 800-457-4570
707-763-1700 Fax 707-763-7121 Email jshaw@mrsgrossmans.com
http://www.mrsgrossmans.com Manufacturer Wholesale (Elementary School)
Ask for 74-page catalog. Peel-off stickers, idea books, and kits include topics on
dinosaurs, nature, ocean life, and animals.

NADA SCIENTIFIC

P. O. Box 1336, Champlain, NY 12919 800-799-NADA Fax 518-298-3063 Email
nadasci@together.net http://www.nadasci.com Manufacturer Distributor (High
School)
Ask for CD-ROM catalog.

NALGE NUNC INTERNATIONAL

Nalgene Labware, P. O. Box 3018, Milwaukee, WI 53201-9253 800-625-4327 Fax
414-355-1072 http://nalgenunc.com Manufacturer Distributor (Elementary
School to Adult)
Ask for catalog. Manufacturer of break-resistant, cost-effective beakers, graduated
cylinders, funnels, flasks, and more for the science classroom.

NASCO

901 Janesville Ave, Fort Atkinson, WI 53538-0901 800-558-9595 920-563-2446
Fax 920-563-0901 or 4825 Stoddard Rd, Modesto, CA 95356-9318 800-558-9595
209-545-1600 Fax 209-545-1669 Email info@nascofa.com
http://www.nascofa.com Distributor Retail (Elementary School to High School)
Ask for 368-page catalog of educational supplies for science.

NATIONAL ASSOCIATION OF GEOSCIENCE TEACHERS, INC.

Contact Robert Christman P. O. Box 5443, Bellingham, WA 98227-5443
360-650-3587 Fax 360-650-7302 Email xman@cc.wwu.edu
This association seeks to foster improvement in teaching earth sciences at all levels.
Ask for information about materials available including slide sets and posters.

NATIONAL BIOLOGICAL LABS, INC.

Anatomical Models, 140-C Tewning Road, Williamsburg, VA 23188
800-248-8830 http://www.NationalBiologicalLabs.com Manufacturer Distributor
(High School to College)
Ask for catalogs. Animal and human anatomical models.

NATIONAL ENERGY FOUNDATION
Contact Gary Swan 5225 Wiley Post Way, Suite 170, Salt Lake City, UT 84116
801-539-1406   Fax 801-539-1451   Email info@nef1.org http://www.nef1.org
(Elementary School to High School)
This nonprofit organization provides programs and materials to help promote an
awareness of energy-related issues. Ask for 15-page catalog of publications and science
kits. Materials include Out of the Rock, a mineral resource and mining education
program for K-8 produced in conjunction with the U. S. Bureau of Mines.

NATIONAL TEACHING AIDS
Division of American Educational Products, 1120 Halbleib Road, P. O. Box 760,
Chippewa Falls, WI 54729 800-323-8368 800-289-9299 715-723-4427 Fax
715-527-3235 http://amep.com Manufacturer Distributor (Elementary School
to High School)
Ask for catalog. Supplier of materials for the classroom.

THE NATURE COMPANY CATALOG
P. O. Box 188, Florence, KY 41022 800-227-1114 http://www.natureco.com
Distributor Retail (Elementary School to Adult)
Ask for this 40-page catalog. Clothing for hiking, bird feeders and houses, binoculars,
electronic pedometer, knives, compasses, Raise and Release Butterfly Kits, tents, kites,
Fossil Fish Kit, toy periscope and binoculars.

NEBRASKA SCIENTIFIC
A Division of Cyrgus Co., Inc., 3823 Leavenworth St, Omaha, NE 68105-1180
800-228-7117 Fax 402-364-2216 Email nescientif@aol.com Retail (Middle School
to High School)
Ask for 134-page catalog of educational supplies for the life science classroom
including preserved specimens.

NEK ENTERPRISES, INC
1111 W. Cedar Lane, Arlington Heights, IL 60005 708-392-3415 Manufacturer
Distributor Retail (Elementary School to High School)
Educational visual aid, Measure-Up, enables students to easily visualize math problems
including fractions.

NERD KARDS
(Names Earning Respect & Dignity) P. O. Box 900, Monroe, CT 06468-0900
203-925-9773 Fax 203-925-9773 Email nerdkards@snet.net
http://www.nerdkards.com (High School to Adult)
This set of 102 Kards features scientists with their major discoveries and inventions.
$ 13.45 per set.

NYSTROM
Division of Herff Jones, Inc., 3333 Elston Ave, Chicago, IL 60618-5898
800-621-8086   773-463-1144   Fax 773-463-0515 http://www.nystromnet.com
Manufacturer Distributor (Elementary School to High School)
Ask for 23-page Science and Health catalog. Manufacturer of Charts, Models, and
Programs, including Earth Science, Physical Science, Life Science, Human Body,
Botany, Zoology, and raised relief maps.

OHAUS CORPORATION
29 Hanover Road, P. O. Box 900, Florham Park, NJ 07932-0900 800-672-7722
973-377-9000 Fax 973-593-0359 Manufacturer (High School to College)
Ask for catalog of electronic and portable precision balances.

OPTICAL SOCIETY OF CHICAGO
Contact George Magerl   640 Pearson St, Suite 200, Des Plaines, IL 60016
800-783-2321   847-298-6692   Fax 847-298-1423   Email info@bea-co.com
http://www.osa.org   Retail distributor.   Single Kits $ 19.95 each.   Retail
(Elementary School to High School)
Ask for information about Optics Classroom Kits from the Optical Society of America.

PARADISE CREATIONS
21789 Town Place Dr, Boca Raton, FL 33433 Manufacturer Phil Seltzer, 11806
Gorham Ave #7, Los Angeles, CA 90049   310-207-4451   Fax 310-207-6320
Distributor (Elementary School to High School)
Ask for brochure. Fully articulated human anatomy skeletons that easily snap together,
including The Skull, 14-inch and 23-inch Skeltons, Male Skelton, Female Skelton, and
Bones-Organs-Muscles. Also Seashell Collector Sets.

PASCO SCIENTIFIC
Contact Ken Nemson   10101 Foothills Blvd, P. O. Box 619011, Roseville, CA
95661-9011 800-772-8700 916-786-3800 Fax 916-786-8905 Email
nemson@pasco.com http://www.pasco.com Retail (High School and College)
Ask for 224-page catalog. Major supplier of quality science education equipment and
supplies, especially physics.

PITSCO
1002 E Adams, P. O. Box 1708, Pittsburg, KS   66762-1708   800-835-0686
800-358-4983 http://www.pitsco.com Fax 800-533-8104 Manufacturer Distributor Retail Mail Order (Elementary School to College)
Ask for 432-page catalog. Major distributor of science materials, including books, new
science toys, video, and more. Over 600 new products.

PLASTIC BAG INFORMATION CLEARINGHOUSE
P. O. Box 2811, Pittsburgh, PA 15230 800-438-5856 Email pbainfo@aol.com
http://www.plasticbag.com (Elementary School)
Ask for brochure. Free materials, curriculum guide, handouts, charts, and teacher's
guide. Supported by the Plastic Bag Association.

PLASTICS IN OUR WORLD
American Plastics Council, 1801 K St, NW, Suite 701-L, Washington, DC 20006
800-243-5790 http://www.plasticsresource.com Free (Elementary School)
Curriculum materials for use with grades K-6 includes How to Set Up a School
Recycling Program, Plastics in Perspective, Classroom Activities K-3 and 4-6, and
American Plastics Council Materials Order Form.

THE POWER HOUSE - LEARNING POWER CATALOG
Commonwealth Edison, 100 Shiloh Blvd, Zion, IL 60099   847-746-7080
http://www.ucm.com/powerhouse Retail (Elementary School to High School)
The Learning Power Catalog is available to teachers. It lists free materials available,
including literature on energy conservation, on the history of electricity, on the
environment, on nuclear issues, and on safety as well as videos available for free loan
on these same topics.

POWERLAB STUDIOS, INC.
616 Ramona Street, Suite 20, Palo Alto, CA 94301 800-843-8769 415-614-0900
Fax 415-614-0909 Email info@powerlab.com http://www.powerlab.com Manufacturer (Elementary School)
Ask for brochure. PowerLab Electricity, a fully integrated curricular unit featuring
multimedia software for grades 3 - 6.

PRIMAL PICTURES LTD.
Ramillies House, 1-2 Ramillies St., London W1V 1DF, United Kingdom
44-171-434-4300 Fax 44-171-494-3670 Email mail@primalpictures.com
http://www.primalpictures.com Manufacturer Distributor (Elementary School
to High School)
Ask for brochure and demo CD-ROM. Manufacturer of Interactive Skeleton CD-ROM.
British Medical Association named this program, Electronic Product of the Year. A
complete 3-D model of the human skeleton and much of the human anatomy.

PRIOR SCIENTIFIC
80 Reservoir Park Drive, Rockland, MA   02370-1062 781-878-8442   Fax
781-878-8736 http://www.prior.com Manufacturer Distributor (High School to
College)
Ask for brochures. Products for photomicrography, including laboratory microscopes,
and stereo zoom microscopes.

PROJECT LEARNING TREE
1111 19th Street N W, Suite 780, Washington, DC 20036 202-463-2462 Fax 202-463-2461 Email info@affoundation.org http://www.plt.org (Elementary School to High School)
Ask for brochure. Project Learning Tree is an award-winning environmental education program for students in pre-K through grade 12.

PROJECT STAR:
A catalog of hands-on materials Contact Jane Sadler Learning Technologies, Inc, 40 Cameron Ave, Somerville, MA 02144 800-537-8703 617-628-1459 Fax 617-628-8606 Email popjsadler@tiac.net http://www.starlab.com Retail (Elementary School to High School)
Ask for catalog of economical lab materials, including astronomy labs. Newsletter: STARLAB News.

PROJECT WET
(Water Education for Teachers) 201 Culbertson Hall, Montana State University-Bozeman, P O Box 170570, Bozeman, MT 59717-0570 406-994-5392 Fax 406-994-1919 Email rwwmb@montana.edu
http://www.montana.edu/wwwwet
Ask for brochure. Project WET is an international, interdisciplinary, water science and education program for formal and non-formal educators K-12. Curriculum, activity guide, and instruction and delivery network.

QUEST AEROSPACE
A division of Toy Biz, Inc. 350 East 18th St, Yuma, AZ 85364 800-858-7302 ext 110 Manufacturer Retail Mail Order (High School)
Ask for 35-page catalog. Rockets and accessories for model rocketry.

ROCKMAN MCLEAN TRADING POST
P. O. Box 7174, Loveland, CO 80537-0174 970-622-0869
http://www.rocksnstuff.com Distributor (Elementary School to High School)
Ask for catalog. Manufacturer of rock and mineral collections for education, including fossils.

SAFE-T PRODUCTS BY EXTRA MEASURES
P. O. Box 316, Bensenville, IL 60106 800-601-2861 Fax 800-529-0252 847-957-0014 Fax 847-957-1658 http://www.exmeasures.com
Ask for brochure. Innovative safe drawing and measuring instruments that allow you to see through to the drawing paper. Products include compasses, protractors, board demonstration tools, rulers, T-squares, scissors, triangles, and Pro-Angle-Ruler.

SARGENT-WELCH A VWR COMPANY

911 Commerce Court, Buffalo Grove, IL 60089-2375 800-SARGENT Fax 800-676-2540 http://www.sargentwelch.com Retail (Elementary School to High School)

Ask for a catalog. Major source of science education equipment and supplies conveniently located in the Chicago area.

SAVI/SELPH

Center for Multisensory Learning, Lawrence hall of Science, University of California, Berkeley, CA 94720 510-642-8941

Email lmalone@uslink4.berkeley.edu http://www.uslink4.berkeley.edu Retail (Elementary School to Middle School)

Ask for catalog of products including books, curriculum materials, videos and science kits. The Center for Multisensory Learning specializes in science curriculum development for all elementary and junior high school students, including students with disabilities.

SCHOOLMASTERS SCIENCE

745 State Circle, P. O. Box 1941, Ann Arbor, MI 48106-1941 800-521-2832 Fax 800-654-4321   Email schscience@aol.com http://www.schoolmasters.com Distributor (Elementary School to High School)

Ask for 131-page science catalog. Distributor of educational science materials, kits, and toys for schools.

SCI TECHNOLOGIES

1716 W Main St, Suite 4, Bozeman, MT 59715 800-622-2091 406-585-9088 Fax 406-585-8840 Email scitech@alpineet.net http://www.jbpub.com/labworks.htm Manufacturer (High School to College)

Ask for 12-page catalog. Manufacturer of LabWorks Learning System software and curriculum support materials that bring affordable research-grade data collection to high school and undergraduate college students.

SCIENCE KIT & BOREAL LABORATORIES

Contact Customer Service   777 E Park Dr, Tonawanda, NY 14150-6782 800-828-7777 Fax 800-828-3299 http://www.sciencekit.com Retail (Elementary School to High School)

Ask for 1000-page catalog. Major supplier of science equipment and science kits for classrooms. Note that chemicals, specimens, and other select products are not available for purchase by individuals and are only available to schools.

THE SCIENCE SOURCE

P. O. Box 727, Waldoboro, ME 04572 800-299-5469
Email scisourc@midcoast.com http://www.thesciencesource.com Manufacturer
Distributor (Elementary School to Middle School)
Ask for 32-page catalog. Design technology products, including the Linx System where
students create their own inventions, as well as tools and basic materials for design and
construction. Also, many related books for young readers are available.

SCIENTIFIC EXPLORER, INC.

4020 E Madison, Suite 326, Seattle, WA 98112 800-900-1182 206-322-7611 Fax
206-322-7610 Email sciex@scientificexplorer.com
http://www.scientificexplorer.com http://www.gettoys.com Manufacturer Retail
Mail Order (Elementary School to Adult)
Ask for 16-page catalog. Manufacturer of science and adventure kits including Fun
with Your Cat, Fun with Your Dog, Smithsonian Adventures Series, Aerial Camera,
High Altitude Launcher, Science of Scent, Make Animal Soaps, Kitchen Science,
Educational Cooking Center, Nature Adventures, Exploring Electronics, Science of
Sound, and many more.

SCIENTIFIC LASER CONNECTION

P. O. Box 433, Glendale, AZ 85311 602-939-6711 Fax 602-939-3369 Distributor
Email sales@siclasers.com http://www.siclasers.com (High School to College)
Ask for 12-page catalog. Lasers, laser technology curricula, and books on lasers.

SCOTT RESOURCES

Division of American Educational Products, 401 Hickory St, Fort Collins, CO
80524 800-446-8767 800-289-9299 Fax 972-484-1198 http://www.amep.com
Distributor Retail (Elementary School)
Ask for Earth Science Catalog and Math Materials Catalog. Earth Science Videolabs,
rock and mineral collection trays, large selection of specific rock and mineral samples,
classroom projects, fossils, environmental materials, Solar Oven, astronomy materials,
solar system simulator, Moon-Earth orbit model, meteorology materials, physical
geography models, Earth history educational materials, educational videotapes.

THE SEISMOLOGICAL SOCIETY OF AMERICA

201 Plaza Professional Bldg, El Cerrito, CA 94530-4003 510-525-5474 Fax
510-525-7204 Email info@seismosoc.org http://www.sesmosoc.org
Ask for brochure describing seismology resources for teachers.

SELSI COMPANY, INC.

P. O. Box 10, 194 Greenwood Ave, Midland Park, NJ 07432-0010 800-275-7357
201-612-9200 Fax 201-612-9548 Manufacturer Wholesale (Elementary School
to Adult)
Quality binoculars, telescopes, student microscope sets, magnifiers, toy kaleidoscopes,
glass prisms, student magnets, compasses, barometers, altimeters, metal detectors.

SHOWBOARD

Contact Mark Oleksak P O Box 10656, Tampa, FL 33679-0656 / 2602 W De
Leon, Tampa, FL 33609 800-323-9189 813-874-1828 Fax 813-876-8046 Email
sales@showboard.com http://www.showboard.com
Ask for 32-page resource catalog of materials for science fair projects and for running
a local science fair, including project display boards, awards & ribbons, science fair
quarterly newsletter, certificates of participation, idea books, and science fair videos.

SKOOLS, INC.

40 Fifth Ave - 15A, New York, NY 10011-8843 800-545-4474 212-674-1150 Fax
212-674-2426 Email skoosinc@aol.com http://www.kinderlink.com Retail Mail
Order (Preschool)
Ask for brochure. Distributor of Kin-der-Link, award winning stools and chairs for
creative classroom environments.

SKY PUBLISHING CORP. CATALOG

Sky Publishing Corp., 49 Bay State Rd, Cambridge, MA 02138 / Sky & Telescope,
P O Box 9111, Belmont, MA 02178-9111 800-253-0245 617-864-7360 Fax
617-864-6117 Email skytel@skypub.com http://www.skypub.com Since 1941.
Ask for 32-page catalog of products for professional and amateur astronomers. Products
include maps, books, videos, globes, posters, software, CD-ROMs, slide sets, star
atlases, and planispheres.

SOCIETY OF PHOTO-OPTICAL INSTRUMENTATION ENGINEERS (SPIE) - CONTINUING EDUCATION CATALOG

P. O. Box 10, Bellingham, WA 98227-0010 360-676-3290
Email education@spie.org   http://www.spie.org
Ask for 75-page catalog, SPIE's Continuing Education Catalog, including programs,
videotapes, broadcasts, and short courses, and SPIE's Publications Catalog. Optical
technology for engineering.

The Lizzadro Museum of Lapidary Art in Elmhurst, Illinois, combines geological minerals and art for both education and viewing pleasure.

Photo Courtesy of the Lizzadro Museum of Lapidary Art

SPACEHAB
1331 Gemini Avenue, Suite 340, Houston, TX   77058   281-282-2235   Fax 281-280-0921   Email campbell@spacehab.com   http://www.spacehab.com Manufacturer (High School)
Ask for brochure. Developers of Space Habitat Modules. Curriculum topics include The Circle of Life-Ecology, Crystal Growth Formation, Fluid Dynamics, Plant Life, Aquatic Animal Life, and Human Anatomy and Physiology.

SQUIRE BOONE VILLAGE
P. O. Box 711, New Albany, IN 47151 800-234-1804 812-941-5900 Fax 812-941-5920 Manufacturer Retail Mail Order (Elementary School to High School)
Ask for 40-page catalog. Manufacturer of earth science related and educational products: experimental kits, mineral and fossil collections, and gemstone jewelry.

SUMMIT LEARNING
P. O. Box 493, Ft. Collins, CO 80522 800-777-8817
http://www.youngexplorers.summitlearning.com Retail Mail Order (Elementary School)
Ask for Science Manipulatives Catalog, Math Manipulatives Catalog, and Young Explorers Catalog. These catalogs are filled with educational materials for math and science including the following categories: Linear Tools; Volume and Capacity; Weights and Measures; Time and Temperature; Problem-Solving; Estimation; Graphs; Probability; Earth Science; Astronomy; Science and Nature, and more.

SWIFT INSTRUMENTS, INC.
Scientific Instruments Division, P. O. Box 562, San Jose, CA 95106 408-293-2380 Fax 408-292-7967 Manufacturer (Elementary School to College)
Ask for catalog. Manufacturer of quality, affordable microscopes.

TASCO
2889 Commerce Parkway, Miramar, FL 33025 / P. O. Box 269000, Pembroke Pines, FL 33026 888-GET-TASCO 954-252-3600 Fax 954-252-3705 http://www.tascosales.com Manufacturer Distributor (Elementary School to Adult)
Ask for 52-page Recreational Optics catalog. Quality optical products for all ages. Children's products include Big Screen Microscope, Binoculars, Periscopes, Magnifiers and more. Adult products include Lasersite Rangefinder, Night Watch Viewing Optics, Binoculars, Zoom Binoculars, Sport Telescopes, Astronomical Telescopes, and more.

TEACHER CREATED MATERIALS, INC.
Contact Steve Mitchell 6421 Industry Way, Westminster, CA 92683 714-891-2273 Fax 714-892-0283 Email alacola@teachercreated.com
http://www.teachercreated.com Manufacturer Wholesale Retail Mail Order (Elementary School)
Ask for catalogs: Teacher Created Materials, Techworks, Curriculum Catalog, and Professional Developmental Seminars. Their goal is to help teachers keep up with new educational trends. Thematic Teaching Resources includes Weather, Human Body, Space/Solar System, and Ancient Civilizations. Techworks helps teachers use whatever hardware and software they have to teach the existing curriculum more effectively.

TEACHER'S DISCOVERY
Science Division, 2741 Paldan Dr, Auburn Hills, MI 48326 888-97-SCIENCE Fax 888-98-SCIENCE 248-340-7220 Distributor (Elementary School to High School) Ask for 68-page science catalog. Materials to make "teaching more exciting and fun." Classroom materials, CD-ROMs, and videos.

TEAM LABS
6390B Gunpark Drive, Boulder, CO 80301 800-775-4357 Fax 303-530-4071 Email pslhelp@teamlabs.com http://www.teamlabs.com Manufacturer (Elementary School to High School to College) Ask for catalog. Manufacturer of Personal Science Laboratory (PSL) software and hands-on materials in the physical sciences.

TESSELATIONS
688 W 1st St, Suite 5, Tempe, AZ 85281 800-655-5341 602-967-7455 Fax 602-967-7582 Email tessella@futureone.com http://tesselations.com Manufacturer Wholesale Retail Mail Order (Elementary School to Adult) Ask for 8-page catalog. Puzzles that creatively combine math, art and fun, including Monkey Business; Spin, Rock & Roll, a 3-D puzzle that creates tops, pendulums, balls, and more; Tessel-Gons; Tessel-Gon Stars; Tessellation Kaleidoscope; Tangrams; Captured Worlds, panoramic projections on polyhedra; and many more. Classroom kits available.

TEXAS INSTRUMENTS
P. O. Box 6118, Temple, TX 76503-6118 800-TI-CARES Email ti-cares@ti.com http://www.ti.com http://www.ti.com/calc Manufacturer (Elementary School to High School to College) See web sites. Manufacturer of calculators.

THREE RIVERS OF BROOKSVILLE, INC.
P. O. Box 10369, Brooksville, FL 34601 800-476-3764 Fax 352-848-0100 Retail (Elementary School) Mail order living amphibians. Ask for brochure including Grow-A-Frog Kit, Frog Friend, Tadpoles, and literature: Pollywogs 'n Frogs.

TIMS PROJECT
(TEACHING INTEGRATED MATHEMATICS AND SCIENCE)
Contact Marty Gartzman, Director of Outreach Institute for Mathematics and Science Education, Room 2075 SEL, University of Illiois at Chicago, 950 S Halsted, Chicago, IL 60607 312-996-2448 Fax 312-413-7411 (Elementary School) Ask the Institute for the Documents Catalog that describes available experiments and the TIMS Tutors for teachers. TIMS, in use since 1974, is a quantitative hands-on approach to K-8 science that uses fun scientific experimental methods and thinking to

integrate math and science. The TIMS Project also has two curricula currently available: Math Trailblazers: A Mathematical Journey Using Science and Language Arts, a full mathematics curriculum for grades K-5; and TIMS Laboratory Investigations, over 150 replacement laboratory experiments for grades 1-8.

TOPS LEARNING SYSTEMS

10970 S Mulino Rd, Canby, OR 97013 Fax 503-266-5200 Email tops@canby.com http://www.topscience.org Manufacturer (Elementary School to High School)
Ask for brochure. Sets of open-ended task cards on science subjects for grades 7-12 and structured activity sheets for grades 3-10, and more.

TREND ENTERPRISES, INC.

300 Ninth Ave, SW, New Brighton, MN 55112 800-328-5540 Fax 612-582-3500 http://www.trendent.com Distributor (Elementary School)
Ask for 88-page catalog. Classroom environments, skill builders, and awards & incentives, including Newton's Apple Science Charts.

UPTOWN SALES INC

33 N Main St, Chambersburg, PA 17201 800-548-9941 Fax 717-264-8123 http://www.hobbyplace.com Distributor (High School to Adult)
Distributor of Estes Model Rockets.

USTOY CONSTRUCTIVE PLAYTHINGS

1227 E 119th St, Gradview, MO 64030-1117 800-448-4115 816-761-5900 Fax 816-761-9295 Email ustoy@ustoyco.com http://www.ustoyco.com Manufacturer Distributor Wholesale Retail Mail Order (Preschool to Elementary School)
Ask for 200-page catalog filled with educational fun for the preschool and elementary school age child including six pages of hands-on science materials.

VAN CORT INSTRUMENTS, INC.

12 Greenfield Rd, P. O. Box 215, South Deerfield, MA 01373-0215 800-432-2678 413-586-9800 Fax 413-665-2300 Email sales@vancort.com http://www.vancort.com Manufacturer Wholesale Retail Mail Order (Elementary School to Adult)
Ask for catalog. Manufacturer of quality telescopes, kaleidoscopes, timepieces, magnifying glasses, and unique instruments including the toy, U-ME, an optical illusion mirror that combines faces. Products handmade in New England.

VERNIER SOFTWARE

Contact Christine Mosier 8565 S W Beaverton-Hillsdale Hwy, Portland, OR 97225-2429 503-297-5317 Fax 503-297-1760 Email cmosier@vernier.com http://www.vernier.com (High School to College)
Ask for 42-page catalog. Software and hardware for the chemistry and physics

laboratory. Ask about workshops for teachers.

VIDEOLABS, INC.
5960 Golden Hills Drive, Golden Valley, MN   55416-1040 800-467-7157
612-542-0061 Fax 612-542-0069 Manufacturer Distributor (Elementary School
to High School)
Ask for catalog. Pioneers of "Gooseneck" camera technology.

WARD'S NATURAL SCIENCE ESTABLISHMENT, INC.
5100 W Henrietta Rd, P. O. Box 92912, Rochester, NY 14692-9012 800-962-2660
716-359-2502   Fax   716-334-6174   Email   customer_service@wardsci.com
http://www.wardsci.com Retail (Elementary School to High School)
Ask for CD-ROM catalog. Major supplier of science education equipment and
supplies.

THE WILD GOOSE COMPANY
375 Whitney Ave, 375 W 1455 S, Salt Lake City, UT 84115   800-373-1498
801-466-1172 Fax 801-466-1186 http://www.widgoosescience.com Manufacturer
Retail Mail Order (Elementary School)
Ask for 16-page catalog. Science materials include Newton's Apple Kits, Teacher
Books, Megalab kits, T-Shirts, Posters, Professional Development Training, and
Student-Centered Programs.

WISCONSIN FAST PLANTS
University of Wisconsin-Madison, Dept. of Plant Pathology, 1630 Linden Dr,
Madison, WI 53706   800-462-7417 http://fastplants.cals.wisc.edu   Retail
(Elementary School to High School)
This source of Brassica Rapa, a plant that takes 34 days growing from seed to seed.
This plant is useful in genetic studies. Also, information on bottle biology for the
classroom.

WTTW STORES OF KNOWLEDGE
Water Tower Place, 7th Flr, 845 N Michigan, Chicago, IL 60611 312-642-6826;
Oak Brook Center, 100 Oak Brook Center, Suite 79, Oak Brook, IL 60521
630-571-4017; Woodfield Mall, L101 Woodfield Shopping Center, Schaumburg,
IL 60173 847-619-9696; Northbrook Court, 2171 Lake-Cook Rd, Northbrook, IL
60062 847-509-9520; Orland Sqare, Orland Park, IL 708-403-9793; Hawthorne
Center, Vernon Hills, IL 60061 847-247-0592.
These well-known stores are filled with educational toys, including many science toys.

YOUNG ENTOMOLOGIST'S SOCIETY, INC.

Contact Gary A. Dunn 1915 Peggy Place, Lansing, MI 48910-2553 517-887-0499
Fax 517-887-0499 Email YESbugs@aol.com http://www.tesser.com/minibeast/
and http://insects.ummc/sa.umich.edu/yes/yes.htm/
Retail Non-profit (Elementary School to High School)
Ask for the 70-page Minibeast Merchandise Catalog including programs and services,
products and materials, and tips for selecting materials. Resource materials include
books, educational games, models, audiovisual materials, and toys. Inquire about
membership.

YOUNG NATURALIST COMPANY

1900 N Main, Newton, KS 67114 316-283-4103 Fax 316-283-9108 **Manufacturer
Distributor (Elementary School to High School)**
Ask for brochure. Products include Leaf Identification Kit, Seed Identification Kit,
Twig Identification Kit, Tree Identification Kit, and more.

ZAHOUREK-SYSTEMS

2198 W 15th St, Loveland, CO 80538-3597 800-950-5025 970-667-9047 Fax
970-667-5025 Email zsi@anatomyinclay.com http://www.anatomyinclay.com
Manufacturer Distributor (Elementary School to High School)
Ask for brochure. The Zoologic System is the study of anatomy using traditional means
combined with the act of forming clay anatomy and positioning it on a precise,
specially-made skeletal model. Quality hands-on system of learning.

ZOMETOOL

1526 South Pearl Street, Denver, CO 80210 888-966-3386 303-733-2880 Fax
303-733-3116 Email sales@zometool.com http://www.zometool.com
Manufacturer (Elementary School to Adult)
The Zome System is a versatile, creative construction toy used by mathematicians,
scientists, engineers and architects. Yet, it is perfect as a classroom teaching tool as
well as creative play. The various possible construction angles reflect the forces of
physics and nature. Teacher kits, student kits, researcher kits, and lesson plans
available.

Chapter

11

Periodicals

Periodical Directories

GENERAL SCIENCE INDEX
H. W. Wilson Co., 950 University Ave, Bronx, NY 10452-4297 212-588-8400
Monthly Bound annually. Available in most major libraries.
Cumulative index to published works in English language periodicals. Articles listed by subject and author with quarterly and annual cumulations published.

THE STANDARD PERIODICAL DIRECTORY
Oxbridge Communications, Inc., 150 Fifth Ave, Suite 302, New York, NY 10011
Published annually. Available in most major libraries.
This guide to United States and Canadian Periodicals alphabetically lists over 90,000 publications under subject categories.

ULRICH'S INTERNATIONAL PERIODICALS DIRECTORY
R. R. Bowker, A Reed Reference Publishing Company, 121 Chanion Rd, New Providence NJ 07974 800-346-6049 Published annually Available in most major libraries.
Published in four volumes, periodicals are alphabetically listed by category.

Periodicals for Parents and Children

One of the nicest gifts a child can receive is a magazine subscription addressed to the child's name. Many of these science magazines for children are equally interesting to adult readers.

3-2-1 CONTACT
Children's Television Workshop, P O Box 51177, Boulder, CO 80322-1177 **Published 10 times per year. $ 16.97 per year.**
A science and technology magazine for young children based on the television series of the same name.

ABRAMS PLANETARIUM SKY CALENDAR
Robert Victor, Editor Abrams Planetarium, Michigan State University, East Lansing, MI 48824 Email victor@pilot.msu.edu http://www.pa.msu.edu/abrams/ **Quarterly $ 9.00 per year.**
For the beginning astronomer, this calendar presents a nightly description of important astronomical events and a simplified chart of the evening sky.

AMERICAN KITE
American Kite Company, P O Box 699, Cedar Ridge, CA 95924-0699 **916-273-3855 Quarterly $ 14.00 per year.**
This quarterly journal is dedicated to kiting.

APPRAISAL: SCIENCE BOOKS FOR YOUNG PEOPLE
Northeastern University, 403 Richards Hall, Boston, MA 02115 **Quarterly $ 55.50 per year.**
Book reviews of new science books for children are presented by both a librarian and a science specialist.

BABYBUG
P O Box 7436, Red Oak, IA 51591-4436 800-827-0227 **$ 32.97 per year for 12 issues.**
Babybug is a listening and looking magazine for infants and toddlers ages 6 months to 2 years. This board-book 24-page magazine has rounded corners and is just the right size for small hands.

BRAINLINK WOW
Publications, 1709 Dryden, Suite 552, Houston, TX 77030 **800-969-4996 713-797-9935 Fax 713-797-9948**
Ask for brochure. Story Books, Explorations, and Teacher's Guide available.

A family enjoys the sea life exhibit with live aquatic creatures in the Oceanarium at the John G. Shedd Aquarium.

Photo Courtesy of The John G. Shedd Aquarium
Photography by Edward G. Lines, Jr.

CHICKADEE MAGAZINE
25 Boxwood Lane, Buffalo, NY 14227-2780 416-971-5275 Fax 416-971-5294
Email owlcom@owl.on.ca Published 10 times each year. $ 17.95 per year.
Children learn about environment, nature and science.

CURRENT SCIENCE
Weekly Reader Corp., 3001 Cindel Dr, Delran, NJ 08370 800-446-3355
Bimonthly $ 7.45 per year.
This news magazine presents topics in science, health and technology for grades 7-9.

THE DOLPHIN LOG
The Cousteau Society, 870 Greenbrier Circle, Suite 402, Chesapeake, VA 23320
804-523-9335 Bimonthly $ 15.00 per year.
Dedicated to oceanography and the environment for ages 7-15.

DRAGONFLY
National Science Teachers Association, P O Box 90214, Washington, DC
20077-7475 800-722-NSTA http://www.muohio.edu/dragonfly/ and
http://www.nsta.org Bimonthly (September - May) $ 14.95
A magazine for young investigators. Grades 3-6.

EXPLORATIONS
Scientific American Explorations, 800-285-5264 Fax 712-755-7118
http://www.explorations.org Quarterly $11.80 per year.
For parents and children. An entertaining medium to explore science and technology.

KITELINES
Contact Valerie Govig Aeolus Press, Inc., 8807 Liberty Road, P O Box 466,
Randallstown, MD 21133-0466 410-922-1212 Fax 410-922-4262
Email kitelines@compuserve.com Quarterly $ 16.00 per year.
This quarterly comprehensive international journal of kiting is endorsed by the
International Kitefliers Association.

MY HEALTH MY WORLD WOW, MY HOME, PLANET EARTH WOW
Publications, 1709 Dryden, Suite 552, Houston, TX 77030 800-969-4996
713-797-9935 Fax 713-797-9948
Ask for brochure. Story Books, Explorations, and Teacher's Guide available.

NATIONAL GEOGRAPHIC WORLD
National Geographic Society, 1145 17th St, NW, Washington, DC 20036-4688
800-447-0647 202-857-7296 Monthly $ 17.95 per year.
A natural history magazine of general interest to children.

ODYSSEY
Cobblestone Publishing, Inc., 7 School St, Peterborough, NH 03458-1470
603-924-7209 Fax 603-924-7380 Published 9 times each year. $ 24.95 per year.
Magazine of astronomy and outer space written for readers ages 8 to 14.

OTTERWISE: FOR KIDS WHO ARE INTO SAVING ANIMALS & THE ENVIRONMENT
Otterwise, Inc., P O Box 1374, Portland, ME 04104 207-283-2964 Newsletter
$ 8.00 per year.
For kids ages 8-13 who love animals and the natural world around them.

OWL
25 Boxwood Lane, Buffalo, NY 14227-2780 416-971-5275 Fax 416-971-5294
Email owlcom@owl.on.ca Published 10 times each year. $ 21.00 per year.
A magazine for children ages 8-14 interested in science and nature.

QUANTUM
Springer-Verlag New York, P. O. Box 2485, Secaucus, NJ 07096 800-SPRINGER
800-722-NSTA 201-348-4033 http://www.nsta.org Bimonthly $ 25.00 per year.
(800-722-NSTA $ 25.00 per year)
Dedicated to state-of-the-art math and science for students (and their teachers), this magazine is also available with NSTA membership.

RADIO CONTROL CAR ACTION
Kable News Fulfillment, P O Box 427, Mt. Morris, IL 61054 800-877-5169
12 issues per year. $ 29.95 per year.
Covers the world of radio-controlled cars including electronics and modeling techniques.

RANGER RICK'S NATURE MAGAZINE
Gerald Bishop, Editor National Wildlife Federation, 8925 Leesburg Pike, Vienna,
VA 22184-0001 800-588-1650 703-790-4000 Fax 703-442-7332
http://www.nwf.org/nwf/rrick 12 issues per year. $ 17.00 per year.
A nature, environment, outdoors magazine for children ages 6-12.

SCIENCE NEWS; THE WEEKLY NEWSMAGAZINE OF SCIENCE
Science News, P O Box 1925, Marion, OH 43305 800-347-6969 Science News,
Science Service, 1719 N Street N W, Washington, DC 20036-2888 800-552-4412
Email scinews@sciserv.org http://www.sciencenews.org Weekly $ 49.50 per year.
Overview of science news in all fields of science.

190 Science Fun in Chicagoland

SCIENCE WEEKLY
Contact Claude Mayberry Science Weekly, Inc., 2141 Industrial Parkway, Suite 202, Silver Spring, MD 20904 800-4-WEEKLY 301-680-8804 Fax 301-680-9240 Email kids@scienceweekly.com Weekly $ 8.95 per year. $ 3.95 per year for 20 or more subscriptions.
Current and high interest science and technology topics for grades K-8.

SCIENCE WORLD
Scholastic Inc., Subscriptions, 2931 E McCarty St, P O Box 3710, Jefferson City, MO 65102-9957 800-SCHOLASTIC 800-246-2986 212-343-6299 Email ScienceWorld@scholastic.com http://www.scholastic.com Biweekly $ 7.50 per school year for orders of 10 or more.
For grades 7 to 10. Science news in general science, nature study, earth science, life and space science.

SCIENCELAND
Scienceland Inc., 501 Fifth Ave, Suite 2108, New York, NY 10017-6165 212-490-2180 Fax 212-490-2187 Published 8 times each year. $ 19.95 per year.
Picture book early reader for preschool children through primary grades, ages 5-10 with vocabulary list. Teacher's manual also available.

SUPERSCIENCE EDITION
Contact Nancy Finton Scholastic Inc., Subscriptions, 2931 E McCarty St, P O Box 3710, Jefferson City, MO 65101-3710 800-631-1586 800-SCHOLASTIC 212-343-6469 Fax 212-343-6333 Email superscience@scholastic.com http://www.scholastic.com Monthly during school year.
$ 5.95 per year for 10 or more subscriptions.
A classroom magazine for students in grades 3-6, including science classroom activities.

TIME FOR KIDS
Time Inc. Principal Office: Time & Life Building, 1271 Avenue of the Americas, New York, NY 10020-1393 800-777-8600 http://www.timeforkids.com 26 issues per year Sept to May. $ 3.95 per student subscription.
Available in both primary and intermediate editions. Each issue includes stories and a teacher's guide for classroom use.

WEATHERWISE
Heldref Publications, 1319 18th St, NW, Washington, DC 20036 800-365-9753 202-296-6267 Bimonthly $ 30.00 per year.
Articles about the weather and its relationship to people presented with color photography.

WILDLIFE CONSERVATION
185th Street and Southern Blvd, Bronx, NY 10460 718-584-2625 Bimonthly
$ 13.95 per year.
Filled with photographs and distinguished articles on animals and wildlife.

WONDERSCIENCE
American Chemical Society, Education Division, 1155 16th St, NW, Washington,
DC 20036 800-209-0423 Fax 800-209-0064 304-728-2170
http://www.acs.org/edugen2/education/conted/conted.htm
Back issues are available. Eight issues per year.
This magazine is in colorful comic book format for grades 4-6. For home or school,
these magazines relate science to technology and are also available in bilingual
(Spanish/English) editions. Telephone to inquire about availability. Ask for The Best
of WonderScience Book, covering 10 years of Wonder Science.

YOUR BIG BACKYARD
Contact Donna Johnson National Wildlife Federation, P O Box 777, Mount
Morris, IL 61054 800-588-1650 703-790-4515 http://www.nwf.org Monthly
$ 15.00 per year.
Simple text and photos about animals and nature help young children, ages 3-6, learn
about science. Includes pull-out guide with activities and crafts for parents and
educators.

ZOOBOOKS
Wildlife Education, Ltd., 9820 Willow Creek Rd, Suite 300, San Diego, CA 92131
619-578-2440 Fax 619-578-9658 Published 10 times each year. $ 20.95 per year.
Written for children, each issue is a full color story about an animal or group of animals.

Periodicals for Teachers

These periodicals and magazines are full of information for science teachers.
Contact your library to see most of these periodicals before subscribing. Sometimes the
publisher will send you a complimentary examination copy.

2061 TODAY
American Association for the Advancement of Science, 1200 New York Ave, NW,
Washington, DC 20005-3920 202-326-6666 http://www.aaas.org/ehr Quarterly
Free.
This bulletin updates the progress of Project 2061, a major national project to improve
science education in the United States by the year 2061.

AAACTION - ISTA NEWSLETTER
Diana Dummitt, ISTA Executive Secretary, Illinois Science Teachers Association University of Illinois, College of Education, 1310 S Sixth St, Champaign, IL 61820 217-244-0173 Fax 217-244-5437 Regular membership includes AAACTION.
This newsletter includes news of ISTA activities and items of interest to science teachers K-12.

AMERICAN JOURNAL OF PHYSICS
American Association of Physics Teachers, One Physics Ellipse, College Park, MD 20740-3845 301-209-3300 Fax 301-209-0845 Email aapt-memb@aapt.org http://www.aapt.org Monthly.
About physics and teaching physics at the college level.

THE AMERICAN BIOLOGY TEACHER
Contact Chris Chantry National Association of Biology Teachers (NABT), 11250 Roger Bacon Dr, #19, Reston, VA 20190-5202 800-406-0775 703-471-1134 Fax 703-435-5582 Email NABTer@aol.com http://www.nabt.org Published 9 times per year. $ 75.00 per year.
This journal includes specific how-to-do-it suggestions for the laboratory, field activities, programs, and review on recent advances in life science.

CAROLINA TIPS
Carolina Biological Supply Co., 2700 York Rd, Burlington, NC 27215-3398 800-334-5551 Fax 800-222-7112 919-584-0381 Email carolina@carolina.com http://www.carosci.com Free.
Ask to be placed on mailing list. Includes articles that present new teaching materals and tips.

JOURNAL OF CHEMICAL EDUCATION
The Division of Chemical Education of the American Chemical Society Inc., Subscription and Book Order Department, P O Box 606, Vineland, NJ 08362-0606 800-691-9846 609-205-9065 Fax 609-696-2130 Email jchemed@aol.com http://jchemed.chem.wisc.edu/ Monthly $ 37 per year.
This journal is dedicated to publishing articles about or relevant to the teaching of chemistry.

CHEMMATTERS
Contact Michael Shea American Chemical Society, Office of High School Chemistry, 1155 16th St, NW, Washington, DC 20036 202-872-6341 Fax 202-833-7732 Email ChemMatters@acs.org http://www.chemcenter.org Published 4 times per year. $ 8.00 per subscription.
This magazine is for high school chemistry students.

CHEMUNITY NEWS
Contact Shirley Mundle American Chemical Society, Education Division, 1155 16th St, NW, Washington, DC 20036 Four-to-five times per year 800-227-5558 202-872-4076 Fax 202-833-7732
The ACS Education Division Newsletter focusing on programs in prehigh school science, high school chemistry, college chemistry, and continuing education.

A CLASS ACT
Argonne National Laboratory, Division of Educational Programs, 9700 S Cass Ave, Argonne, IL 60439 630-252-6925
This newsletter is an Argonne Community of Teachers (ACT) publication that includes news items for science teachers. ACT's purpose is one of linking research and education.

COMPRESSED AIR MAGAZINE
253 E Washington Ave, Washington, NJ 07882-2495   908-850-7817   Fax 908-689-3095 Published 8 times per year. Free.
A magazine with interesting articles on applied technology and industrial management. Published by a division of Ingersoll-Rand. Fun reading for teachers, students and those interested in science. Request a subscription application.

SCIENCE DISCOVER MAGAZINE SCHOOL PROGRAM
105 Terry Drive, Suite 120, Newtown, PA 18940-3425 800-416-5140 Fax 215-579-8589 Email think@edumedia.com http://www.discover.com
This program provides strategies for using the magazine, Discover, in the classroom.

EDUCATION PROGRAMS
Science and Education Department, Museum of Science & Industry, 57th St and Lake Shore Drive, Chicago, IL 60637 773-684-1414 http://www.msichicago.org Published three times a year. Free.
Teachers, ask to be put on the mailing list of this newsletter for educators. It covers upcoming programs, exhibits, and events at the Museum.

ENC UPDATE
Eisenhower National Clearinghouse for Mathematics and Science Education, The Ohio State University, 1929 Kenny Rd, Columbus, OH 43210-1079 800-621-5785 614-292-7784 Fax 614-292-2066 Email editor@enc.org http://www.enc.org
Newsletter of the Eisenhower National Clearinghouse for Mathematics and Science Education. Request to be placed on mailing list.

GEOTIMES
American Geological Institute, Communications Department, 4220 King St, Alexandria, VA 22302 703-379-2480 Email agi@agiweb.org http://www.agiweb.org/ Monthly $ 36.95 per year.
This journal reports events, research, meetings, and developments in geoscience education, political activities, and technological advances.

GIRLS IN SCIENCE - NEWSLETTER
American Association for the Advancement of Science, 1200 New York Ave, NW, Washington, DC 20005-3920 http://www.aaas.org/ehr 4 issues $ 4.00
Focuses on activities, resources, and opportunities in science and mathematics for girls and the adults who work with them in schools or community-based organizations.

INSECT WORLD
Young Entomologist's Society, Inc. Contact Gary A. Dunn 1915 Peggy Place, Lansing, MI 48910-2553 517-887-0499 Fax 517-887-0499 Email YESbugs@aol.com   http://www.tesser.com/minibeast/ and http://insects.ummc/sa.umich.edu/yes/yes.htm/ Non-profit.
One-year educator membership includes various resources and a one-year subscription to Insect World, $ 48.00. Ask for the 70-page Minibeast Merchandise Catalog including programs and services, products and materials, and tips for selecting materials. Resource materials include books, educational games, models, audiovisual materials, and toys.

JOURNAL OF COLLEGE SCIENCE TEACHING
Contact Michael Byrnes National Science Teachers Association, 1840 Wilson Blvd, Arlington, VA 22201-3000 800-722-NSTA 703-312-9232 Fax 703-243-7177 Email Michael.Byrnes@nsta.org http://www.nsta.org/pubs/jcst Monthly.
Dedicated to college introductory science teaching, this journal is available with NSTA membership. It includes ideas for classroom teachers.

JOURNAL OF GEOSCIENCE EDUCATION
Contact Robert Christman National Association of Geoscience Teachers, Inc., P O Box 5443, Bellingham, WA 98227-5443 360-650-3587 Fax 360-650-7302 Email xman@cc.wwu.edu Published 5 times each year. $ 35 per year includes membership.
This journal seeks to foster improvement in teaching earth sciences at all levels.

JOURNAL OF RESEARCH IN SCIENCE TEACHING
Journal for the National Association for Research in Science Teaching (NARST) John Wiley & Sons, Inc., Journals, 605 Third Ave, New York, NY 10158-0012 212-850-6000 Published 10 times per year.
Articles on research related to the teaching of science.

JOURNAL OF SCHOOL SCIENCE AND MATHEMATICS
Contact Norman G. Lederman School Science and Mathematics Association, Oregon State University, 237 Weniger Hall, Corvallis, OR 97331-6508 541-737-1818   Fax 541-737-1817   Email   ssm@ucs.orst.edu http://www.orst.edu/Dept/sci_mth_education/SSM/ Quarterly.
Founded in 1901, the purpose of this association is to disseminate research findings and its implications for school practice. Topics in science and mathematics education at the elementary and high school levels.

JOURNAL OF SCIENCE TEACHER EDUCATION
Contact Dr. Joe Peters Association for the Education of Teachers in Science (AETS), University of West Florida, 11000 University Pkwy, Pensacola, FL 32514-5753 850-474-2860 Fax 850-474-2856 Email jpeters@uwf.edu http://science.coe.uwf.edu/aets/aets.html Quarterly.
This journal serves as a forum for presentation and discussion of issues relating to professional development in science teaching.

JOURNAL OF TECHNOLOGY EDUCATION
Dr. James LaPorte, Techology Education Program, 144 Smyth Hall, Virginia Tech, Blacksburg, VA 24061 703-860-2100 http://www.iteawww.org Biannual $ 8 per year.
A scholarly journal that provides a forum for discussion on technology education. Conceptual as well as research-based articles are published.

LEARNING AND LEADING WITH TECHNOLOGY
Contact Anita Best International Society for Technology in Education, 1787 Agate St, Eugene, OR 97403-1923 800-336-5191 541-346-4414 Fax 541-346-5890 Email anita_best@ccmail.uoregon.edu http://www.iste.org/publish/learning
This professional organization is dedicated to the improvement of all levels of education through the use of computer-based technology.

NSTA REPORTS!
National Science Teachers Association, 1840 Wilson Blvd, Arlington, VA 22201-3000 703-243-7100 http://www.nsta.org Bimonthly Included with NSTA membership.
This newspaper format bulletin contains over 50 pages of news items relevant to science teaching.

NSTA'S EDUCATIONAL HORIZONS
Elsie Diven Weigel, NSTA's Educational Horizons, Code FE, 300 E St, SW, Washington, DC 20546-0001 202-358-1533 http://www.nsta.org Quarterly Free.
Ask to be placed on the mailing list of this NSTA educational newsletter that includes current NASA news, educational division activities, and lists of educational materials.

THE PHYSICS TEACHER

Cliff Swartz, Editor American Association of Physics Teachers, One Physics Ellipse, College Park, MD 20740-3845 516-632-8019 Fax 301-209-0845 Email cswartz@sunyb.edu http://www.aapt.org Monthly.

About teaching introductory physics at the high school and college level.

QUANTUM

National Science Teachers Association, 1840 Wilson Blvd, Arlington, VA 22201-3000 800-722-NSTA http://www.nsta.org Six issues per year. $ 25.00 per year.

Dedicated to state-of-the-art math and science for students (and their teachers), this magazine is also available with NSTA membership.

SCIENCE ACTIVITIES

Contact Caroline Schweiter Heldref Publications, Inc., 1319 18th St, NW, Washington, DC 20036-1802 800-365-9753 202-296-6267, ext 254 Fax 202-296-5149 Email sa@heldref.org http://www.heldref.org Quarterly $ 32.00 per year individual. $ 58.00 per year institutional.

Articles on classroom science projects for teachers of science.

SCIENCE AND CHILDREN

National Science Teachers Association, 1840 Wilson Blvd, Arlington, VA 22201-3000 800-722-NSTA http://www.nsta.org Monthly.

Dedicated to preschool through middle school science teaching, this journal is available with NSTA membership. It includes ideas for classroom teachers.

SCIENCE EDUCATION

John Wiley & Sons, Inc., Journals, 605 Third Ave, New York, NY 10158-0012 212-850-6000 Fax 212-850-6088 Bimonthly $ 324.00 per year. Since 1916

This journal reports research on practices, issues and trends in science instruction as well as on the preparation of science teachers for the science classroom and laboratory.

SCIENCE EDUCATION NEWS

Janet Aldrich, Editor Directorate for Education and Human Resources (EHR), American Association for the Advancement of Science, 1200 New York Avenue, NW, Washington, DC 20005-3920 202-326-6670 Bimonthly 4 pages.

Email jaldrich@aaas.org http://www.aaas.org/ehr Available by controlled subscription and on the World Wide Web.

This newsletter is an online, interdisciplinary tool to inform readers of science education activities. EHR offers a free Guide to Publications and Resources at http://www.aaas.org/ehr.

**This tour group enjoys Garfield Park Conservatory in Chicago,
one of the most beautiful botanical gardens under glass.**

Photo Courtesy of Garfield Park Conservatory

SCIENCE SCOPE
National Science Teachers Association, 1840 Wilson Blvd, Arlington, VA 22201-3000 800-722-NSTA http://www.nsta.org Monthly.
Dedicated to middle school science teaching, this journal is available with NSTA membership. It includes ideas for classroom teachers.

THE SCIENCE TEACHER
National Science Teachers Association, 1840 Wilson Blvd, Arlington, VA 22201-3000 800-722-NSTA http://www.nsta.org Monthly.
Dedicated to middle and high school science teaching, this journal is available with NSTA membership. It includes ideas for classroom teachers.

SCIENCELINES
Susan Dahl, Editor Teacher Resource Center, Fermi National Accelerator Laboratory, Leon M. Lederman Science Education Center, Teacher Resource Center, P. O. Box 500 MS 777, Batavia, IL 60510-0500 630-840-8258 Email sdahl@fnal.gov http://www.ed.fnal.gov/trc/sciencelines_online/sciencelines.html Quarterly newsletter Free.
This newsletter contains current information about science education. resources, reviews, activities and scientist interviews as well as articles about Fermilab.

SCIENCELINK NEWSLETTER
Contact Evelyn Ernst National Science Resources Center (NSRC), Smithsonian Institution, MRC 403, Arts & Industries Building, Room 1201, Washington, DC 20560 202-287-2064 202-287-7247 Fax 202-287-2070 Email outreach@nas.edu http://www.si.edu/nsrc
Ask to be placed on the mailing list for the NSRC ScienceLink Newsletter. NSRC disseminates information about effective science teaching, develops curriculum materials, and sponsors outreach and leadership development activities.

SPECTRUM
- JOURNAL OF THE ILLINOIS SCIENCE TEACHERS ASSOCIATION
Diana Dummitt, ISTA Executive Secretary, University of Illinois, College of Education, 1310 S Sixth St, Champaign, IL 61820 217-244-0173
Fax 217-244-5437 Quarterly $ 25.00 regular membership includes SPECTRUM.
This journal includes news of ISTA activities, articles on science and science education, and items of interest to science teachers K-12.

SSMARRT NEWSLETTER
Contact Michael Grote School Science and Mathematics Association, Deparment of Education, Ohio Wesleyan University, Delaware, OH 43015 614-368-3561 Fax 614-368-3553 Email mggrote@cc.owu.edu Monthly.
Founded in 1901, the purpose of this association is to disseminate research findings and its implications for school practice. Topics in science and mathematics education at the elementary and high school levels.

TECHNOLOGY AND CHILDREN
International Technology Education Association, 1914 Association Dr, Suite 201, Reston, VA 20191-1539 703-860-2100 Fax 703-860-0353 Email itea@iris.org http://www.iteawww.org Quarterly $ 40 per year.
Each issue is packed with practical, innovative, and creative articles and activities for the elementary teacher.

TECHNOLOGY AND LEARNING
Available from the International Society for Technology in Education, 1787 Agate St, Eugene, OR 97403-1923 800-336-5191 541-346-4414 Fax 541-346-5890 http://iste.org/publish/learning
This professional organization is dedicated to the improvement of all levels of education through the use of computer-based technology.

THE TECHNOLOGY TEACHER
International Technology Education Association, 1914 Association Dr, Suite 201, Reston, VA 20191-1539 703-860-2100 Fax 703-860-0353 Email itea@iris.org http://www.iteawww.org Monthly $ 65 per year.
Each issue provides ideas for the classroom, project activities, resources in technology, and current trends in technology education.

THE UNIVERSE IN THE CLASSROOM
Astronomical Society of the Pacific, 390 Ashton Ave, San Francisco, CA 94112 415-337-1100 Email membership@aspsky.org http://www.aspsky.org Quarterly.
Features articles, resource lists, and teaching ideas for astronomy teachers.

Science Periodicals

This list is for anyone and everyone interested in science. Periodicals exist for almost every science topic. The periodicals and magazines listed here are just a few of the many found in your local public library.

200 Science Fun in Chicagoland

AIR & SPACE /SMITHSONIAN
420 Lexington Ave, New York, NY 10170 800-766-2149 202-287-3733 Fax
202-287-3163 Bimonthly $ 18.00 per year.
Includes articles on aviation, aviation history and space travel.

AMERICAN SCIENTIST
Sigma Xi, Scientific Research Society, Box 13975, 99 Alexander Dr, Research
Triangle Park, NC 27709 800-282-0444 919-549-0097 Fax 919-549-0090 Email
editors@amsci.org http://www.amsci.org Bimonthly $ 28.00 per year.
Sigma Xi is an honor society for scientists and engineers. Articles concentrate on all
fields of research in science and technology and are written for the lay reader.

ARCHAEOLOGY MAGAZINE
Archaeological Institute of America, 135 Williams St, New York, NY 10038
800-829-5122 212-732-5154 Bimonthly $ 19.97 per volume.
Articles include topics on archaeological discoveries and relevant issues.

ASTRONOMY MAGAZINE
Kalmbach Publishing Co., 21027 Crossroads Circle, P O Box 1612, Waukesha,
WI 53187-1612 800-446-5489 Monthly $ 30.00 per year.
Covers all aspects of astronomy. Articles include reviews such as "Best Astronomy
Books for Kids."

AUDUBON
National Audubon Society, 700 Broadway, New York, NY 10003 212-979-3000
http://www.audubon.org   http://www.audubon.org/bird/watch/kids/index.html
Bimonthly $ 20.00 per year.
This magazine of the National Audubon Society covers wildlife, wilderness and
environmental topics.

BROOKFIELD ZOO PREVIEW
Brookfield Zoo/Chicago Zoological Society, 3300 S Golf Rd, Brookfield, IL 60513
708-485-0263, ext 361 www.brookfield-zoo.mus.il.us Quarterly Free to members.
Preview includes news about Brookfield Zoo, its exhibits, and its programs for children
and the public.

COSMIC QUARTERLY
Chicago Astronomical Society, P. O. Box 30287, Chicago, IL   60630-0287
Quarterly.
This newsletter is included with membership in the Chicago Astronomical Society.

DISCOVER - DISCOVERY CENTER MUSEUM
711 N Main St, Rockford, IL 61103 815-963-6769 Fax 815-968-0164
Email discoverycentermuseum@discoverycentermuseum.org
http://wwwdiscoverycentermuseum.org Quarterly.
Newsletter of the Discovery Center Museum, published quarterly, containing Museum news, special events, and science topics. The Museum has over 200 hands-on science exhibits inside the museum and even more in the outdoor science park.

DISCOVER
114 Fifth Ave, New York, NY 10011 800-829-9232 Monthly $ 29.95 per year.
Science topics in an illustrated magazine format for the general public.

EVANSTON ECOLOGY CENTER NEWSLETTER
Evanston Environmental Association, Evanston Ecology Center,
2024 McCormick Blvd, Evanston, IL 60201 708-864-5181 Quarterly.
Newsletter of the Evanston Environmental Association that describes current programs and events at the Center.

FACTS ON FILE SCIENTIFIC YEARBOOK
Facts on File, Inc., 11 Penn Plaza, 15th Floor, New York, NY 10001-2006
800-322-8755 Fax 800-678-3633 212-683-2244 http://www.factsonfile.com
Published annually. $ 30.00 per year.
The year's scientific achievements and developments described for high school students.

GARDEN TALK - CHICAGO BOTANIC GARDEN
Chicago Horticultural Society, P. O. Box 400, 1000 Lake Cook Road (at Edens Expressway), Glencoe, IL 60022 847-835-5440 http://www.chicago-botanic.org
Monthly.
This newsletter of the Chicago Botanic Garden includes news, events calendar, and gardening topics.

GEONEWS
Illinois State Geological Survey, 615 E Peabody Dr, Champaign, IL 61820-6964
217-333-4747 Fax 217-244-0802 http://www.isgs.uiuc.edu Quarterly.
Newsletter of the Illinois State Geological Survey. Includes articles and   lists publications available.

HORTICULTURE
Horticulture, Inc., 98 N Washington St, Boston, MA 02114-1922 617-742-5600
617-482-5600 Fax 617-482-9487 Published 10 times per year. $ 26.00 per year.
The Magazine of American Gardening.

I.C.E. CUBE

Computer Update Bulletin for Educators (CUBE), Illinois Computing Educators (ICE), 8548 145th St, Orland Park, IL 60462-2839 847-940-7132 http://www.iceberg.org Monthly $ 25.00 per year, includes membership.
This organization focuses on utilizing computer technology in the classroom. This newsletter includes information about computer bulletin boards, information on grants, reviews of software, announcements about meeting where public domain software is traded.

ILLINOIS STATE ACADEMY OF SCIENCE TRANSACTIONS

Contact Pat Zimmerman   Illinois State Museum, Spring & Edwards Sts, Springfield, IL 62706 217-782-6436 Fax 217-782-1254
Email zimmerma@museum.state.il.us   http://www.museum.state.il.us/isas/
Articles about new developments in science written by members of the academy. Inquire about membership. Annual meetings of the Academy are held at a College or University or Industrial Institution.

ISIS

University of Chicago Press, Journals Division, 5720 S Woodlawn Ave, Chicago, IL 60637-1603 312-702-7600 Fax 312-702-0694 Quarterly $ 57.00 per year.
Covers the history of science and its cultural influence.

THE JOURNAL

Institute of Environmental Sciences and Technology, 940 E Northwest Hwy, Mt. Prospect, IL 60056 847-255-1561 Bimonthly $ 80 per year includes membership.
Areas of interest included in this Journal are knowledge pertaining to environmental sciences, product design, and contamination control.

LIFE SCIENCES

Pergamon Press, Inc., Journals Division, 660 White Plains Rd, Tarrytown, NY 10591-5153 914-592-7700 Fax 914-592-3625 Weekly.
International, scholarly publication on new work in the bio-medical sciences.

MERCURY

Astronomical Society of the Pacific, 390 Ashton Ave, San Francisco, CA 94112 415-337-1100 Email membership@aspsky.org http://www.aspsky.org Bimonthly Magazine to Members.
Features articles, resource lists, news bulletins, new photographs on astronomy for readers not trained in science.

THE MORTON ARBORETUM - THE MEMBER'S NEWSLETTER
The Morton Arboretum, 4100 Illinois Route 53 (just north of interstate 88), Lisle, IL 60532-1293 630-719-2468 http://www.mortonarb.org Bimonthly.
A 12-page newsletter of news, events, activities, and plant information. To request a copy call 630-719-2465.

THE MORTON ARBORETUM QUARTERLY
The Morton Arboretum, 4100 Illinois Route 53 (just north of interstate 88), Lisle, IL 60532-1293 630-719-2400 http://www.mortonarb.org Quarterly.
A 30-page journal with articles about the horticulture of woody plants.

NATURAL ENQUIRER
Contact Mary Rice Spring Valley Nature Sanctuary, 1111 E Schaumburg Rd, Schaumburg, IL 60194 847-985-2100 Fax 847-985-9692 Bimonthly.
Newsletter of the Spring Valley Nature Sanctuary with natural history topics, news, and events at the Sanctuary.

NATURAL HISTORY
Contact Cary Castle American Museum of Natural History, Central Park West at 79th St, New York, NY 10024-5192 212-769-5500 Fax 212-769-5511 Email nhmag@amnh.org Monthly $ 28.00 per year.
Articles written by scientists on social and natural science.

NATURE
Nature America, Inc., 345 Park Avenue South, 10th Floor, New York, NY 10010-1707 800-524-0384 212-726-9200 Fax 212-696-9591 Weekly $ 145.00 per year.
Articles about new discoveries and research in all fields of science.

NATURE'S NOTES - CHICAGO ACADEMY OF SCIENCES
2060 N Clark St, Chicago, IL 60614 773-549-0606 http://www.chias.org Quarterly.
A newsletter on exhibits, field trips, programs and special events.

NEW SCIENTIST
Magazines, Specialist Magazine Group, King's Reach Tower, Stamford St, London SE1 9LS ENGLAND 071-261-7301 Weekly $ 130.00 per year.
Comprehensive coverage of new science research and discoveries in all fields of science.

PHILOSOPHY OF SCIENCE
Philosophy of Science Association, Michigan State University, Department of Philosophy, 503 S Kedzie Hall, East Lansing, MI 48824-1032 517-353-9392 Quarterly $ 60.00 per year.
Philosophical analysis of concepts or words used in science.

PHYSICS TODAY
American Institute of Physics, American Center for Physics, One Physics Ellipse, College Park, MD 20740-3843 301-209-3040 Monthly $ 35.00 per year with affiliated society membership.
News about current physics research or research related to physics as well as topics on physics of interest to the general reader.

POPULAR SCIENCE
Times-Mirror Co., 2 Park Ave, New York, NY 10016-5675 212-779-5000 800-289-9399 Monthly $ 13.94 per year.
Written for the general reader, this magazine describes new products and ideas from science and technology.

RE-ACTIONS
Contact Sharon Kerrick 555 N Kensington Ave, La Grange Park, IL 60525 800-323-3044 708-579-8230 Fax 708-352-0499 Email skerrick@ans.org http://www.ans.org Published four times each year. Free Published since 1954.
Published by the American Nuclear Society, this bulletin is for educators interested in learning and teaching about various peaceful uses of nuclear science and careers in the field.

SCIENCE
American Association for the Advancement of Science, 1200 New York Ave, NW, Washington, DC 20005-3920 202-326-6400 http://www.aaas.org/membership Weekly $ 108.00 per year, includes membership.
This prestigious weekly journal of science contains articles and reports on original research and science news.

SCIENCE BOOKS & FILMS
by the American Association for the Advancement of Science, 1200 New York Ave, NW, Washington, DC 20005-3920 202-326-6400 http://www.aaas.org/ehr Online version http://SBFonline.com Nine issues per year. $ 45.00 per year.
This periodical reviews scientific accuracy and presentation of print, audiovisual, and electronic resources intended for educational use.

SCIENCE ILLUSTRATED
8428 Holly Leaf Dr, McLean, VA 22102 Bimonthly $ 15.00 per year.
Popular reading about science news.

SCIENCE NEWS
Science Service, Inc., 1719 N St, NW, Washington, DC 20036-2888 800-552-4412
202-785-2255 P O Box 1925, Marion, OH 43305 800-347-6969 Email
scinews@sciserv.org http://www.sciencenews.org Weekly $ 49.50 per year.
Overview of science news in all fields of science.

THE SCIENCES
New York Academy of Sciences, 655 Madison Ave, 16+th Floor, New York, NY
10021-0003 212-838-6727 Fax 212-888-2894 Bimonthly $ 18.00 per year.
This periodical is written by scientists for both the scientist and the non-scientist.

SCIENTIFIC AMERICAN
Scientific American, Inc., 415 Madison Ave, New York, NY 10017-1179
212-754-0550 http://www.sciam.com Monthly $ 36.00 per year. Since 1845
This magazine is about a broad range of science topics presented at a technical level
for persons in professional positions.

THE SCIENTIST
Scientist, Inc., 3600 Market St, Suite 450, Philadelphia, PA 19104-2641
215-386-9601 Fax 215-387-7542 Biweekly $ 58.00 per year.
News, politics of science, and career information for science professionals.

SCITECH BOOK NEWS
Book News, Inc., 5600 NE Hassalo St, Portland, OR 97213-3640 503-281-9230
Fax 503-287-4485 Monthly $ 45.00 per year.
Reviews of new science books written primarily for librarians.

SKY & TELESCOPE
Sky Publishing Corp., 49 Bay State Rd, Cambridge, MA 02138 800-253-0245
617-864-7360 Fax 617-864-6117 Email skytel@skypub.com
http://www.skypub.com Monthly $ 37.95 per year.
Ask for 32-page catalog of products for professional and amateur astronomers. Articles
and information on astronomy, space science and telescopes.

SMITHSONIAN
Smithsonian Institution, Office of Public Affairs, ASI 2410, MRC421,
Washington, DC 20560 202-357-2888 Fax 202-786-2564 Monthly $ 22.00 per
year.
History of sciences in all fields including social sciences.

TODAY'S CHEMIST AT WORK
American Chemical Society, 1155 16th Street NW, Washington, DC 20036-4899 202-872-4600 Fax 202-872-6005 Bimonthly $ 17.00 per year.
Articles of news about current developments in chemistry.

TODAY'S SCIENCE ON FILE
Facts On File News Service, 11 Penn Plaza, 15th Floor, New York, NY 10001-2006 800-363-7976, ext 348 Fax 800-363-7978 212-290-8090 Fax 212-967-9051 Email tsof@facts.com http://www.facts.com http://www.facts.com/tsof.htm Monthly.
This science news digest is published monthly and assembles The Science News Digest and Cumulative Index and Glossary in a three ring binder for ready reference.

YEARBOOK OF SCIENCE AND THE FUTURE
Encyclopaedia Britannica, 310 S Michigan Ave, Chicago, IL 60604-4293 312-347-7000 Published annually in book form.
Annual developments in science summarized for the biological, physical and social sciences.

ZOO REVIEW
The Lincoln Park Zoological Society, 2200 N Cannon Drive, Chicago, IL 60614 312-742-2000 http://www.lpzoo.com Free to members.
This magazine is published and distributed to members of the Society.

Chapter

12

Safety

Science Education Safety Resources

Use this list to obtain various reference books, materials, and programs related to safety in science.

BEST'S SAFETY DIRECTORY
**Thomas Leader, Editor A. M. Best Co., Inc., Ambest Rd, Oldwick, NJ 08858
908-439-2200 Fax 908-534-1506 Email leadert@ambest.com
http://www.ambest.com Annually $ 49.95 plus shipping.**
A buying guide and manual of safety practices safety supervisors. Contains a Buyer's Guide of Safety and Security Products, OSHA standards, and articles on safety-related topics.

CHEMICAL SAFETY
**Goldstein & Associates, 1150 Yale St, # 12, Santa Monica, CA 90403-4734
310-828-1309 Bimonthly**
Information on training, research and products.

GREATER CHICAGO SAFETY COUNCIL
1 N LaSalle, Chicago, IL 60602 312-372-9756
Ask about how schools may become members. Rental safety films are available to members at discount rates. Ask about monthly safety programs.

HAZARDOUS MATERIALS COMPLIANCE POCKETBOOK

J. J. Keller & Associates, Inc., P O Box 368, Neenah, WI 54957-0368
800-558-5011 800-327-6868 Fax 800-727-7516 920-722-2848 Fax 920-727-1998
Email editors@jjkeller.com http://www.jjkeller.com 512 pages
This comprehensive pocket reference was written for the transportation industry.

NATIONAL SAFETY COUNCIL - LIBRARY

Robert J. Marecek, Manager Contact the Reference Desk National Safety
Council, 1121 Spring Lake Dr, Itasca, IL 60143-3201 630-775-2199 Fax
630-285-0765 Email bob-nsc@dupagels.lib.il.us http://www.nsc.org
This library is open to the public and contains a comprehensive collection of 140,000
documents on health and safety. Fees apply to researchers requiring extensive
assistance. It is best to telephone ahead for an appointment.

NATIONAL SAFETY COUNCIL

1121 Spring Lk Dr, Itasca, IL 630-775-2500, 1815 Landmeier Rd, Elk Grove
Village, IL 847-981-0250 800-621-7619 Fax 630-258-0797 http://www.nsc.org
This nonprofit, nongovernmental organization offers a library, safety videos, training
materials, and safety training instruction.

OCCUPATIONAL SAFETY AND HEALTH ADMINISTRATION (OSHA) TRAINING INSTITUTE

1555 Times Dr, Des Plaines, IL 60018 847-297-4810 http://www.osha-slc.gov
Ask for catalog of audiovisual safety video cassettes for schools. This training center
includes a safety equipment laboratory and a 3,000 volume reference library.

THE POWER HOUSE - EDUCATIONAL PROGRAMS

Commonwealth Edison, 100 Shiloh Blvd, Zion, IL 60099 847-746-7492
http://www.ucm.com/powerhouse
Teachers and schools can request a program that visits schools, Safety and Electricity,
for grades K-3. Ask for brochure on tours and educational programs.

SAFETY IN THE ELEMENTARY SCIENCE CLASSROOM

by Dean, Dean, Gerlovich, and Spiglanin Produced and distributed by the
National Science Teachers Association 800-722-NSTA 1993 22 pages $ 5.95
Easy-to-read flip chart covers the important safety topics for the classroom.

TEACHING CHEMISTRY TO STUDENTS WITH DISABILITIES - 3RD EDITION

Contact Ronald J. Sykstus American Chemical Society, Chicago Section, 7173
N Austin, Niles, IL 60714 847-647-8405 Fax 847-647-8364 (Contact national
ACS office for career pamphlets at 800-227-5558.) 1993 46 pages Free
Ask for this excellent information and resource booklet.

THE TOTAL SCIENCE SAFETY SYSTEM
- ELEMENTARY & SECONDARY EDITIONS
Contact   Jack Gerlouich   JaKel, Inc., 585 Southfork Dr, Waukee, IA 50263
515-225-6317 Fax 515-222-9554 Email jakel@netins.net
http://www.netins.net/showcase/jakel
This computer software is an information data base about safety & science teaching,
legal issues, safety assessment, and safety equipment resources. Request a brochure
giving pricing. Developed by Dr. Jack Gerlovich, Professor of Science Education,
Drake University.

WASTE MANAGEMENT AND RESEARCH CENTER
One E Hazelwood Dr, Champaign, IL 61820 217-333-8940 Fax 217-333-9844
http://www.hazard.uiuc.edu/wmrc/library/hwricpub.htm
Ask for Clearinghouse Reports and Publications List of available free publications or
see web site for up-to-date list.

Mail Order Suppliers of Safety Equipment

ALDRICH SAFETY PRODUCTS
Aldrich Chemical Company, P. O. Box 2060, Milwaukee,   WI 53201-0355
800-558-9160 Retail (High School to Adult)
Ask for 200-page catalog of laboratory equipment and supplies.

CLEAN HARBORS
1501 Washington St, Braintree, MA 02184 800-282-0058 Fax 718-849-1561
http://www.cleanharbors.com
Clean Harbors is a nationwide hazardous waste disposal and transportation company.
As a Clean Harbors customer, you will have your choice of a variety of service plans
and pickup schedules.

FLINN CHEMICAL CATALOG REFERENCE MANUAL
Flinn Scientific Inc., P. O. Box 219, Batavia, IL 60510 800-452-1261 688 pages
Retail (High School to Adult)
This catalog, for science teachers only, lists new products, chemicals, chemical solution
preparation, Apparatus & Laboratory Equipment, Books, Computer Software, Satety
Storage Cabinets & Fume Hoods, Safety Supplies & Equipment, Right to Know Laws,
Mystery Substance Identification, Chemical Inventory & Storage, and Chemical
Disposal Procedures.

J. J. KELLER & ASSOCIATES, INC.

P O Box 368, Neenah, WI 54957-0368 800-558-5011 800-327-6868
Fax 800-727-7516 920-722-2848 Fax 920-727-1998 Email editors@jjkeller.com
http://www.jjkeller.com
Ask for 175-page Full Line Catalog of books, software, and materials used for handling hazardous materials. Products for DOT, OSHA, EPA compliance and workplace safety.

LAB SAFETY SUPPLY INC.

P. O. Box 1368, Janesville, WI 53547-1368 800-356-0783 Info 800-356-2501
Fax 800-543-9910 http://www.labsafety.com Retail (High School)
Ask for 900-page catalog of laboratory equipment and supplies dedicated to personal environmental safety for industry, hazardous waste, and school science laboratories.

Chapter

13

Science Fairs

Steps to a Winning Project Experiment

Good science fair projects include eleven steps...

1. Making a study of other projects that win.

2. Choosing a topic idea or problem to study and clearly stating the problem.

3. Stating the purpose, or value, of the experiment.

4. Conducting a literature search of related work in books and talking to professional experts.

5. Doing preparatory work, selecting materials, and organizing the experiment.

6. Collecting raw experiment data in a notebook.

7. Analyzing data, by creating tables, diagrams, graphs, photographs and drawings.

212 Science Fun in Chicagoland

8. Examining sources of error. Thinking.
   Drawing the best conclusions.

9. Preparing a written report and
   a brief oral presentation.

10. Constructing a science fair exhibit.

11. Participating in the science fair and
    the science fair judging process.

Science Fair Project Ideas

These books contain good ideas for science fair projects. Contact your local public library. The library should have an excellent collection of books on science fair project ideas and books on how to develop an experiment. Some libraries conduct workshops on how to succeed with your science fair project.

1001 IDEAS FOR SCIENCE PROJECTS
by Marian Brisk 1992 250 pages Ages 12+ ($ 12.95 Showboard 800-323-9189)
This book lists supplies needed and time required and has ideas for all levels. One chapter is devoted to writing clear reports.

ALL ABOUT SCIENCE FAIRS
96 pages Ages 7-12 ($ 11.95 Showboard 800-323-9189)
This book includes Teacher's Guide, Parent's Packet, Student Handbook and Worksheets, Scientific Method, Reproducibles.

GUIDE TO THE BEST SCIENCE FAIR PROJECTS
160 pages 1997 Ages 8-12 ($ 14.95 Showboard 800-323-9189)
A single resource for everything from how to pick a topic to how to put together an eye-catching display.

HAROLD WASHINGTON LIBRARY CENTER
Contact Mary Elizabeth Isom, Science Fair Library Collection Librarian, 4th Floor, Science and Technology, 400 S State St, Chicago, IL 60605 312-747-4447
The Harold Washington Library Center has a large collection of books on science fair projects.

A student with his science fair project at a regional science fair
in Chicago. Science fair projects teach methods of scientific
investigation, increase knowledge, and build self confidence.

Photo printed with permission. © 1998 Allan Reisberg

SCIENCE EXPERIMENTS AND PROJECTS FOR STUDENTS
by Cothron, Giese, and Rezba   Distributed by the National Science Teachers
Association 800-722-NSTA 1996 195 pages $ 17.95
An interactive book that requires students to progress through the several levels of
activity necessary for science fair project completion.

214 Science Fun in Chicagoland

SCIENCE EXPERIMENTS BY THE HUNDREDS
by Cothron, Giese, and Rezba   Distributed by the National Science Teachers Association 800-722-NSTA 1996 148 pages $ 17.95
For use by students and teachers at home and in the classroom with many practical suggestions and methods.

SCIENCE FAIR CENTRAL
Contact Dr. Paul Dolan Northeastern Illinois University, 5500 N St. Louis Ave, Chicago, IL 60625 773-794-2539 Email P-Dolan@neiu.edu
http://www.neiu.edu/~pjdoland/
Middle school students, high school students, and their parents can attend Saturday meetings in the fall of the year for general ideas on science fair project ideas. Inquire about current meetings.

SCIENCE FAIR PROJECT INDEX 1973-1980
Akron-Summit County Public Library,   Scarecrow Press, Inc., 1983. 729 pages Out of print.
This reference lists hundreds of science fair project ideas found in books and magazines published from 1973 to 1980. Check with your local public library to see this major reference.

SCIENCE FAIR PROJECT INDEX 1981-1984
by Bishop and Crowe Akron-Summit County Public Library, Scarecrow Press, Inc., 1986. 692 pages Out of print.
This reference lists hundreds of science fair project ideas found in 135 books and five magazines published from 1981 to 1984. Check with your local public library to see this major reference.

SCIENCE FAIR WORKSHOP
43 pages Ages 7-12 ($ 7.99 Showboard 800-323-9189)
This book includes step-by-step science project guide, student workbook, reproducibles.

SCIENCE FAIR: A RESOURCE GUIDE
28 pages Ages 9-13 ($ 4.95 Showboard 800-323-9189)
This book takes the student from choosing a topic to the final display, including judge's worksheet and reproducibles.

SHOWBOARD - SCIENCE FAIR RESOURCE CATALOG
Contact Mark Oleksak P O Box   10656, Tampa, FL 33679-0656 / 2602 W De
Leon, Tampa, FL 33609 800-323-9189   813-874-1828 Fax 813-876-8046
Email sales@showboard.com   http://www.showboard.com
Ask for 32-page catalog of materials for science fair projects and for running a local
science fair, including project display boards, awards & ribbons, science fair quarterly
newsletter, certificates of participation, idea books, and science fair videos.

STUDENTS AND RESEARCH - PRACTICAL STRATEGIES FOR SCIENCE CLASSROOMS AND COMPETITIONS
by Cothron, Giese, and Rezba Second Edition Distributed by the National
Science Teachers Association 800-722-NSTA 1993 280 pages $ 25.95
Field-tested teaching strategies for developing research skills in students at all grade
levels. Teacher's Guide to Local Science Fairs

Teacher's Guide to Chicago Area Science Fairs

CHICAGO NON-PUBLIC SCHOOLS' SCIENCE EXPOSITION INC.
Sponsored by Region 2 of the Illinois Junior Academy of Science. Contact Julia
Ferrari 815-254-4005   Fax 815-436-5238
This regional science fair welcomes its participating schools from Chicago and the
surrounding metropolitan area. The exposition is held annually in March at the
Museum of Science & Industry. Students who exhibit are from grades 7-12.

CHICAGO PUBLIC SCHOOLS ANNUAL STUDENT SCIENCE FAIR
Sponsored by Chicago Public Schools Student Science Fair, Inc., P. O. Box 29546,
Chicago, IL 60629 312-535-7978 and the Department of Curriculum &
Instruction, Chicago Public Schools, 1819 W Pershing Rd, 6 East (s), Chicago, IL
60609 773-535-8860
Held annually in the spring, this exposition is sponsored by major corporations in the
Chicago area. For answers to questions about student registration and project support
contact this resource and ask for publications, including the Student Science Fair
Program Guide to Projects, Information for Judges, Organizational Handbook for
Administrators and Coordinators, and the Participant Handbook.

ILLINOIS JUNIOR ACADEMY OF SCIENCE
State-wide organization consisting of 11 regions through out Illinois.
Founded in 1927. Contact Ken Priban, President for 1999-2000, at 847-679-8861.
Contact Jackie Naughton, President for 2001-2002, at 847-299-4166.
Students from all over the state of Illinois present projects at regional expositions. The
best of these are invited to present their projects at the University of Illinois,
Champaign/Urbana, in May of each year. Contact the Illinois Junior Academy of

Science about how your students may participate.

INTERNATIONAL SCIENCE AND ENGINEERING FAIR
Contact Sharon Manley Science Service, Inc., 1719 N St, NW, Washington, DC 20036 202-785-2255 Fax 202-785-1243 Email smanley@sciserv.org Email youth@sciserv.org http://www.sciserv.org http://www.tss-inc.com/sciserv/
For over forty years Science Service has administered the International Science and Engineering Fair. More than 1100 students participate from over 30 different countries. Students in grades 9-12 are eligible and two student finalists and a team of up to three are selected from each of the 485 regional science fairs. Sponsored by Intel.

MUSEUM OF SCIENCE AND INDUSTRY - SCIENCE FAIRS
Museum of Science and Industry, 57th St and Lake Shore Drive, Chicago, IL 60637 773-684-1414 http://www.msichicago.org
The Chicago Public Schools student science fair is the premier science fair in the United States. The top projects, from about 300 students are displayed at the Museum. The Museum is also the site of the annual Non-Public Schools Science Fair. Contact the Museum with questions concerning scheduling of these two fairs.

SCIENCE FAIRS AND PROJECTS - GRADES 7-12
Published and distributed by the National Science Teachers Association 800-722-NSTA 1988 72 pages $ 9.50
This book is for the teacher and explains all aspects of how to develop a successful science fair.

Chapter

14

Video

Film and Video Sources

These sources provide great films on science subjects in VHS format as well as interactive media on CD-ROM's and laserdiscs.

AIMS MULTIMEDIA
9710 DeSoto Ave, Chatsworth, CA 91311 800-367-2467 Fax 818-341-6700 Email info@aims-multimedia.com http://www.aims-multimedia.com
Ask for 58-page Educational Technology Catalog. Distributor of video, CD-ROMs, Laserdisc, and teaching modules.

AMERICAN ASSOCIATION OF PHYSICS TEACHERS - AAPT PRODUCTS CATALOG
American Association of Physics Teachers, One Physics Ellipse, College Park, MD 20740-3845   301-209-3300   Fax 301-209-0845   Email aapt-memb@aapt.org http://www.aapt.org
Ask for this 28-page catalog. The 1997-98 catalog lists 85 books on physics and physics education. It also offers Physics of Technology Modules, computer software, videodiscs, videotapes, materials for teachers, gift items, workshop materials, and posters.

AMERICAN CHEMICAL SOCIETY
- SATELLITE TELEVISION AND VIDEO CATALOG
American Chemical Society, Department of Continuing Education, 1155 16th St, NW, Washington, DC 20036 800-209-0423 Fax 800-209-0064 304-728-2170 http://www.acs.org/edugen2/education/conted/conted.htm
Ask for 44-page catalog. Educational satellite TV seminars and video courses for chemistry educators and students.

ANNENBERG/CPB CHANNEL
c/o Harvard-Smithsonian Center for Astrophysics, 60 Garden St, MS-82, Cambridge, MA 02138 800-228-8030 617-495-9798 Fax 617-496-7670 Email channel@learner.org http://www.learner.org/channel
This satellite channel of programs is fed to public television stations, public access cable stations, schools, colleges, and other commercial organizations that have equipment to receive a DigiCipher II satellite signal. Ask for schedule of current programs.

ANNENBERG/CPB PROJECT
901 E Street, NW, Washington, DC 20004-2037 800-LEARNER
http://www.learner.org
Ask for brochure. Educational television series in science include: Teaching Modules/The Brain, Against All Odds/Inside Statistics, For All Practical Purposes, Algebra, Earth Revealed, The Mechanical Universe, The World of Chemistry, The Power of Place, and Human Geography.

BILL NYE THE SCIENCE GUY
KCTS/Seattle, Outreach Department, 401 Mercer St, Seattle, WA 98109 206-624-1915 http://nyelabs.kcts.org
The wild and wacky style of this program provides an entertaining approach to science for the younger viewer. Ask for 42-page teacher's guide and educational materials available to schools, including off-air recording rights expiration chart. To purchase videotapes contact PBS at 800-752-9727, or Disney Educational Productions, 105 Terry Drive, Suite 120, Newtown, PA 18940 800-295-5010.

BLOCKBUSTER VIDEO
(See your telephone directory for store locations.)
Video rental. See Science and Nature Section which includes Audubon videos, Cousteau videos, National Geographic Video series, NOVA series, and PBS Home Video.

CAREERS FOR CHEMISTS VIDEO
American Chemical Society, Department of Continuing Education, 1155 16th St, NW, Washington, DC 20036   800-209-0423   Fax 800-209-0064   304-728-2170 http://www.acs.org/edugen2/education/conted/conted.htm $ 24.95
This video looks at various professional careers in the chemical sciences. Features 15 chemists from diverse backgrounds talking about their day-to-day responsibilities.

JOURNAL OF CHEMICAL EDUCATION
- PUBLICATIONS/SOFTWARE CATALOG
University of Wisconsin-Madison, Department of Chemistry, 1101 University Avenue, Madison, WI   53706-1396   800-991-5534 (Software)   800-691-9846 (Subscriptions)   Email jcesoft@chem.wisc.edu (Software) and jce@aol.com (Subscriptions) http://jchemed.chem.wisc.edu/
Request 47-page catalog of videos, CD-ROM, Online, Multimedia, Print, Software, and Books.

CHEMICAL EDUCATIONAL FOUNDATION
1525 Wilson Blvd, Suite 750, Arlington, VA 22209   703-527-6223   Fax 703-527-7747 http://www.chemed.org
Distributes information about chemical products through web site, videos, publications, and training. More than 13,000 videos have been distributed to schools.

COLLEGE VIDEO CORPORATION
Project Worldclass, 4455 Connecticut Ave, N W, Suite B100, Washington, DC 20008 800-852-5277 800-253-4663 http://www.acas.com
Students enrolled in college credit video courses, such as the Center for Open Learning, City Colleges of Chicago, 30 E Lake St, 11th Floor, Chicago, IL 60601, via Channel 20 TV, telephone 312-553-5970, may rent the entire educational video series from College Video Corporation for a period of four months. Inquire about available video series and rental rates.

COMPUTER CHRONICLES
2410 Charleston Rd, Mountain View, CA 94043 http://www.cmptv.com Program tapes $ 19.95 each, 888-310-2850
This television program is broadcast on WYCC/Chicago Channel 20 and summarizes current advances in personal computers and software.

CONNECTICUT VALLEY BIOLOGICAL
82 Valley Road, P O Box 326, Southhampton, MA 01073 800-628-7748 Fax 800-355-6813 413-527-4030 Manufacturer Distributor Retail Mail Order
Ask for 450-page catalog. Major source of science materials, including living botanical and zoological material, microscope slides, biological displays, books, and video tapes.

220 Science Fun in Chicagoland

CSY, INC.
111 East Capitol Street, Suite 465, Jackson, MS 39201 800-352-0477 Email mis@csy.com http://www.csy.com Manufacturer Distributor
Ask for brochure. Minorities in Science, a supplemental science videodisc program.

DISCOVERY CHANNEL SCHOOL - EDUCATOR GUIDE & CATALOG
Discovery Channel School, P O Box 970, Oxon Hill, MD 20750-0970 888-892-3484 Fax 301-567-9553 http://www.discoveryschool.com
Ask for 60-page catalog that includes videos, classroom programs, Internet resources, and CD-ROMs.

DISNEY EDUCATIONAL PRODUCTIONS
105 Terry Drive, Suite 120, Newtown, PA 18940 800-295-5010 Fax 215-579-8589
Ask for 46-page videos & videodiscs catalog. This catalog has 16 pages on science, math, health, safety, and computers, including videos: Bill Nye the Science Guy, Wonders of Life Series, Minnie's Science Field Trip Series, Nature Classics Series, and many more.

EDUCATION EXCHANGE - VIDEO LEASING LIBRARY
Disney Educational Productions, 500 S Buena Vista St, Burbank, CA 91521-6677 800-295-5010
Inquire about membership for schools and classrooms. Associated with The Disney Channel on cable television.

THE EDUCATION GROUP
9312 Nightingale Dr, Los Angeles, CA 90069 310-276-1122 Fax 310-276-7330 Email edgroup@wavenet.com
Manufacturer of The Video Encyclopedia of Physics Demonstrations. 600 physics demonstrations on laserdisc.

EDUCATIONAL ACTIVITIES, INC.
Contact Alan Stern P. O. Box 392, Freeport, NY 11520 800-645-3739 516-223-4666 Fax 516-623-9282 Email learn@edact.com http://www.edact.com
Ask for science brochure including software, videos, and CD-ROMs.

EDUCATIONAL VIDEO NETWORK
Dr. Kenneth L. Russell, President 1401 19th St, Huntsville, TX 77340 800-762-0060 Fax 409-294-0233 http://www.edvidnet.com
See Internet web site for complete catalog of video tapes for sale.

EDUCATORS GUIDE TO FREE FILMS, FILMSTRIPS AND SLIDES
57th Edition Contact Kathy Nehmer Educators Progress Service, Inc., 214 Center St, Randolph, WI 53956-1497 888-951-4469 920-326-3126 Fax 920-326-3127 1997 225 pages $ 36.95
This book lists and describes free audiovisuals available to educators. Revised annually.

EDUCATORS GUIDE TO FREE SCIENCE MATERIALS - 38TH EDITION
Edited by Mary H. Saterstrom Contact Kathy Nehmer Educators Progress Service, Inc., 214 Center St, Randolph, WI 53956-1497 920-326-3126 888-951-4469 Fax 920-326-3127 1997 256 pages $ 29.95
This book lists and describes free science materials, including films, filmstrips, slides, videotapes, and printed materials by category of science subject area. Revised annually.

EDUCATORS GUIDE TO FREE VIDEOTAPES
44th Edition Contact Kathy Nehmer Educators Progress Service, Inc., 214 Center St, Randolph, WI 53956-1497 888-951-4469 920-326-3126 Fax 920-326-3127 1997 407 pages $ 27.95
This book lists and describes free videotapes available to educators. Revised annually.

FASE PRODUCTIONS
Park Mile Plaza, 4801 Wilshire Blvd, Suite 215, Los Angeles, CA 90010 800-404-FASE Order Fax 317-579-0402 Credit card orders 800-270-6363 http://www.fasenet.org
Ask for 12-page catalog. VHS cassettes of Teacher Talk (Staff Development), Living and Working in Space, Math..Who Needs It?, Interactions: Career Series, Futures with Jaime Escalante Series, The Eddie Files Series, and more.

THE FIELD MUSEUM - THE NEW EXPLORERS MATERIALS DEPOSITORY
The Field Museum, Roosevelt Road at Lake Shore Drive, Chicago, IL 60605-2497 312-922-9410, ext 853 http://www.fmnh.org
The popular television series, The New Explorers with Bill Kurtis, is made available to teachers along with educational materials. This collection is found in the Harris Educational Loan Center on the Museum ground floor.

FILMS FOR THE HUMANITIES & SCIENCES
P O Box 2053, Princeton, NJ 08543-2053 800-257-5126 609-275-1400 Fax 609-275-3767 Email custserv@films.com http://www.films.com
Ask for catalog in a specific science subject, eg. physics. Video and CD-ROM programs.

GPN MATH AND SCIENCE CATALOG
P O Box 80669, Lincoln, NE 68501-0669 800-228-4630 Fax 800-306-2330 Email gpn@unlinfo.unl.edu http://gpn.unl.edu (Elementary, Secondary, Professional Development) GPN is a service agency of KUON-TV, University of Nebraska-Lincoln.
Ask for 38-page catalog filled with video, videodisc, CD-ROM, World Wide Web video programs available for purchase. Programs include programs from 3-2-1 Contact, Backyard Safari, By The Numbers, Discovering, Earth Revealed, The Earth Science Video Library, Exploring the Internet, Field Trips, National Teacher Training Institute Video Series, Newton's Apple, Reading Rainbow Science, Universe: The Infinite, and many more.

HAWKHILL ASSOCIATES, INC.
215 E Gilman St, P. O. Box 1029, Madison, WI 53701-1029 800-422-4295 608-251-3434 Fax 608-251-3924 Email hawkhill@inxpress.net
http://www.hawkhill.com
Ask for 15-page catalog of video tapes on science topics.

HOLLYWOOD VIDEO
(See your telephone directory for store locations.)
Video rental. Look for many science and nature videos.

INSIGHT MEDIA
Contact Customer Service 2162 Broadway, New York, NY 10024-6620 800-233-9910 212-721-6316 Fax 212-799-5309
Ask for brochure of video cassettes and CD-ROMs on all science topics for the high school classroom.

INVENTING THE FUTURE:
AFRICAN-AMERICAN CONTRIBUTIONS
TO SCIENTIFIC DISCOVERY AND INVENTION
American Chemical Society, Department of Continuing Education, 1155 16th St, NW, Washington, DC 20036 800-209-0423 Fax 800-209-0064 304-728-2170 http://www.acs.org/edugen2/education/conted/conted.htm 202-452-2113 VHS Video $ 20.00 per set of two.
Overview of historic African science including almanacs, astronomical measurements, and railroad communication covering the mid 1970's to the mid 1900's. This video includes a 12-page teacher's guide of biographical material as well as hands-on science activities. Sold as set with another video, Tracing the Path: African-American Contributions to Chemistry in the Life Sciences.

Waterways Exhibit at the Chicago Children's Museum located at Navy Pier in Chicago.

Photo Courtesy of the Chicago Children's Museum

THE LPD VIDEO JOURNAL OF EDUCATION
8686 S 1300 E, Sandy, UT 84094 800-572-1153 Fax 888-566-6888
http://www.videojournal.com
Ask for 58-page catalog. Faculty and staff development videos including The Technology-Infused Classroom, Technology to Enhance Learning, Utilizing the Internet in the Classroom, and many more.

MUSEUM OF SCIENCE AND INDUSTRY - NEW EXPLORERS
Museum of Science and Industry, 57th St and Lake Shore Drive, Chicago, IL 60637 773-684-1414 http://www.msichicago.org
The popular television series, The New Explorers with Bill Kurtis, is made available to teachers along with educational materials. Workshops and tape support groups also are provided for teachers.

PBS NATIONAL AUDUBON SOCIETY SPECIALS
Home Video, 1320 Braddock Place, Alexandria, VA 22314-1698 800-645-4727 Fax 703-739-8131 http://www.pbs.org/shop VHS $ 59.95 each
This PBS series for grades 4-12 examines the wonder and beauty of nature's rarest creatures. Each program is accompanied by a 1-5 page teacher resource.

NATIONAL GEOGRAPHIC SOCIETY MEMBER CATALOG
1145 17th Street, NW, Washington, DC 20036-4688 Orders: P O Box 400401, Des Moines, IA 50340-0401 888-225-5647 Fax 515-362-3345
Ask for 24-page catalog. Gift catalog includes numerous National Geographic Videos, CD-ROMs, and gift items.

THE NEW EXPLORERS WITH BILL KURTIS
Produced by Kurtis Productions Ltd. for the A&E Cable Network. Original productions in this series are seen monthly on A&E; reruns are broadcast weekly on Saturday afternoons. To order *The New Explorers* home videos, call 800-423-1212. For information on educational materials and videos, call eld!n, the Electronic Long Distance Learning Network, 1420 N Meacham Road, Schaumburg, IL 60173 847-843-1299 Email info@eldln.com http://www.eldln.com
This science-adventure series goes around he world to highlight today's scientists in the never-ending pursuit of discovery.

NEWTON'S APPLE
Twin Cities Public Television, 172 4th Street E, Saint Paul, MN 55101 612-222-1717
Telephone for information about Newton's Apple resources. Hands-On Science Kits 800-373-1498, CD-ROM's 800-219-9022, Video Tapes 800-228-4630, Videodisc Multimedia 800-368-2728, Science Charts 800-328-5540.

NSTA SCIENCE EDUCATION SUPPLIERS

A Supplement to: Science & Children, Science Scope, and The Science Teacher, National Science Teachers Association, 1840 Wilson Blvd, Arlington, VA 22201-3000 800-722-NSTA Published annually. 165 pages $ 5.00 per additional copy

List of educational video producers and distributors. The most current and comprehensive list of manufacturers, publishers and distributors of science education materials. See Media Producers. In 1998, 261 media producers were listed.

OPTICAL DATA CORPORATION - SCHOOL MEDIA

512 Means St, N W, Suite 100, Atlanta, GA 30318-9716 800-524-2481 Fax 800-953-8691 http://opticaldata.com

Ask for 32-page catalog. Products include multimedia science program, Windows on Science, on video discs and video tapes: Primary Science, Life Science, Earth Science, Physical Science, The Living Textbook, and more.

PBS HOME VIDEO - CATALOG

1320 Braddock Place, Alexandria, VA 22314-1698 800-645-4727 Fax 703-739-8131 http://www.pbs.org/shop

Ask for 64-page catalog. PBS television series and programs are available for purchase on VHS cassettes. This catalog contains many quality science programs.

PHYSICS CURRICULUM & INSTRUCTION

22585 Woodhill Dr, Lakeville, MN 55044 612-461-3470 Fax 612-461-3467

Ask for 18-page catalog of physics demonstrations and concepts on videocassette and laserdisc, as well as computer software.

PITSCO

1002 E Adams, P O Box 1708, Pittsburg, KS 66762-1708 800-835-0686 800-358-4983 http://www.pitsco.com Fax 800-533-8104 Manufacturer Distributor Retail (Elementary School to College)

Ask for 432-page catalog. Major distributor of science materials, including books, new toys, video, and more.

THE POWER HOUSE - LEARNING POWER CATALOG

Commonwealth Edison, 100 Shiloh Blvd, Zion, IL 60099 847-746-7080 http://www.ucm.com/powerhouse Retail Mail Order

The Learning Power Catalog is available to teachers. It lists free materials available, including literature on energy conservation, on the history of electricity, on the environment, on nuclear issues, and on safety as well as videos available for free loan on these same topics.

PUBLICATIONS CATALOG FOR THE TECHNOLOGY TEACHER
International Technology Education Association, 1914 Association Dr, Suite 201, Reston, VA 20191-1539 703-860-2100 Fax 703-860-0353 Email itea@iris.org http://www.iteawww.org
Ask for 35-page catalog of publications, classroom materials, videos, resources, and computer software.

RAINBOW EDUCATIONAL MEDIA
4540 Preslyn Drive, Raleigh, NC 27616-3177 800-331-4047 Fax 919-954-7554
Manufacturer Distributor
Ask for 110-page catalog. Videocassettes, videodiscs, and CD-ROM's in Earth Science, Environment, Health, Life Science, Physical Science, and more.

SCIENCE BOOKS & FILMS
by the American Association for the Advancement of Science, 1200 New York Ave, NW, Washington, DC 20005-3920 202-326-6400 http://www.aaas.org/ehr Online version http://SBFonline.com Nine issues per year. $ 45.00 per year
This periodical reviews scientific accuracy and presentation of print, audiovisual, and electronic resources intended for educational use.

PBS SCIENCELINE
1320 Braddock Place, Alexandra, VA 22314 703-739-7538 Email sciencecline@pbs.org   http://www.pbs.org/learn/scienceline
Created for K-5 science teachers, this professional development program concentrates on innovations in science teaching. A collaborative effort of PBS and the National Science Teachers Association.

SCIENTIFIC AMERICAN FRONTIERS
School Program, 105 Terry Drive, Suite 120, Newton, PA 18940 800-315-5010 Email saf@pbs.org   http://pbs.org/saf/
This television series takes you on excursions into the furthest realms of scientific investigation. A free 16-page teaching guide, with classroom activities related to the PBS television series hosted by Alan Alda, are available to middle and high school science teachers. Underwritten by GTE Corporation.

SKY PUBLISHING CORP. CATALOG
Sky Publishing Corp., 49 Bay State Rd, Cambridge, MA 02138 / Sky & Telescope, P O Box 9111, Belmont, MA 02178-9111 800-253-0245 617-864-7360
Fax 617-864-6117 Email skytel@skypub.com http://www.skypub.com Since 1941.
Ask for 32-page catalog of products for professional and amateur astronomers. Products include maps, books, videos, globes, posters, software, CD-ROMs, slide sets, star atlases, and planispheres.

TEACHER'S DISCOVERY
Science Division, 2741 Paldan Dr, Auburn Hills, MI 48326 888-97-SCIENCE Fax 888-98-SCIENCE 248-340-7220 Distributor
Ask for 68-page science catalog. Materials to make "teaching more exciting and fun." Classroom materials, CD-ROMs, and videos.

TEACHER'S VIDEO COMPANY
P O Box SCG-4455, Scottsdale, AZ 85261 800-262-8837 Fax 602-860-8650 Distributor Retail Mail Order
Ask for 80-page science catalog. Quality videos in all areas of science, including National Geographic Video, NOVA, Eyewitness Video, Discovery Channel Video, Smithsonian Video, and many more. Every video $ 29.95. Buy 4, get 1 free.

THE PROBLEM SOLVERS:
PEOPLE WITH DISABILITIES IN ENGINEERING CAREERS
American Association for the Advancement of Science, 1200 New York Ave, NW, Washington, DC 20005-3920 800-222-7809 http://www.aaas.org/ehr 1992 1993 26 minutes 20-page guide $ 20.00
Documentary focuses on 24 people with disabilities who study and work in various fields of engineering.

UNIVERSITY OF CALIFORNIA EXTENSION CENTER FOR MEDIA AND INDEPENDENT LEARNING
2000 Center St, Suite 400, Berkeley, CA 94704 510-642-0460
Email cmil@uclink.berkeley.edu
Films and Video: http://www-cmil.unex.berkeley.edu/media
Request Film & Video Sales Catalog and Film/Video Rental Catalog offering videos like When the Bay Area Quakes, the series General Chemistry Laboratory Techniques, and the series Understanding Space and Time.

WEIRD SCIENCE VIDEO
Lee Marek, Instructor. Naperville North High School, 899 N Mill St, Naperville, IL 60563-8998 630-420-6513 Fax 630-420-3246 Email lmarek@aol.com Email lmarek@fnal.gov
The Weird Science Kids now make chemistry fun on wild, mad science video demonstrations. You may have seen Lee Marek squirt television's David Letterman with a fire extinguisher, cover him with shredded Styrofoam and blind him with burning magnesium. Inquire about Weird Science Video including Chemistry Classics, Weird Science Show, etc.

228 Science Fun in Chicagoland

WGBH BOSTON VIDEO
P O Box 2284, S. Burlington, VT 05407-2284 800-255-9424 Fax 802-864-9846
617-492-2777, ext 2652 Email WGBH_Materials_Request@wgbh.org
http://www.wgbh.org Wholesale Orders: 800-367-6228
Ask for 16-page catalog of VHS video tapes. Science programs include NOVA,
Frontline, and NOVA Classroom Field Trips. Classroom activity guides are available
for each currently aired program.

MR. WIZARD INSTITUTE
Contact Cathy Loudon A Division of Prism Productions, 1960 W. West Maple,
Walled Lake, MI 48390 800-992-8388 248-669-8093, ext 109 Fax 248-669-7515
Ask for brochure that describes Mr. Wizard's World Science Video Library, available
on videocassettes and Teacher to Teacher with Mr. Wizard video tapes. The very best
of Mr. Wizard's World, the popular children's television program seen on Nickelodeon.

ZTEK CO.
P. O. Box 11768, Lexington, KY 40577-1768 800-247-1603 606-281-1611 Fax
606-281-1521 Email info@ztek.com http://www.ztek.com
Ask for 32-page catalog of educational multimedia on CD-ROM, software, and
videodiscs, as well as multimedia equipment.

Index

232 Science Fun in Chicagoland

About the Author

Thomas W. Sills has been associated with Wright College, one of the City Colleges of Chicago, since 1989, and with the City Colleges since 1981. He has held several teaching positions over the years and has worked on course and lab development. He currently holds the position of professor of physical science.

His diverse professional career in science education includes test development, science toy design, science teacher training, reviewing college physics textbooks, and acting as science consultant to programs for the gifted. He is also faculty coordinator of telecourses on Channel 20/Chicago educational television, including *The Mechanical Universe* and *Planet Earth.*

In high school he received an award at the International Science Fair for his student science project on learning and memory. In 1967 he taught college physical science for elementary teachers as his first teaching assignment. In 1977 he received his Ph.D. in physics and education at Purdue University.

Dr. Sills is a serious collector of books and manuscripts on science and technology. But most of all, he enjoys going to new places to meet new people in order to stimulate ideas. "Doing adventuresome things is just plain fun."